Understanding the Costs of Environmental Regulation in Europe

Understanding the Costs of Environmental Regulation in Europe

Edited by

Michael MacLeod

Researcher, Scottish Agricultural College, Edinburgh, Scotland

Paul Ekins

Professor of Energy and Environment Policy, King's College, London, England

Robin Vanner

Visiting Fellow, Policy Studies Institute, London, England

Dominic Moran

Senior Environmental Economist, Scottish Agricultural College, Edinburgh, Scotland

Edward Elgar
Cheltenham, UK • Northampton, MA, USA

Published by
Edward Elgar Publishing Limited
The Lypiatts
15 Lansdown Road
Cheltenham
Glos GL50 2JA
UK

Edward Elgar Publishing, Inc.
William Pratt House
9 Dewey Court
Northampton
Massachusetts 01060
USA

A catalogue record for this book
is available from the British Library

Library of Congress Control Number: 2008939743

Mixed Sources
Product group from well-managed
forests and other controlled sources
www.fsc.org Cert no. SA-COC-1565
© 1996 Forest Stewardship Council
FSC

ISBN 978 1 84720 492 9

Printed and bound in Great Britain by MPG Books Ltd, Bodmin, Cornwall

Contents

Contributors

Cécile Des Abbayes
BIO Intelligence Service, Ivry-sur-Seine, France

Kev Bevan
Scottish Agricultural College, Edinburgh, Scotland

Paul Ekins
King's College, London, England

Winston Harrington
Resources for the Future, Washington DC, USA

Salman Hussain
Scottish Agricultural College, Edinburgh, Scotland

Diane Huybrechts
VITO (Flemish Institute for Technological Research), Boeretang, Belgium

Jochem Jantzen
TME (Institute for Applied Environmental Economics), Nootdorp, The Netherlands

Onno Kuik
IVM (Institute for Environmental Studies), Amsterdam, The Netherlands

Manuel Lago
Scottish Agricultural College, Edinburgh, Scotland

Michael MacLeod
Scottish Agricultural College, Edinburgh, Scotland

Erika Meynaerts
VITO, Boeretang, Belgium

Dominic Moran
Scottish Agricultural College, Edinburgh, Scotland

Richard D. Morgenstern
Resources for the Future, Washington DC, USA

Robin Vanner
Policy Studies Institute, London, England

Andrew Venn
Policy Studies Institute, London, England

Peter Vercaemst
VITO, Boeretang, Belgium

Preface and acknowledgements

Environmental regulation is an area of considerable debate. Protests are frequently made that 'red tape' (a pejorative term derived from the tape used to hold together English legal documents) is placing an undue burden on business. These are countered with claims that regulation, far from being a drag on the economy, can stimulate innovation and help the market function more efficiently.

One of the areas of contention is the accuracy of regulatory cost estimates: do the predicted costs used to develop and implement policy turn out to be correct? A range of theories have been proposed to explain why costs will tend to be overestimated or underestimated. While the arguments concerning regulatory costs are interesting from a theoretical perspective, they are also central to the practical process of implementing regulation. Identifying the optimum level of regulatory intervention requires an understanding of the costs and benefits. Inaccurate assessment of the costs (or benefits) can lead to too much or too little regulation, which in turn can hinder economic growth, deplete the natural resource base and impact on human health.

In recognition of the importance of cost estimation, several studies have recently been commissioned by the UK Department for Environment, Food and Rural Affairs (Defra) and the European Commission's Environment Directorate. This book draws together the findings of these studies with the wider evidence. It should be of interest to several groups. Firstly, for those with an academic interest in the economics of environmental regulation, there is a comprehensive review of the literature, detailed analyses of specific sectors and a discussion of the role of innovation. Secondly, it is hoped that the practical suggestions for improving the accuracy of regulatory cost estimates will be of interest to economists grappling with regulatory and other impact assessments. Finally, the rationale for regulation is outlined in the belief that a knowledge of the ideas that underpin regulation will help non-economists (for example from regulated industries and non-governmental organisations) to engage in the wider debate about environmental regulation.

The authors would like to acknowledge the support of the UK Department for Environment, Food and Rural Affairs, which funded one of the research projects on which this book is based (*Comparing the ex ante and ex post costs of complying with regulatory changes* (EPES 0405–19)). Original text © Defra, 2006.

The authors would also like to acknowledge DG Environment, the Environment Directorate-General of the European Commission, for permission to draw on the results of the project *Ex post estimates of costs to business of EU environmental policies.* Some of the content of this book is based on and adapted from the following reports and case studies from this project, which are published on the European Communities' Europa website.

1. *Ex post* estimates of costs to business of EU environmental policies: report of workshop at the European Commission, 10 October 2005.
2. *Ex post* estimates of costs to business of EU environmental policies: a case study looking at ozone depleting substances, final draft: 28 November 2005.
3. Costs of compliance case study: Packaging & Packaging Waste Directive 94/62/EC. Final report submitted by GHK, June 2006.
4. Literature review on *ex post* assessment of costs to business of environmental policies and legislation, final version, September 2005.
5. *Ex post* estimates of costs to business of EU environmental legislation. Final report, 2006.

Original texts © European Communities, 2005/2006.

We are grateful to the following for permission to reproduce copyright material from other sources:

The Carbon Trust (Figure 15.1)
The Institute for Applied Systems Analysis (Figure 15.3).

We would like to thank the Scottish Agricultural College, the Policy Studies Institute and the Scottish Government Rural and Environment Research and Analysis Directorate for supporting the writing of this book. We would also like to thank the referees for their helpful comments on the draft manuscript and the staff at Edward Elgar for their help throughout.

PART I

Rationale and overview

1. Introduction

Paul Ekins, Michael MacLeod and Dominic Moran

Government regulation is an important fact of economic life in all developed economies. It has become more pervasive as economies have become more complex, as technologies have become more powerful and potentially hazardous, and as consumer expectations of product and environmental safety and quality have increased.

Regulations are, of course, supposed to deliver benefits to society at large. They also usually impose costs on those who are regulated and their administration results in further social costs. If the regulations are justified, then their social benefits will exceed their costs, but even where this is the case it will always be desirable to keep regulatory costs as low as possible, consistent with the desired social benefits being achieved.

Given that many environmental effects are not taken account of by markets, the task of government is to achieve socially desirable levels of environmental quality and to moderate harmful development patterns with appropriate interventions, including regulations that set standards and compliance rules. There is a range of regulatory levers that the government can use to deliver sustainable growth. Environmental policy is an evolving area of policy with a tendency to look for market-based solutions rather than traditional standard-setting regulations, which can be less flexible and more costly.[1] The challenge is to identify the right amount of regulatory intervention. Too much, and growth and innovation can be hindered. Too little, and growth can be bought at the expense of the natural resource base including human health and well being.

In theory the right amount of regulation balances the marginal costs and benefits to determine an optimal level of intervention. The practice of calculating costs and benefits to identify this optimal level is more challenging. Government can at best make a reasonable approximation of this theoretical optimum. But in the strictest sense there is always likely to be too much or too little regulation. This fact, and the fact that any social optimum is essentially unobservable, leads to claims of disproportionate cost being borne by the various affected parties. For example, the study of regulation in the US, EU,

Australia and New Zealand by Chittenden *et al.* (2002) suggests that small businesses bear a disproportionate share of the costs of regulation.

The importance of identifying the optimal level of intervention, and hence of predicting costs accurately, is heightened by the present scale of regulation and the rate at which it has increased since the 1960s. Dudley and Warren (2004, p 1) used 'the expenditures of federal regulatory agencies . . . as a barometer of regulatory activity'. Their figures indicate that federal regulatory spending in the US (measured in year 2000 Dollars) increased from \$2.5bn per annum in 1960 to \$37bn per annum in 2003. Note that this more than ten-fold increase is in inflation-adjusted terms. Spending by the environmental agencies was (in 2003) the second largest component of this (after Homeland Security) at \$5.8bn. The cost of environmental protection to the US overall has been estimated to be in excess of \$150bn per annum, representing about 2 per cent of GDP (Morgenstern *et al.* 1998). The total cost of all regulation (not just environmental regulation) has been estimated to be 10–12 per cent of GDP in the USA and the Netherlands, and is thought to be about the same in the UK (Better Regulation Task Force 2005). However, regulatory costs are difficult to determine accurately; as the OECD noted (1997: quoted in Better Regulation Task Force 2005, p 12), 'many governments have no idea how much of their national wealth they are spending through regulation'.

In response to concerns about regulatory burden (often characterised as 'red tape'), many countries now require some kind of impact assessment when new policies are being drawn up. A new system of Impact Assessment (IA) was introduced in the European Union (EU) in 2002 (EC 2002). In the UK, government departments are required to undertake an Impact Assessment (prior to 2007 these were called Regulatory Impact Assessments – RIAs) when introducing any policy change that places a burden on businesses, charities, the voluntary sector or individuals.[2] Part of this assessment involves the appraisal of the costs (and benefits) associated with complying with all the available options as well as the wider economic costs.

The calculation and scale of regulatory costs comprise the subject matter of this book, and in particular the comparison of calculations of regulatory costs before the regulations have been introduced (called *ex ante* calculations) with those after their introduction and implementation (called *ex post* calculations). The chapters in this book explore in detail how these costs are calculated, how *ex post* and *ex ante* calculations seem to be related, and why this might be.

Evidence from a recent policy evaluation commissioned by the UK Department for the Environment, Food and Rural Affairs (Defra) (Watkiss *et al.* 2004) suggested that in one case, the compliance costs, when assessed *ex post*, were lower than the *ex ante* assessment made beforehand. It is unclear whether this outcome is unusual or typical for regulatory changes introduced across Defra's policy areas. In order to shed more light on the validity of RIA cost estimates and identify ways of improving their accuracy, Defra decided to commission a study comparing the *ex ante* and *ex post* costs of complying with regulatory changes.

This book draws on the case studies undertaken during the Defra study – along with the accompanying analysis – and on the results of two other projects commissioned at the European level. The seven Defra case studies, five of which are summarised in the chapters that follow, concerned: the packaging regulations for hazardous substances; the UK Air Quality Strategy (Chapters 4 and 5); regulations to control major hazards (Chapter 8); groundwater regulations (Chapter 12); regulations on the welfare of farmed animals (Chapter 13); food safety regulations (Chapter 14); and meat handling regulations. The final report of the Defra project, the main conclusions of which are included in Chapters 3 and 16, is referenced here as MacLeod *et al.* (2006).

At about the same time as the Defra study, DG Environment of the European Commission commissioned a consortium of European institutes to investigate the same topic through a literature review and six case studies, five of which are summarised in the chapters which follow: regulation of car emissions from road transport in the Netherlands (Chapter 6); the Large Combustion Plants Directive (Chapter 7); the Integrated Pollution Prevention and Control Directive (Chapter 9); the Montreal Protocol and the EU regulations on ozone depleting substances (Chapter 10); the Nitrates Directive (Chapter 11); and the Directive on Packaging and Packaging Waste. The final report of this European project, the main conclusions of which are also included in Chapters 3 and 16, is referenced here as Oosterhuis (2006a).

Clearly the choice of case studies was an important element of the projects. For the Defra project, a long list of potential case studies was generated after undertaking a literature review and consulting with experts and policy makers. A range of selection criteria was then used to create a provisional short list of suitable case studies. The basic criteria were that: a) there was a robust RIA document containing detailed *ex ante* cost estimates; b) a sufficient amount of time had elapsed for the main body of each regulation to be implemented; and c) there was some form of *ex post* compliance costing, preferably estimated or compiled by an independent analyst. In fact, a lack of rigorous *ex post* evaluations meant that some *ex post* data had to be collected as part of the project. In the case of the project for DG Environment, the choice of case studies was made following discussions with experts in the European Commission, and focused on six important pieces of EU environmental legislation.

As will be seen, a consistent theme that emerges from the case studies is that a major cause of uncertainty in the *ex ante* estimation of regulatory costs is the role to be played by innovation in meeting new regulations. It is to be expected that the more innovation that the regulations bring about, the less the cost of meeting them will be, but this is very difficult to judge in advance for at least two reasons. First, innovation is inherently unpredictable, so that it is uncertain whether it will take place and what its economic implications will be. Second, it is not known with any assurance what kind of regulations (or other policy instruments) are most likely to stimulate an innovatory response. A synthesis paper from the project formed the basis of a workshop at the European Commission in June 2006 (Ekins and Venn 2006), and also provides the basis for Chapter 15. The final report from the project (Oosterhuis 2006b) was published in November 2006.

This book therefore draws on a rich empirical base of varied case studies, with associated analysis which is both recent and not very well known. Together the projects underlying the book added significantly to the understanding of regulatory costs, why calculations of them differed before and after the event, and how they could be reduced. This book pulls together the insights from these projects into a single integrated narrative for the first time. The next chapter gives the theoretical basis and rationale for regulation. Chapter 3 draws together the insights and conclusions from the wider evidence base on regulatory costs. The case studies then follow. The extended Chapter 15 presents the results and case study summaries of the project on innovation dynamics, and Chapter 16 concludes. It is the editors' hope that this book will both strengthen the case for appropriate regulation and help policy makers, regulators and those who are regulated to understand how the costs of regulation may both be calculated before and after the event, and kept to a minimum.

NOTES

1. Economically inefficient, which means that the overall costs are not minimised irrespective of who bears them.
2. See: www.berr.gov.uk/employment/research-evaluation/ria/index.html, accessd 22 April 2008.

REFERENCES

Better Regulation Task Force (2005) *Regulation: Less is More*. London: Cabinet Office.

Chittenden, F., Kauser, S. and Poutziouris, P. (2002) *Regulatory Burdens of Small Business: A Literature Review.* London: Small Business Service (available at: www.berr.gov.uk/files/file38324.pdf, accessed 5 April 2008).

Dudley, S. and Warren, M. (2004) *Regulators' Budget Continues to Rise: An Analysis of the U.S. Budget for Fiscal Years 2004 and 2005.* Arlington, VA/St Louis, MO: Mercatus Center/Murray Weidenbaum Center on the Economy, Government, and Public Policy (available at: http://mercatus.org/repository/docLib/MC_RSP_RA-BudgetContinuestoRise_ 040716.pdf, accessed 5 April 2008).

EC (European Commission) (2002) *Communication from the Commission on Impact Assessment,* COM(2002) 276 final. Brussels: European Commission (available at: http://eur-lex.europa.eu/LexUriServ/LexUriServ.do?uri=COM:2002:0276:FIN:EN:PDF, accessed 5 April 2008).

Ekins, P. and Venn, A. (2006) *Assessing Innovation Dynamics Induced by Environmental Policy,* report of workshop at the European Commission on 21 June (available at: http://ec.europa.eu/environment/enveco/pdf/workshop_report.pdf, accessed 5 April 2008). See http://ec.europa.eu/environment/enveco/activities.htm for documents from the project.

MacLeod, M., Moran, D., Aresti, M.L., Harrington, W. and Morgenstern, R. (2006) *Comparing the Ex Ante and Ex Post Costs of Complying with Regulatory Changes: Final Report to DEFRA, contract number EPES 0405-19* (available at: http://www.defra.gov.uk/science/project_data/DocumentLibrary/SD14011/SD1 4011_3366_FRP.pdf, accessed 5 April 2008).

Morgenstern, R.D., Pfizer, W.A. and Shih, J.-S. (1998) *The Cost of Environmental Protection,* Discussion Paper 98-36, Washington: Resources for the Future.

Oosterhuis, F. (ed.) (2006a) *Ex-post Estimates of Costs to Business of EU Environmental Legislation: Final Report to DG Environment* (available at: http://ec.europa.eu/environment/enveco/ex_post/pdf/costs.pdf, accessed 5 August 2008).

Oosterhuis, F. (ed.) (2006b) *Innovation Dynamics Induced by Environmental Policy: Final report to DG Environment,* IVM Report E-07/05 (available at: http://ec.europa.eu/environment/enveco/policy/pdf/2007_final_report_conclusions.pdf, accessed 5 April 2008).

Watkiss, P., Baggot, S., Bush, T., Cross, S., Goodwin, J., Holland, M., Hurley, F., Hunt, A., Jones, G., Kollamthodi, S., Murells, T., Stedman, J. and Vincent, K. (2004) *An Evaluation of the Air Quality Strategy: Final Report to Defra, December 2004.* Didcot: AEA Technology.

2. The origins and appraisal of regulation

Michael MacLeod, Dominic Moran, Salman Hussain and Kev Bevan

This chapter introduces the concept of regulation, the reasons why it exists and the many forms that it can take. This is followed by an examination of the methodologies used by government to assess the impact of regulation and discussion of the debates surrounding regulation and its appraisal.

2.1 WHAT IS REGULATION AND WHY DO WE HAVE IT?

In order to understand why society has and indeed needs regulation, we first need to step back and examine the context – economic agents acting in a market. By 'economic agents', we are referring to both consumers and producers of goods and services. The need for intervention arises because the 'best' course of action for the private agent might not coincide with what is 'best' for society.

The conventional economic assumption about firm behaviour is that firms attempt to maximise profits. They weigh up the (expected) private costs and benefits of different alternative courses of action. This appraisal sometimes does not take into account the impacts on other agents in society, that is, the social costs and benefits.

Take as an example emissions of sulphur dioxide. If left unregulated, the private profit-maximising firm would simply use the cheapest available disposal method, that is, direct untreated emissions to air, with no private expenditure on reducing these emissions. In economic terms, such an unregulated state is a type of market failure – in this case an externality – in that the costs of this pollution are borne by other agents in society in the form of acid rain. Without regulatory intervention, there is a chronic over-supply of this negative externality – the social cost is not internalised into the private cost-benefit appraisal of the polluting firm. Society would be better off were this polluter forced to internalise this pollution externality, and that is in essence what the sulphur-trading programme across US power-generating utilities is all about.

In a similar vein, there can be positive externalities. These occur if the actions of some private agent lead to a positive change in the wellbeing of others but this private individual is not compensated for this social benefit. Take by way of example the case of immunisation for polio. When someone is immunised, that person not only reduces his or her chance of suffering the disease (the private benefit) but also reduces the chances of other non-immunised people catching polio (the social benefit). The greater the percentage of the population that is immunised, the lower is the chance of an epidemic. Left to the unregulated free market, there would be less immunisation than would be socially optimal. This is why immunisation programmes are either free or heavily subsidised in many countries. This is a legitimate form of regulatory intervention in that it addresses a type of market failure.

A second instance of market failure is anti-competitive behaviour. If a firm can earn substantial private profits by reducing competition – by acting as a monopoly – then it has an incentive to do so. The consequences of this can be higher prices to consumers and thus reduced social welfare, and again the regulator intervenes in such cases to protect the public interest. Strongly enforced anti-trust regulation is thus a necessary form of regulatory intervention, as it is set up to protect the interests of the consumer.

There are of course other forms of regulatory intervention that are discussed in this book, but there is a fundamental principle that underpins each and every form of intervention: if the market is functioning properly, leave well alone. Regulation that is well-conceived, well-designed and well-implemented is clearly *not* about simply adding bureacratic 'red tape' for the sake of it. Throughout this text we will sometimes be discussing instances where regulation is in fact poorly thought out, but we must not lose sight of the fact that regulation is required, as unfettered market operation can and does lead at times to outcomes that society does not want. Table 2.1 outlines some recent instances where regulatory intervention in the market has been required (or at least considered) to address different types of market failure.

The responses set out in Table 2.1 are, in the broadest sense, all forms of regulation, a term that can take a number of meanings. A straightforward definition is given in Bannock *et al.* (2003, p 329): 'The supervision and control of the economic activities of private enterprise by government in the interest of economic efficiency, fairness, health and safety'. In practice, this elegant definition covers a wide range of government interventions. The overall approaches to regulation, and some of the specific interventions

Table 2.1   Examples of regulatory responses to problems

Problem	Cause	Response
CO_2 emissions from power stations	*Negative externality*: environmental and social cost of the effects of CO_2 emitted not fully reflected in the price of electricity	EU Emissions Trading Scheme
Maintaining high value farmed ecosystems	*Positive externality*: the value of the biodiversity gain due to grazing is not received by the farmer	Payments to farmers in Natura 2000 sites (EU protected areas) for carrying out agreed actions
Traders concealing the condition of used vehicles	*Informational failure*: the purchaser has limited information on the condition (and hence value) of the vehicle prior to purchase	Provision of the Citizens' Advice Bureau UK Sale of Goods Act 1979
Large volume grocery retailers (allegedly) exploiting suppliers	Concentration of market power leading to a *lack of competition*, and depressed prices	The UK Competition Commission's 2006 Inquiry into the operation of the groceries market

that can be employed are shown in Table 2.2. This Table illustrates the complexity of the decisions facing policy makers, who have to weigh up alternative options – with all their potential advantages and disadvantages – and make some appraisal of what unintended consequences might arise.

Table 2.3 gives some examples of the approaches that have been taken in addressing two issues in the UK: (a) the reduction of diffuse aquatic pollution from agricultural sources, and (b) the reduction of the social costs arising from the consumption of alcohol. In both cases a wide range of regulatory options has been deployed, which perhaps is unsurprising given the scale and complexity of these issues. However, it should be borne in mind that the number of initiatives is not necessarily a good measure of the (political) commitment to solving a problem, or the effectiveness of the interventions.

Even if the aggregate expenditure on a particular issue is known, low cost does not automatically equate to 'the most economically desirable outcome'. An economic appraisal balances the costs and benefits of any course of action at what is termed the 'margin'. Marginal analysis is

Table 2.2 Summary of the Better Regulation Task Forces Guidance on Alternatives to Regulation

	No intervention	Information and education	Self-regulation	Incentive-based structures	Classic regulation and its variants
Types of intervention		• Government-provided information • Labelling schemes • Reporting and disclosure (voluntary or mandatory) • Naming and shaming	• Codes of practice • Co-regulation (codes with Government involvement)	• Creating markets; tradeable permits; quotas • Price caps; targets • Taxes • Rewards: tax credits; subsidies; awards	• This covers a wide range of statutory measures, often backed up with monitoring, enforcement and sanctions, e.g. prohibiting activities, prior permissions, technical/quality standards etc.
Advantages		• Allow individuals and business to make informed decisions • Leave decisions to individuals and managers • Improve the working of the market • A less intrusive form of regulation	• Offer a cheaper alternative to classic regulation • More adaptable to change in society • Exclude the courts (thus, cheaper for society)	Many, in theory, e.g.: • Increase efficiency and lower costs; reduce prices for consumers • More flexible than classic regulation • Simulate the virtues of the market where a natural monopoly exists	• Provide a level playing field; clarity • The principal way of implementing an EU Directive • Act as a visible sign that Government is 'doing something' about a problem

Table 2.2 (continued)

No intervention	Information and education	Self-regulation	Incentive-based structures	Classic regulation and its variants
Disadvantages	• No better than classic regulation – requiring the provision of information can be costly and bureaucratic • A barrier to entry • Too much of a good thing – information overload	• Toothless, especially if the relevant trade association is weak, or if large companies dominate • Anti-competitive, providing a barrier to entry for smaller firms	Many, in theory, e.g.: • Upheaval to businesses • Tricky to set up, disputes about initial allocations • Ineffective in preventing harm if the value of the activity is worth more than the tax	• Costly and bureaucratic • Unenforceable • A burden, especially on small businesses • Inflexible, difficult or slow to change • Unintended consequences

Source: Better Regulation Task Force (2004).

Table 2.3   Examples of regulatory measures

INCREASING LEVEL OF INTERVENTION ▬ ▬ ➤

	Do nothing	Inform and educate	Self-regulation	Incentive-based structures	Classic regulation and its variants
Example 1: Reducing diffuse pollution from UK farming		• Educational campaigns in catchment planning • EA Catchment Sensitive Farming Initiative • PEPFAA Code	• The Voluntary Initiative	• Payments for meeting the requirements of the CAP, i.e. keeping land in GAEC	• General Binding Rules and provisions for the registration and licensing of farms within the Controlled Activities Regulations 2005
Example 2: Regulating alcohol consumption in the UK		• Poster and TV adverts, e.g. seasonal drink-driving campaigns	• The Portman Group's Code of Practice	• Duty on alcohol, e.g. for spirits £19.56 duty was payable per litre of pure alcohol from 1999–2007	• Driving under the influence of alcohol is banned under the Road Traffic Act 1991 • The Licensing Acts require possession of a licence to sell alcohol

Notes: EA: Environment Agency; CAP: Common Agricultural Policy; GAEC: Good Agricultural and Environmental Condition; PEPFAA: Preventing Environmental Pollution From Agricultural Activities.

concerned with how much extra cost or benefit is associated with a particular choice. Thus, in an appraisal of economic efficiency the marginal cost of (say) a drink-driving advertising campaign in the media would be set against an estimate of the reduction in accidents that this campaign would bring about. In turn, an economist would measure the total value of these avoided accidents in monetary terms in order to make a like-for-like comparison. These costs would include not only the repair costs for the vehicles involved but also any costs of illness or mortality.[1]

Another economic approach is cost-effectiveness analysis. Whereas efficiency is concerned with analysing costs and benefits at the margin, cost-effectiveness analysis only looks at the costs of different regulatory interventions that can contribute to achieving a given policy goal. Taking the example of drink-driving again, the state might decide that it wants to reduce road deaths involving drink-drivers by 500 deaths per year. The alternative means of achieving this goal are set out in Table 2.3. The analysis would still be at the margin. In this case, we might ask 'what is the estimated reduction in drink-driving road deaths that arises from spending £100 000 on education campaigns versus spending this same sum on extra resourcing for the police to monitor and enforce the Road Traffic Act 1991?' A general economic rule-of-thumb is that more and more policing (or campaigning) realises less and less marginal benefit. Cost-effectiveness analysis takes this into account and is concerned with finding the least-cost solution to achieving a pre-ascribed benefit (in this case reduced road deaths) by carrying out analysis at the margin.

Regulation is not of course only driven by such economic arguments. It is often conditioned by what is palatable to the stakeholders that are affected by the regulation. Less interventionist approaches such as providing information and advice are often politically palatable as, by seeking to correct informational failures and/or encourage more socially desirable behaviour, they raise fewer concerns about civil liberties and 'red tape'. With respect to diffuse pollution in Scotland, it has been argued (D' Arcy *et al.* 2006, p 199) that 'Promotion of best practice will continue to be the standard means of diffuse pollution control from rural areas. However, the expense of educational initiatives is the hidden cost of light touch regulation'. The latter point is an important one: even low intervention regulation has a cost and, because of the way it is funded, may not be consistent with the polluter pays principle.[2] It could be argued that in the case of diffuse pollution, the emphasis on the promotion of best practice is due to the logistical difficulties of enforcement and the political unattractiveness of imposing further costs on the struggling farming industry.

While self-regulation may be a desirable option, it is better suited to some issues and industries than others. Self-regulation of diffuse pollution raises problems because of the nature of the issues (attributing pollutant loads to specific polluters is difficult) and of the structure of the industry, which consists of many small, independent firms. While self-regulation may present challenges, these are not necessarily insurmountable. The Voluntary Initiative is an example of how an industry (in this case farming) can undertake self-regulation (with associated costs) in the face of the threat of statutory controls. In order to avoid a pesticides tax, the UK industry set up the Voluntary Initiative in 2001. Its aim is to reduce the impact of pesticides, particularly on water quality and biodiversity, through a programme of research, training, communication and stewardship. The annual cost of the scheme is estimated to be around £13m, compared to a pesticides tax which could have cost £125m per year, so there is a strong financial incentive to make self-regulation work. Self-regulation is less problematic in industries that have greater concentration and vertical integration, such as the drinks industry, and therefore more scope for co-ordinated action, monitoring and enforcement. For example, most firms in the drinks industry have signed up to the Portman Group Code of Practice, a code devised and implemented by the industry, which sets and enforces standards on matters such as alcohol advertising and promotion.

Incentive-based structures, such as markets, taxes and subsidies, should in principle provide more economically efficient solutions by setting out targets (as opposed to processes), thereby providing scope for innovation. However they are difficult to set up, and require careful consideration of initial allocations, tax and subsidy levels and so on. Despite these difficulties, there has been increasing use of incentive-based structures in recent years. Environmental regulation in particular is an evolving area of policy with a tendency to look for incentive-based structures rather than traditional command-and-control regulations. Recent examples include the European Union Greenhouse Gas Emission Trading Scheme and the US Environmental Protection Agency's Water Quality Trading Policy.

Classic (or command-and-control) regulation refers to the myriad statutory measures (for example, prohibiting actions or requiring prior permissions such as licensing) that are used to control activities. They have key advantages, for example, they provide a level playing field and act as a visible sign that Government is 'doing something' about a problem. However, they also tend to be costly, bureaucratic and inflexible, and can lead to unintended consequences. Despite these shortcomings, it has been argued that classic regulation is the default position, particularly when risk to the public is involved: 'Contradictory pressures on those in the regulation business – they are criticised both for intervening and failing to act – have served to emphasise classic regulation as the default response' (Better Regulation Commission 2006, p 3).

2.2   THE IMPACT OF REGULATION

Government has the responsibility for delivering sustainable growth. This means that it must determine appropriate standards and compliance rules for (say) 'acceptable' levels of environmental quality or 'moderately' harmful development patterns. The ultimate objective is that growth stays within ecological limits.

Government can use a variety of regulatory approaches in its efforts to deliver sustainable growth (see Table 2.2). However, the use of these is often cri-ticised by industry, which perceives a growing regulatory burden that is unnecessary and bureaucratic, and undermines their competitiveness. For example, in its submission to the Scottish Parliament's Inquiry into the Transposition and Implementation of European Directives, the Federation of Small Businesses Scotland (FSBS) commented that 'the feeling remains amongst small businesses that regulations are implemented in a more rigor-ous manner in the UK than elsewhere in the EU' (Scottish Parliament 2006). However, the same sentence also stated: 'We cannot offer any specific exam-ples of regulations being implemented more onerously in Scotland than in England and Wales . . . let alone elsewhere in the UK or Europe'. The FSBS's position – of believing that over-implementation occurs without being able to provide any conclusive evidence to support its claim – is common. Nevertheless, the perception that there is an unfair regulatory burden has led to considerable lobbying in certain industries. For example, there is an ongoing debate regarding the influence that regulation – and EU-derived legislation in particular – has on the performance of Scottish agriculture (see Box 2A).

In a recent report (Ambler *et al.* 2005), the British Chamber of Commerce criticised regulation as a means of covert taxation. They argued that there is a 'consistent transfer of financial responsibility for govern-ment policies that benefit the Exchequer and the taxpayer at the expense of business' (Ambler *et al.* 2005, p 19) and used the Money Laundering Regulations 2003 to illustrate their argument. However, to dismiss all redis-tribution of costs to business as taxation is a simplification. In certain cir-cumstances, such changes may reflect a move towards a more equitable distribution of costs and benefits. For example, it could be argued that the Air Quality Strategy represents an attempt to shift the costs of air pollu-tion from public health and the environment to those that produce the pol-lution, that is, the road transport sector and the electricity supply industry.

Not all regulation is resisted by business. Some suggest that regulation stimulates innovation, although the relationship between regulation, inno-vation and competitiveness is difficult to disentangle (see Example 2B and Chapter 15). Specific measures may be supported because they help the industry as a whole or provide a strategic advantage to some businesses.

BOX 2.1   EXAMPLE 2A: THE REGULATORY BURDEN ON BRITISH FARMING – RHETORIC OR REALITY?

British farming is one of the sectors where the debate about the appropriate level of regulation has been most vigorous. Claims such as 'Red tape may be final straw for Scots farming' (Buglass 2007) may be overheated, but they indicate that the current level of regulation is (at least perceived to be) problematic. The National Farmers' Union of Scotland (NFUS) has led the call for a new regulatory model which puts 'common sense back at the heart of the government's approach to European regulation' (National Farmers' Union of Scotland 2006). Regulation appears to be viewed as anything from an unwelcome intrusion to part of a Government-led anti-rural agenda.

Over-implementation

It is often suggested that the UK administrations tend to 'gold plate' legislation, that is, they deliberately make regulations more rigorous (and hence costly) than they need to be. The NFUS has argued that 'There is a strong perception, and evidence, that European Directives are implemented more strictly in the UK than elsewhere in the EU' (Scottish Parliament 2006). In fact gold plating is only one of the ways in which governments can over-implement regulation. It can also result from 'double banking' (that is, policy overlap caused by a failure to streamline existing legislation) and from over-zealous enforcement, or 'regulatory creep' (Davidson 2006, p3). The term 'over-implementation' implies a comparison between the present level of regulation and some benchmark. Common benchmarks are (a) the level of regulation in competitor countries and (b) the minimum required by EU law. While these may provide useful comparisons, it should not be assumed that a regulation is necessarily inappropriate simply because it exceeds the legal minimum or the level in other countries. For example, the greater commitment to implementing the Drinking Water Directive in Scotland may have arisen quite properly in response to local circumstances, for example, a greater proportion of people on private supplies in parts of Scotland and the greater incidence of E coli 0157. As Davidson (2006, p1) notes 'It is sometimes beneficial for the UK economy to set or maintain regulatory standards which exceed the minimum requirements of European legislation'. A

more useful concept may be that of 'inappropriate over-implementation', where the costs of implementing a regulation are significantly higher than the benefits accruing from it.

Claims of over-implementation are not restricted to the farming
industry. A study commissioned by the Federation of Small
Businesses Scotland (Schaefer and Young 2006) claimed to have
evidence of gold plating; however, its findings are rendered trivial by
flawed methodology and selective interpretation of evidence.
Blackburn and Hart (2002) recognised that such business surveys
are often based on biased samples. Their survey, based on a more
representative sample of small businesses, found that the biggest
constraints on business performance facing small firms were 'competition, followed by labour market factors and then government
legislation or regulations' (Blackburn and Hart 2002, p60). One-third
of respondents cited regulation as a constraint and one in six cited
it as the main constraint.

In response to claims that regulation is damaging business, the
Trades Union Congress (TUC) (2003, p1) has argued that 'anti-red
tape rhetoric of this kind is essentially bogus' given that 'the international evidence is very persuasive and shows that the UK still
has a very lightly regulated labour market with low levels of business taxation'. They draw the conclusion that 'employers' preju-
dices are more influential in shaping their responses than a sober
assessment of the real business impact' (TUC 2003, p6). Many
other countries have significantly less stringent laws in areas such
as pollution, working conditions or animal welfare (see for example
Metcalfe 2000). These are highlighted as examples of an 'uneven
playing field' that needs to be levelled. However, truly evening out
the playing field could also involve removing farm subsidies and/or
lowering agricultural wages below the current legal minimum as
part of a 'race to the bottom'. The Scottish Trades Union Congress
has argued that such a strategy could put the UK at a disadvantage as it would force firms to compete on cost rather than innovation (Scottish Parliament 2006).

While the regulatory regime in the UK imposes costs on business,
these should be balanced against the significant benefits it provides
to business by, for example: strengthening the competition regime;
protecting consumers; encouraging people to take paid employment; and reducing the costs of accidents and ill health (Keter 2004,
p43). A detailed evaluation of these costs and benefits is complex;
however, the World Bank ranks countries in terms of how conducive
they are to doing in business in their *Doing Business: Economy*

Rankings (World Bank 2007b). The fact that the UK ranks sixth best out of 175 suggests that the regulatory regime may not be as great a barrier to business success as some claim.

Will the Cost of Regulation Put Many Farmers out of Business?

The Department for the Environment, Farming and Rural Affairs (Defra) has attempted to quantify the cumulative impact of forthcoming regulation on farming in England. Its research calculated that the burden 'would equate to a total increase in annual production costs of about 1.5% for the average farm over the next decade' (Defra 2006 p2). The study concluded that 'Regulatory effects are barely discernible from the baseline trend (in costs) and are minimal when compared with potential exchange rate effects' (Defra 2006 p3). However, it should be noted that while the overall costs for the industry appeared modest, sectors such as pigs and poultry were expected to face significant cost increases.

These findings, while interesting, should be treated with some caution, as estimating the costs of new regulations is difficult and therefore subject to considerable uncertainty. In addition, some key costs, such as the time taken to familiarise oneself with new regulations, are easily underestimated. It should also be borne in mind that the financial cost of regulation is only one of its impacts. Part of the problem is that there seems to be a high 'business irritation' factor associated with the regulation of farming. The Agricultural Development and Advisory Service (ADAS 2005) found that 75 per cent of farmers agreed with the statement that 'The main impact of regulations is irritation and hassle rather than financial'.

Conclusions

1. Farmers and their representatives complain that the competitiveness of UK farming is under threat from a growing regulatory burden. Their protests are echoed by other sectors of industry.
2. The evidence indicates that the cost to farmers of complying with regulations is in general small, and World Bank reports rank the UK as having a relatively benign regulatory environment for business.
3. Business irritation appears to be a more important impact of regulation than direct financial cost.

BOX 2.2   EXAMPLE 2B: REGULATION AND
              INNOVATION

Government is generally reluctant to regulate and most forms of industrial regulation are resisted or condemned for hindering economic performance. But the evidence of whether environmental regulation promotes or reduces international performance is sometimes contradictory. The picture on aggregate performance is obscured behind a range of counter claims that derive from anecdotal evidence at micro (firm) rather than macro (regional or country) levels. The true macro picture has yet to be proven.

Economic theory of profit maximisation is unambiguous about the impact of regulation. Firms that fail to maximise profits face bankruptcy. A firm should rationally and systematically appraise the private costs borne and the private benefits accrued across strategic options, and choose the option that maximises the private net benefit. Decisions pertaining to environmental performance are carried out in a similar fashion. Since firms are assumed to be at their 'efficiency frontiers', any regulation then imposes a cost to firms and therefore a cost to society. Thus, the comparative static analysis amounts to comparing these private costs with the social benefits of any regulatory intervention.

The Porter hypothesis (PH) challenges this assumption (Porter and van der Linde, 1995). The PH suggests that this is a 'static' model that fails to recognise that firms are not in reality perched on the edge of their efficiency frontiers but actually display gross inefficiencies in their decision making in the environmental domain. More stringent environmental legislation can then force firms to search for efficiency improvements. In so doing, the PH suggests that firms are likely to find options that are 'win-win' in nature, that is, not only does environmental performance improve, but also net profitability. Further, the PH suggests that firms that are subject to such stringent environmental legislation might then have a 'first mover advantage' in the development, and potential future sale, of environmental techniques, technologies and applications.

The PH is highly controversial and has been extensively tested and criticised. For instance, Palmer *et al.* (1995) cite data from the US Environmental Protection Agency register to show that the gross environmental spend exceeds the pollution offsets achieved by a significant factor. Hussain (2003) contends that firms might achieve these pollution offsets but that there are significant transactions costs which imply that firms' managers have less time to search for efficiency gains that are non-environmental. The implication is that there is no 'free lunch'.

One of the problems associated with testing the validity of the PH is that the environmental spend is generally a small proportion of total R&D expenditure and an even smaller segment of the profitability 'bottom line'. Thus studies have relied on case study appraisal that fails to capture the entirety of the effects of more stringent legislation.

If the costs of complying with environmental regulation put companies at a competitive disadvantage, one might expect those countries with less rigorous environmental regimes to gain market share by becoming 'pollution havens' as the compliance costs of their competitors increases. Goodstein and Hodges (1997) tested this hypothesis by studying the relationship between (environmental) regulatory burden and market share. They found that there was little evidence for the existence of pollution havens: on the contrary, 'industries facing higher environmental costs actually faced less intense import competition' (Goodstein and Hodges 1997, p13). This could be interpreted as evidence for the PH, or that regulation can help industries by creating import barriers. In contrast, Jenkins *et al.* (2002) have argued that the context-specific character of firms' responses to regulation makes it difficult to detect any regulation-competitiveness relationships at the aggregate level. To overcome this, they carried out detailed case studies of three industries: leather tanning, iron and steel production and the fertiliser industry. These studies found no evidence for the PH: 'none of the three industries studied here provides any significant examples of innovation offsets' (p305). Furthermore, the authors conclude: 'our case studies lead us to reject the view that environmental regulation does not affect competitiveness and the global distribution of industrial activity' (p312).

Ekins and Venn (2006) also carried out detailed analyses of individual sectors in their examination of innovation induced by environmental policy. Of their five case studies, 'only one clear example emerges in favour of the Porter hypothesis' (p31): there is strong evidence that the hazardous chemicals legislation in Germany created a 'first mover advantage' for the chemical industry there. The evidence, discussed in detail in Chapter 15, would seem to suggest that while regulation can lead to innovation and competitive advantages in particular circumstances, it is by no means certain.

The Montreal Protocol is often cited as an example of a regulation that provided an opportunity for some firms, notably DuPont, to gain a competitive advantage. However, as the Stockholm Environment Institute (1999, p 36) notes: 'the situation can of course to be more precarious if benefits of regulation do not accrue to "loser" industries'. In addition, some counterarguments have been made in favour of regulation by workers' representatives. Britain's Trades Union Congress (TUC) has argued that antipathy towards regulation arises because its economic impacts are not fully understood or because it is a way to deflect attention from Government and management failures to improve productivity and competitiveness (Trades Union Congress 2003).

2.3   DEREGULATION AND REGULATORY IMPACT ASSESSMENT

Regardless of the rights and wrongs of the debate, the goal of reducing the burden of regulation on business, often characterised as an assault on 'red tape', is a recurrent theme amongst politicians. The EC's enterprise commissioner, Günter Verheugen, made a fairly typical declaration of intent shortly after taking up his new post:

> Cutting red tape shall be my trademark. Reducing red tape, removing unnecessary restrictions, screening the existing legislation – whether or not we need it, whether we can simplify it. We should not bring forward legislation without proper impact assessment. (Parker and Laitner 2004)

The political imperative to 'cut red tape' has found expression in the formation of a plethora of regulatory reform initiatives and associated strategies, guidelines and principles. These range from international initiatives, such as the OECD's *Guiding Principles for Regulatory Quality and Performance* (2005) and the EC's Action Plan *Simplifying and Improving The Regulatory Environment* (European Commission 2002) via national measures to local initiatives such as the UK's planned Local Better Regulation Office (LBRO). Two examples are given in Table 2.4.

These initiatives are part of what Froud *et al.* (1998) have called the 'Deregulation Initiative'. This can be traced back to the early 1980s, when President Reagan, in response to the increasing levels of regulation and the prevailing political climate in the USA, promised to reduce the burden of regulation on small business. In order to achieve this he passed Executive Order 12291, requiring Regulatory Impact Assessments (RIA) to be carried out on new regulations. Many countries have since adopted some form of RIA. However the character of these can vary from the cost-benefit analyses employed in the USA, with their emphasis on quantification, to the

Table 2.4   Examples of principles of good regulation

OECD Guiding Principles for Regulatory Quality and Performance (OECD 2005)	**The Five Principles of Good Regulation (Better Regulation Task Force 2005, p51)**
Good regulation should: (i) serve clearly identified policy goals, and be effective in achieving those goals; (ii) have a sound legal and empirical basis; (iii) produce benefits that justify costs, considering the distribution of effects across society and taking economic, environmental and social effects into account; (iv) minimise costs and market distortions; (v) promote innovation through market incentives and goal-based approaches; (vi) be clear, simple, and practical for users; (vii) be consistent with other regulations and policies; (viii) be compatible as far as possible with competition, trade and investment-facilitating principles at domestic and international levels.	*Proportionality:* Regulators should only intervene when necessary. Remedies should be appropriate to the risk posed and costs identified and minimised. *Accountability:* Regulators must be able to justify decisions and be subject to public scrutiny. *Consistency:* Government rules and standards must be joined up and implemented fairly. *Transparency:* Regulators should be open and keep regulations simple and user-friendly. *Targeting:* Regulation should be focused on the problem and minimise side effects.

'more impressionistic account of the expected costs and benefits of proposals' in the Swedish system (Froud *et al.* 1998, p 10). The OECD (2007) describes the RIA process as 'an information based analytical approach to assess probable costs, consequences, and side effects of planned policy instruments (laws, regulations etc). It can also be used to evaluate the real costs and consequences of policy instruments after they have been implemented'.

RIA has evolved over the past 20 years to become a more sophisticated tool for measuring the impact of regulation. Both the OECD and the World Bank noted the influence of the Dutch in this evolution. The World Bank has recently reviewed the Dutch government's 2003–07 Administrative Burdens Reduction Programme. The Programme was expected to reduce the cost of regulations on Dutch business by € 4 billion by 2007. Key to achieving this big reduction were: the targeted 25 per cent reduction in regulatory costs, a link between regulatory reforms and the budget cycle, and the establishment of ACTAL (the Dutch Advisory Board on Administrative Burden) as an independent watchdog on the reforms (World Bank, 2007a).

Other countries have drawn on the Dutch experience. The Standard Cost Model (SCM), developed in the Netherlands, has been particularly important. In 2003, several European countries, including the UK, formed the SCM Network.[3] The SCM measures the administrative cost of a regulation by breaking it down into informational obligations and activities in a systematic way, thereby enabling inter- and intra-country comparison. In the following section, the development of RIA in one country (the UK) is examined.

2.4   REGULATORY IMPACT ASSESSMENT IN THE UK

Concern about the red tape burden on business and the wider debate about the effects of Government intervention (driven by neo-liberal economic policies in the 1980s and 1990s) led to considerable support for deregulation in the UK. In August 1998 the Prime Minister announced that 'no proposal for regulation which has an impact on business, charities or voluntary bodies should be considered by Ministers without a regulatory impact assessment being carried out' (Regulatory Impact Unit 2003, p 1). RIAs were a development of the Compliance Cost Assessment system that was developed in the mid-1980s (see Froud *et al.* 1998). Chittenden *et al.* (2002) have interpreted this announcement as reflecting a change in emphasis within the Government from deregulation to better regulation. Initially RIAs were carried out for about 75 per cent of the regulations that, under UK law, should have an associated RIA. Coverage has increased significantly in the intervening period and by 2005 was reported to have reached about 95 per cent.[4] Between 1999 and 2003 an average of 183 RIAs were undertaken each year. During the period from 1 July 2003 to 30 June 2004 the departments that produced the most RIAs were the Department for Trade and Industry (DTI), the Department for Environment, Food and Rural Affairs (Defra), the Department of Transport and the Department of Health (see Table 2.5).

According to the UK Government: 'an RIA is a framework for analysis of the likely impacts of a policy change and the range of options for implementing it' (Better Regulation Executive 2007b), which should be applied to any form of regulation, including codes of practice and information campaigns. In principle, they should consider their scope as wide and should consider the potential economic, social and environmental impacts and the distribution of impacts, that is, which groups will be affected. Government guidance sets out the RIA structure (see Box 2.3). However, it

Table 2.5   *The number of RIAs produced by selected UK Government departments from 1 July 2003 – 30 June 2004*

Department	Number of RIAs	% of total RIAs produced
Dept of Trade and Industry	43	19.3
Dept for Environment, Food and Rural Affairs	33	14.8
Dept of Transport	32	14.3
Dept of Health	27	12.1
Other departments	88	39.5

Source: Ambler *et al.* (2005).

BOX 2.3   CABINET OFFICE GUIDANCE ON RIA STRUCTURE

1. Title of proposal
2. Purpose and intended effect
3. Consultation
4. Options
5. Costs and benefits
6. Small Firms Impact Test
7. Competition assessment
8. Enforcement, sanctions and monitoring
9. Implementation and delivery plan
10. Post-implementation review
11. Summary and recommendation
12. Declaration and publication

Source: Adapted from Better Regulation Executive (2007a).

---

is left to the discretion of the civil servants undertaking the RIA to decide on the precise contents and degree of analysis.

The summary and recommendation involves the responsible minister signing off the final RIA with the statement: 'I have read the Regulatory Impact Assessment and I am satisfied that the benefits justify the costs' (Cabinet Office, 2005). The signing off statement implies that an RIA is a full cost-benefit analysis (COBA). However, UK Regulatory Impact Assessments typically focus on the market costs of the measures. Medhurst (2005) identified three levels of assessment (see Table 2.6):

Table 2.6　Levels of analysis of costs and benefits

Level of assessment	Costs and benefits included	Example: Phasing out of organophosphate (OP) sheep dips
1. Partial equilibrium analysis	The market costs and benefits of regulation to the regulated firm	The financial costs and benefits borne directly by the regulatee, e.g.: • time spent learning about regulation • the cost of disposing of banned dips and of switching to more expensive alternatives • reduced sheep growth rates due to less effective dips
2. Full/general equilibrium analysis	The market costs and benefits to the regulated firm and the wider economy	Also includes the wider economic effects, e.g.: • reduced lamb production leading to reduced business for abbatoirs • lost revenue for OP manufacturers and increases for suppliers of alternatives
3. Social cost benefit analysis	The full social costs and benefits, i.e. the market costs and benefits (both to the regulated firm and economy-wide) plus the non-market costs and benefits of the regulation	Includes potential wider impacts such as: • improvements in human health • impacts in aquatic biodiversity, arising from changed dipping regime • animal welfare effects arising from changed dipping regimes and efficacy

1. Market costs (and benefits) to business (partial equilibrium analysis)
2. Level 1 plus market costs (and benefits) to the economy (full equilibrium analysis)
3. Levels 1 and 2 plus social (including environmental) costs and benefits.

Criticisms of UK Regulatory Impact Assessment

Despite the development of regulatory impact assessment, it has been argued that the costs of regulation tend to outweigh the benefits. The National Farmers' Union Scotland (see Example 2A) have complained that 'there is no apparent cost/benefit analysis of implementation plans. As a result there is a widespread presumption that regulatory measures are effectively revenue-raising measures, rather than genuine vehicles for delivering public benefit' (Scottish Parliament 2006). Clearly, the analyses undertaken in RIAs are perceived to be inadequate. There is evidence that some key EU policies (notably the Landfill Directive, the Bathing Water Directive and the Water Framework Directive) fail a cost-benefit test (Pearce 2004). However, the assessment of benefits is notoriously difficult and the underestimation of benefits is less likely to be challenged and corrected than the underestimation of costs to business.

Wilkes (2004) has argued that the present system of RIA systematically overestimates the (net) costs of regulation by failing to account fully for the wider economic benefits of environmental legislation. This raises the question of where RIAs should draw the boundaries of their analysis. The same policy can have different net costs depending on where the boundaries are drawn and which costs and benefits are included (see Wilkes 2004, pp 9–10). The Environmental Audit Committee (2005 p 22) has criticised the narrow scope of RIAs and their failure to take into account 'the huge positive role which regulation has played in delivering environmental and social improvements'. However, it is important to note that the resources for conducting RIAs are limited and that most RIAs are in some sense incomplete. That is, they offer a partial picture of the effects of a regulation (relative to a baseline) that cannot always account for wider social effects. They can generally only make rudimentary assumptions about changes through time.

Parker (2006) highlighted a number of areas in which the RIA process could be improved:

- Most of the regulatory burden on business comes from existing regulations. More effort should therefore be invested in assessing the actual impact of existing regulations in terms of their original goals.
- RIAs tend to focus on the quantitative effect of regulations. Suitable attention should also be given to measuring the qualitative impact.
- Risk assessment could be improved by examining alternatives to regulation more closely. Sensitivity analysis is also underused in quantifying the impact of regulations.
- The use and quality of RIAs varies across government departments, with the National Audit Office finding major deficiencies in the way some RIAs are completed.
- Few RIAs result in the decision to impose new regulations being overturned.

In a recent study, Jacobs (2007, p 115) found that Regulatory Impact Unit staff had the following broad concerns regarding RIAs: 'unclear objectives; lack of evidence to support conclusions; failure to consider alternatives;

weak monitoring and evaluation; and the need for an earlier introduction of RIA'. In April 2007, the Cabinet Office announced a new Impact Assessment process to replace RIA. Among the stated aims of the new process are: to increase transparency and clarity; to place more emphasis on post-implementation reviews; and to embed Impact Assessments from the earliest stage of policy making (Cabinet Office Press Office, 2007). If the new Impact Assessments meet the aspirations of the Cabinet Office, they will go some way to overcoming the criticisms of the RIA process, in particular the lack of post-implementation reviews.

In theory, reviews of RIAs were meant to be carried out in order that, amongst other things, consideration was given to 'whether the costs and benefits in the original RIA were correct' (Regulatory Impact Unit 2003, p 29). Pre-implementation estimates are termed *ex ante* evaluations. In addition there was meant to be 'systematic post-implementation reviews of major pieces of legislation' (Regulatory Impact Unit 2003 p 30). In practice, these guidelines were 'interpreted broadly'.[5] Reflecting this, Hampton (2004, p 20) recommended that 'there is a strong case for post-implementation reviews to be undertaken more systematically, not only to review the effectiveness of the regulation, but also to *test and strengthen the cost estimations made when regulations are proposed*' (our italics). This is what is termed *ex post* evaluation. Despite the general lack of reviews, there are some examples of regulations that have been the subject of detailed *ex post* evaluation, such as the Control of Major Accident Hazards (COMAH) Regulations 1999 (Risk Solutions 2005). In addition, there are occasional examples of industry carrying out *ex post* reviews (for example, British Coatings Federation Ltd, 2003). Notwithstanding the exceptions noted above, there are limited *ex post* cost data in the UK against which the validity of original estimates could be tested and the process of *ex ante* cost estimation in RIAs improved.

The lack of *ex post* data is important because one of the key criticisms of RIAs and impact assessment in general regards the (in)accuracy of the *ex ante* cost estimates. On the one hand, pro-regulation groups (such as, environmental NGOs, the environmental technology industry) often argue that *ex ante* estimates systematically overestimate the costs of implementing measures. This can happen because, for example, the estimates use data supplied by industry (which is based on conservative assumptions) or because they fail to account fully for the effects of regulation-induced innovation. On the other hand, business interests often argue that regulators have a vested interest in underestimating the cost of measures so that they can get their legislation passed more easily. They also argue that the opportunity cost of compliance is rarely taken into account. This is an important debate, as the type and amount of regulation passed depends in part on predictions of how much it will cost. Whatever the truth may be, this perception can contribute to general scepticism about the impartiality of appraisal in government decision making. The challenge is to estimate the costs accurately to enable the optimal level of regulatory intervention to be found.

The next chapter reviews existing studies in order to see if the accusations of systematic bias in *ex ante* cost estimates are supported by the evidence.

NOTES

1. Economists routinely have to grapple with the issue of valuing life itself. Clearly, all human life is in essence priceless, or to put it another way each life has infinite value. But if regulations in society were to be designed around an infinite value for human life then all regulation would be tied to minimising the chances of death. In such a worldview, there would for instance be no cars at all (and no alcohol for that matter), which is clearly untenable. Thus economists in cost-benefit analysis generally input a value for life which is the amount that insurance companies pay out in the event of accidental death.
2. The polluter pays principle originated in the OECD in the 1970s. Although it is a principle grounded in economic theory, it means what one would expect it to mean, that is, polluters ought to pay for the externality damage they impose on society. The economic argument is that this then gives firms a private incentive to reduce their pollution to socially desirable levels.
3. See www.administrative-burdens.com.
4. Personal communication from M. Barnes, Better Regulation Executive, Cabinet Office, London, 1 April 2005.
5. See www.administrative-burdens.com.

REFERENCES

ADAS (2005) *Study on the Impacts of Regulation on Agriculture: A Supporting Document for Partners for Success – a Farm Regulation and Charging Strategy.* London: Defra.

Ambler, T., Chittenden, F. and Hwang C. (2005) *Regulation: Another Form of Taxation? UK Regulatory Impact Assessment in 2003/04.* London: British Chamber of Commerce.

Bannock, G., Baxter, R.E. and Davis, E. (2003) *The Penguin Dictionary of Economics*, 7th Edition. London: Penguin Books.

Better Regulation Commission (2006) *Risk, Responsibility and Regulation – Whose Risk Is It Anyway?* London: Better Regulation Commission.

Better Regulation Executive (2007a) *Regulatory Impact Assessment Guidance*, London: Better Regulation Executive.

Better Regulation Executive (2007b) *RIA Overview.* London: Better Regulation Executive.

Better Regulation Task Force (2004) *Alternatives to Regulation.* London: Better Regulation Task Force.

Better Regulation Task Force (2005) *Regulation: Less is More.* London: Better Regulation Executive.

Blackburn, R. and Hart, M. (2002) *Small Firms' Awareness and Knowledge of Individual Employment Rights*, DTI: Employment Relations Research Series No. 14. London: DTI.

British Coatings Federation Ltd (2003) *BCF CHIP 3 Compliance Costs Survey.* Leatherhead: British Coatings Federation Ltd.

Buglass, D. (2007) Red tape may be the final straw for Scots farming. *The Scotsman* 19 February, p 31.

Cabinet Office Press Office (2007) *New Impact Assessments will Increase Transparency and Improve Regulation*, CAB/030/07. London: Cabinet Office.

Chittenden, F., Kauser, S. and Poutziouris, P. (2002) *Regulatory Burdens of Small Business: A Literature Review*. London: Small Business Service, www.berr.gov.uk/Files/File38324.pdf, accessed 5 April 2008.

D'Arcy, B.J., Schmulian, K. and Wade, R. (2006) Regulatory options for the management of diffuse pollution. In L. Gairns, K. Crighton and B. Jeffrey (eds), *Agriculture and the Environment VI: Managing Rural Diffuse Pollution* Edinburgh: SEPA/SAC.

Davidson, N. (2006) *Davidson Review Implementation of EU Legislation: Final Report*. London: Cabinet Office.

Defra (2006) *Cumulative Impact of Forthcoming Regulatory Proposals on the Economics of Farming: Update 2*. London: Defra.

Ekins, P. and Venn, A. (2006) *Assessing Innovation Dynamics Induced by Environmental Policy: Combined Methodological and Case Study Synthesis Discussion Paper*. London: Policy Studies Institute.

Environmental Audit Committee (2005) *Pre-Budget 2004 and Budget 2005: Tax, Appraisal, and the Environment*. London: The Stationery Office.

European Commission (2002) *Communication from the Commission: Action Plan 'Simplifying and Improving the Regulatory Environment'*. Brussels: European Commission.

Froud, J. Boden, R., Ogus, A. and Stubbs, P. (1998) *Controlling the Regulators*. London: Macmillan.

Goodstein, E. and Hodges, H. (1997) Polluted data. *The American Prospect* 8(35), www.prospect.org/cs/articles?articleId=4757, accessed 5 April 2008.

Hampton, P. (2004) *Reducing Administrative Burdens: Effective Inspection and Enforcement*. London: HM Treasury.

Hussain, S.S. (2003) Eco-innovations and industrial organisation: a review of complementary explanations of unsustainable economic paths. *International Journal of Agricultural Resources, Governance and Ecology* 2(3/4): 243–261.

Jacobs, C. (2007) The evolution and development of regulatory impact assessment in the UK. In Colin Kirkpatrick and David Parker (eds), *Regulatory Impact Assessment: Towards Better Regulation?* Cheltenham: Edward Elgar pp 106–31.

Jenkins, R., Barton, J., Bartzokas, A., Hesselberg, J. and Knutsen, H.M. (2002) *Environmental Regulation in the New Global Economy: The Impact on Industry and Competitiveness*. Cheltenham: Edward Elgar.

Keter, V. (2004) *Small Firms: Red Tape,* House of Commons Library Research Paper 04/52. London: House of Commons.

Medhurst, J. (2005) Ex-post estimates of costs to business of EU environmental policies, Presentation given at the *European Commission Workshop*, Brussels, 10 October 2005.

Metcalfe, M. (2000) *Environmental Regulation and Implications for the US Hog and Pork Industries*. PhD Thesis, Raleigh: North Carolina State University.

National Farmers' Union of Scotland (2006) *Industry plan for dealing with EU law*. News Article No. 25/06, www.nfus.org.uk/news_detail.asp?newsID=765, accessed 7 April 2008.

OECD (2005) *OECD Guiding Principles for Regulatory Quality and Performance*, www.oecd.orgdataoecd/19/51/37318586.pdf, accessed 7 April 2008.

OECD (2007) *Cutting Red Tape: National Strategies*, OECD Observer Policy Brief. Paris: OECD.

Palmer, K., Oates, W.E. and Portney, P.R. (1995) Tightening environmental standards: the benefit-cost or the no-cost paradigm. *Journal of Economic Perspectives* 9(4): 119–132.

Parker, D. (2006) Regulatory Impact Assessment. *Management Focus: Bi-annual Journal of Cranfield School of Management* 24: 4–7.

Parker, G. and Laitner, S. (2004) Promise to reduce burden of environmental red tape. *Financial Times*, 9 December.

Pearce, D. (2004) Does European Union environmental policy pass a cost-benefit test? *World Economics* 5(3): 115–37.

Porter, M.E. and van der Linde, C. (1995) Towards a new conception of the environmental-competitiveness relationship. *Journal of Economic Perspectives* 9(4): 97–118.

Regulatory Impact Unit (2003) *Better Policy Making: A Guide to Regulatory Impact Assessment.* London: Cabinet Office.

Risk Solutions (2005) *Impact Evaluation of the Control of Major Accident Hazards (COMAH) Regulations 1999*, www.hse.gov.uk/research/rrpdf/rr 343.pdf, accessed 7 April 2008.

Schaefer, S. and Young, E. (2006) *Burdened by Brussels or the UK? Improving the Implementation of EU Directives.* London: The Foreign Policy Centre.

Scottish Parliament, European and External Relation Committee (2006) *Inquiry into the Transposition and Implementation of European Directives in Scotland: Written Submissions*, http://www.scottish.parliament.uk/business/committees/europe/inquiries/tied/eur-tied-evidence.htm, accessed 13 March 2007.

Stockholm Environment Institute (1999) *Costs and Strategies Presented by Industry During the Negotiation of Environmental Regulations.* Stockholm: Stockholm Environment Institute.

Trades Union Congress (2003) *Unravelling the Red Tape Myths*, http://www.tuc.org.uk/em_research/tuc-6257-f0.cfm, accessed 14 March 2007.

Wilkes, A. (2004) *Regulatory Impact Assessments: Memorandum of Evidence for the Environmental Audit Committee's Pre-Budget 2004 Inquiry.* London: House of Commons Library.

World Bank (2007a) *Review of the Dutch Administrative Burden Reduction Program*, www.doingbusiness.org/documents/DBdutch_admin_report.pdf, accessed 7 April 2008.

World Bank (2007b) *Doing Business: Economy Rankings*, http://www.doingbusiness.org/EconomyRankings/, accessed 13 March 2007.

3. Evidence on regulatory cost estimates and reasons for *ex ante/ex post* variation

Michael MacLeod and Dominic Moran

The case studies in the following chapters will explore the relationship between *ex ante* and *ex post* estimations of regulatory costs. However, these case studies represent only a small part of the evidence base in this area. This chapter briefly reviews the rest of the evidence base, before moving on to an analysis of the various reasons for the discrepancies between *ex ante* and *ex post* estimates that have been found.

The studies summarised in Appendix 3.1 report the findings of research carried out, primarily in the USA and Europe, on behalf of Government Departments, NGOs and academic institutions to investigate whether there was any evidence for systematic divergence in *ex ante* and *ex post* cost estimates. The studies vary in terms of their scope and methodologies; some are reviews of other studies, while some attempt primary analyses bases on modelling, extrapolation and surveys. Overall, most of the studies reported *ex ante* costs to be overestimated relative to *ex post* costs. However, the temptation to conclude that *ex ante* evaluations are inevitably overestimated, as some have suggested (for example, International Chemical Secretariat ICS 2004; Wilkes 2004), should be resisted as there are notable exceptions to this trend. For example, while Harrington *et al.* (1999) found that the *ex ante* unit costs of 12 of the 26 rules they examined had been overestimated, they also concluded that 8 were accurate and 6 had been underestimated. A recent review of *ex ante* cost estimation in Denmark found the accuracy of (administrative) cost estimates to be 'acceptable in light of the inevitable complexity and uncertainties involved' (OECD 2004, p 33). Other authors have suggested that in certain circumstances, *ex ante* costs may be systematically underestimated (James jr 1998). Clearly, the picture appears to be more complex than some studies imply.

Further mixed evidence emerges from analysis carried out for *ex ante* and *ex post* estimates undertaken in respect of the Dutch National Environmental Policy Plan (NEPP, VROM 1989). A model was built

Table 3.1   Comparison of the ex ante *and* ex post *assessment of direct environmental costs of implementing the first NEPP in the Netherlands*

	Ex ante Million € (2001)	Ex post Million € (2001)	Ex ante compared to ex post %
Total	12 356	10 935	13
Per policy theme			
Acidification	1 928	918	110
Climate change	454	617	−26
Eutrophication	1 082	599	81
Hazardous substances (air, water, soil)	2 549	2 014	27
Waste management	3 566	4 004	−11
Soil sanitation	672	648	4
Disturbance	679	561	21
Other	1 426	1 574	−9

Sources: *Ex ante* assessment Jantzen (1989), *ex post* assessment RIVM (2000), cited in Oosterhuis (2006, p. 6).

comprising about 400 environmental measures, each linked with the implementation of certain pieces of regulation. Data were taken from a variety of studies on potential technologies that could be applied to reduce environmental pressure. Specific attention was given to the calculation principles, to enable comparison and ensure harmonisation with the statistics on environmental costs of the Central Statistical Bureau of the Netherlands (CBS).

In addition, considerable effort was made to clarify the physical implications of certain pieces of regulation (the intended emission reduction for example) and the business populations affected. About 12 years after the *ex ante* estimate (which covered the period 1988–2010), RIVM (the National Institute for Public Health and the Environment) published an overview of the realised costs (in co-operation with the CBS). Table 3.1 summarises the results of the *ex ante* and *ex post* estimates. To enable comparison, the initial *ex ante* assessment was inflated using the consumer price index.

This example provides further evidence that *ex ante* cost estimates do not always overestimate to a large extent. On the other hand, it should be noted that, in this case, as early as 1979 onwards, good statistics were available on cost, making their *ex ante* estimation easier, and this is likely to have contributed to their relative accuracy. Furthermore, a number of detailed studies were also available at the time of the preparation of the NEPP, enabling detailed estimates for various parts of environmental policy.

3.1   REASONS FOR DIFFERENCES BETWEEN *EX ANTE* AND *EX POST* COST ESTIMATES

The range of reasons that have been proposed to explain the disparities between *ex ante* and *ex post* costs estimates are summarised in Table 3.2. It has been assumed that *ex post* estimates (while still very much estimates) are more likely to be accurate than *ex ante* estimates. This is because *ex post* estimates, with the benefit of hindsight, should be based on fewer assumptions and should therefore have a lower level of uncertainty. Therefore *ex ante/ex post* discrepancies should tend to be due to inaccuracies in the *ex ante*. The sources of disparity have been categorised as either random (r) or systematic (s). Random errors are those that can lead to both overestimation and underestimation, while systematic errors can lead only to either overestimation or underestimation.

3.1.1   Sources of Error that can Lead to Over- or Under-estimation

Post-estimate changes in the regulation

Cost estimation is part of the process of policy formulation and implementation, so *ex ante* estimates are usually made on regulations that are, to some extent, provisional. Sometimes the consultative and political processes bring about modifications to proposals for regulatory change. As a consequence, the policy ultimately adopted is not necessarily the same as the one for which the costs were estimated. These changes to scope, timing, technology or standard may affect the aggregate costs of compliance and in turn generate differences between *ex ante* and *ex post* assessments. For example, Harrington (2003) reports how for the USA's Clean Water Act 'the regulations were relaxed considerably between the contractor's report and the final promulgated standards'. Moreover, the way in which the policy or legislation is implemented and the instruments chosen (for example, incentive-based instruments versus command-and-control measures) may strongly affect the *ex post* costs. For example, the compliance costs of the USA's 1990 Clean Air Act Amendments turned out to be substantially lower than anticipated initially, partly because the early proposals mandated scrubbers at many units and allowed little emissions trading, whereas the actual policy substantially reduced costs by allowing emissions trading and leaving the choice of reduction devices open to the private firms (Ellerman 2003).

Table 3.2   Categories of reasons for disparities between ex ante *and*
                ex post *estimates*

Overestimation of *ex ante* relative to *ex post*	Random or systematic
Post-estimate changes in the regulation	random
Uncertainty	random
Compliance issues	random
Strategic behaviour by regulatees	systematic
Asymmetric correction of errors	systematic
Static assumptions leading to the underestimation of innovation	systematic
Underestimation of *ex ante* relative to *ex post*	
Post-estimate changes in the regulation	random
Uncertainty	random
Compliance issues	random
Strategic behaviour by regulators	systematic
Cost turbulence and selection bias	systematic

Ex ante estimates therefore often reflect the proposed version of a regulation rather than the enacted version. This can of course introduce significant differences between *ex ante* and *ex post* estimates of costs.

Uncertainty
Ex ante cost estimates are forecasts and can therefore be subject to a high degree of uncertainty. They entail the quantification of many parameters about which the regulator may have little or no reliable data. There is often a time gap between carrying out the estimation and implementation, so even when good quality baseline data are available, it is often necessary to make predictions about how key parameters will change over time. They may be subject to gradual change (such as trends in herd size or rates of car ownership) or one-off unforeseen events (such as major disease outbreaks or oil price changes).

Predictions about future compliance costs require assumptions regarding the future development of prices and costs. The cost of a technology may decrease as a result of innovations and economies of scale. Furthermore, the cost of compliance may be strongly affected by changes in, for example, the energy price. This is especially relevant for technologies to reduce CO_2 emissions. These technologies deserve special attention because their cost structure differs considerably from more traditional environmental technologies (like waste water treatment, scrubbers and so on). When applying 'traditional' environmental technologies, in most cases only additional costs occur (capital costs, costs of operation and

Table 3.3   Additional costs, fuel savings and net costs of a hybrid car as a function of the price of petrol (including taxes)

Fuel price (€ / litre)	0.8	1.0	1.2	1.5	2.0
Gross costs per year (€ /year)	1200	1200	1200	1200	1200
Savings (fuel) (€ /year)	800	1000	1200	1500	2000
Net costs per year (€ /year)	400	200	0	−300	−800
Cost-effectiveness of CO_2 reduction (€ / kg CO_2 reduced)	0.168	0.084	0.000	−0.127	−0.338

maintenance). However, technologies aiming at reducing energy or replacing fossil fuels by wind, sun, hydropower and so on, also include an economic benefit, as the (fossil) energy inputs are reduced or energy is produced. The net costs of the policy therefore depend to a large extent on the price of fossil fuels. Table 3.3 gives an example calculation of the costs of CO_2 reduction by the transport sector by using a hybrid passenger car. The additional investment is about €8000, which is equivalent to about €1200 annual costs (for depreciation, interest and maintenance). On the basis of 20 000 km a year, 1000 litres of fuel can be saved compared to a normal petrol car (that runs 1 litre on 10 km, leading to an annual petrol use of 2000 litres).

This simple calculation shows that depending on the assumed petrol price, the costs vary from a net cost of €400 per year to a cost saving of €800 per year. In other words, when the petrol price reaches a level of over €1.20, the total costs of the technology (including fuel savings) are nil. A higher fuel price would even give a financial profit to the owner of the car, compared to the choice of a regular car. Also, in cases where the car runs more than 20 000 km per year, the technology becomes more profitable or less costly. The example shows that in the case of energy-saving technologies, savings in expenditure on (fossil) fuels form an important part of the cost equation. This makes it more difficult to apply general cost functions for the (uncertain) future. The cost function should include additional variables in order to incorporate price changes that heavily affect outcomes (especially for energy, but more generally also for water, raw materials and so on).

In some cases, the implementation of the regulation may itself induce changes. For example, the introduction of a minimum wage will increase the wage bill within industries where low pay is common. However, the minimum wage may also change other parameters by, for example, leading to alterations in the size of the sector, averting industrial action or reducing the number of working days lost due to absenteeism. In such cases, the costs should be measured relative to the counterfactual, that is, the *ex post* costs should be measured relative to the situation that would have existed had the policy not been implemented (see Example 3A below).

Compliance issues – noncompliance, undercompliance and overcompliance
Many *ex ante* estimates assume that compliance will be 100 per cent even when historic compliance levels tell a different story. While assuming 100 per cent compliance may not be realistic, it is often a political necessity. This is important as low compliance rates can lead to the total costs (and total benefits) of a regulation being much lower than predicted, even if the unit costs turn out as predicted. In addition to noncompliance, undercompliance and overcompliance can also lead to discrepancies between *ex ante* and *ex post* estimates. These can occur when a regulation contains ambiguities or loopholes. Undercompliance refers to regulatees complying with the letter rather than the spirit of a policy and will reduce the unit and total costs. Overcompliance is likely to occur when the guidance is not clear and the penalties for noncompliance significant.

3.1.2 Sources of Error that can Lead to Overestimation of the *Ex Ante* Relative to the *Ex Post* Costs

Strategic behaviour by regulatees, for example, lobbying or deliberately overestimating costs leading to estimates of maxima rather than means
It is frequently suggested that those being regulated engage in strategic behaviour in order to reduce the impact of regulation on their activities. Bailey *et al.* (2002) characterised compliance as a 'negotiated process rather than an event', a process in which firms engage 'in an attempt to shape the regulations in ways that would minimize the costs of compliance'. This can be done by simply making representations during the formal consultation. Alternatively, regulatees may engage in the process informally, as for example when the Formula One Association is alleged to have successfully lobbied the UK Government in order to delay the introduction of the tobacco advertising ban in 1997. Regulatees can also exert influence as a result of their possession of information. Estimating the costs of regulation is complex and it can often be difficult for the regulator to obtain the required information. It is therefore not unusual for *ex ante* estimates to be based, at least in part, on the regulated industries' data. Industries may err on the cautious side when estimating costs (thereby inflating them), or even deliberately overestimate them.

Asymmetric correction of errors
A related problem is asymmetric correction of errors. Harrington *et al.* (1999 p 22) have argued that 'gross underestimates of costs are more likely

to be brought to the regulator's attention by worried members of the regulated community' than overestimates, leading to 'an upward bias in regulatory cost estimates'. Thus it is possible for systematic bias to influence cost estimates, even when the parties involved are acting in good faith.

Static assumptions leading to the underestimation of innovation and adaptation

One of the most commonly cited reasons for overestimation is that static assumptions are employed in carrying out *ex ante* cost estimates (for example, ICS 2004; Harrington 2003; Hammitt 2000). It is argued that in many cases it is difficult to predict accurately the extent to which industry can innovate and adopt cost-minimising strategies in response to regulation. In the face of this uncertainty, rather conservative assumptions about innovation tend to be made. These may be encouraged by the fact that regulators often have to rely on regulatees to provide estimates of the likely costs of regulations. In such circumstances, regulatees have little incentive to do anything other than provide conservative estimates based on current costs. It should be noted that the apparent importance of static assumptions may in part be due to the types of regulations that have been examined in the studies. Some regulations are more amenable to innovation and technological fixes than others, in particular, those regulations employing incentive-based measures rather than command-and-control measures.

The extent to which regulation can stimulate innovation and provide firms with (first mover) advantages has been the subject of extensive debate and was discussed in Chapter 2 (see Example 2B); it and is explored in more detail in Chapter 15.

3.1.3   Sources of Error that can Lead to Underestimation of the *Ex Ante* Relative to the *Ex Post* Costs

Strategic behaviour by regulators

It is commonly assumed that those undertaking or commissioning research can influence the results in order to serve their interests. In the case of regulatees, the tendency will be to overestimate the costs of compliance in order to minimise the impact of legislation. On the other hand, it has been suggested that regulators can also be prone to bias, for example James Jr (1998 p 331) has argued that 'OSHA has an incentive to underestimate the full compliance cost of its proposed regulations in order to ensure that the proposed rules are finalized'. However this is refuted by Harrington *et al.* (1999 p 16), who note that 'our data does not support the notion of systematic underestimation of regulatory costs'. Note that while strategic behaviour by regulators has been characterised as systematically leading to *ex ante* cost underestimates, it could also, in theory, lead to *ex ante* overestimates. This could occur if civil servants wished to stymie a particular regulation proposed by their political masters, or 'if the costs of compliance are thought to be modest, if underestimation of the costs risks embarrassment, or if court challenge seems likely' (Harrington *et al.* 1999 p 21).

Cost turbulence and selection bias
Harrington *et al.* (1999) asked why 'the nonstrategic explanations for cost underestimation in investment projects – cost turbulence and selection bias[1] – should not in principle apply to regulatory cost estimation as well'. This is an interesting question, and may be relevant to complex regulations, particularly those that have been developed in ways similar to large investment projects, that is, from suites of options that provide the opportunity for selection bias. While there appears to be little evidence of these processes influencing regulatory cost estimates, this may be due to the inevitable difficulty of detecting such processes.

3.2 GENERAL LESSONS: ESTIMATING AND COMPARING REGULATORY COSTS

There are a number of factors that can influence cost estimates, notably: the definition and attribution of costs; the scope of the estimate, that is, which costs are included and excluded; and the methodology used to calculate the costs. As the Stockholm Environment Institute (1999, p 38) notes:

> The term 'cost' has many different meanings in everyday language and within technical discussions. This wide usage provides an opportunity for differing interpretations and re-interpretations of the cost of an environmental regulation – a problem that can be mitigated only by adopting rigorous and agreed rules, in advance, for comparative costing exercises. The issues relate to where the boundaries of the activity undertaken are to be drawn, cost estimation and auditing procedures, discount rates, interest and exchange rates, and their change over time, external costs and the form in which costs are (or have been) presented.

3.2.1 Unit Costs and Total Costs

When comparing the *ex ante* and *ex post* costs, it is important to state precisely which particular definition of cost is being measured, that is: total cost or unit cost; average cost or marginal cost; gross cost or net cost. Costs can be expressed in absolute, aggregate terms (for example, total cost for the regulated community or for a specific sector) or they may be expressed in relative terms, related to a relevant parameter (for example, per tonne of product or of emission abated, or as a percentage of profit or turnover). It is important to keep this distinction in mind when comparing *ex ante* and *ex post* cost estimates. For example, if total costs turn out to be (*ex post*) a certain percentage lower than *ex ante*, this may be due to an unforeseen decrease in the polluting activity by that percentage, whereas the cost per unit of activity was in fact predicted accurately. Whether unit costs or total costs should be used depends on the purpose of the cost estimate. In cost-benefit and cost-effectiveness analysis, total costs should be compared to the overall environmental impact. On the other hand, if the cost figure is intended to show the relative weight of the environmental costs (for example, compared to overall production costs) then the unit cost figure should be used. Costs expressed as a percentage of profit or turnover of a firm or sector are sometimes used to show the affordability of the policy. The importance of this is highlighted in Harrington *et al.* (1999), where comparison of the unit costs and the total costs lead to different conclusions for 7 of the 26 case studies. As they point out, low compliance rates can lead to lower than predicted total costs (and lower benefits) even if the unit costs are predicted accurately or underestimated.

3.2.2 Attributing Costs to Measures

A related problem is that of attributing costs to measures. Can we be confident that the costs arising from a regulation are actually additional, that is, they do not include the costs of measures that the regulatees would have undertaken anyway, either voluntarily or in response to other legislation? Often proposed policies will impact on businesses already subject to previous regulation, with new changes modifying, tightening or complementing previous legislation. The complexity of different levels, vintages and types of policy interactions not only makes it difficult to estimate costs, it also makes it difficult to attribute costs to specific policy changes. The continuing evolution of air quality standards and related measures (for example, emissions abatement, fuel quality standards) on certain industries (for example, refineries, vehicle producers, power plants) is one example where attribution is often difficult. This issue is also partly related to the timing of policy and hence to what is termed the counterfactual, that is, what do we think would have happened if we had retained existing policies?

An *ex post* assessment of the Waste Packaging Directive (GHK 2006) demonstrates the difficulties. In some EU Member States, similar policies had been enacted prior to the Directive (which are therefore included in the counterfactual or baseline). Other Member States introduced policies only after the Directive and thus these are attributable to it. The attribution may become even more difficult where businesses are subject to a host of environmental (and other interrelated) legislation. For instance, a particular piece of capital equipment might be necessitated in order to implement a HACCP (Hazard Analysis and Critical Control Point) approach to food safety, but it also might contribute to meeting other statutory responsibilities. What proportion of this capital cost should then be attributed to HACCP?

Colatore and Caswell (2000) (reported in Romano *et al.* 2005) distinguish between three types of compliance cost: (a) total cost of the system adopted; (b) minimum costs required to comply with the regulations; and (c) incremental cost of the system adopted (the minimum cost minus the cost of any measures that the regulatees would have adopted anyway (that is, the additional cost of the regulation). Measures of the total cost should be interpreted with care as they increase the likelihood of double counting occurring. For example, measures undertaken by European farmers in response to the Nitrates Directive may also be attributed to the Water Framework Directive, in which case the costs of the measures would be counted twice.

3.3   THE IMPORTANCE OF THE COUNTERFACTUAL

Assessing the impacts arising from regulation is complicated by the fact that not all business activity is the result of Government intervention; tasks such as record keeping may be required to meet customer requirements or as a means of improving business management. When The UK Agricultural Development and Advisory Service (ADAS 2005 p 24) carried out a survey of farmers, they found that half of the respondents agreed with the statement 'The records you have to keep for Government regulation are necessary anyway to help manage your business'. This result raises an important point regarding the way in which the costs of regulation are assessed. The costs of any policy should be measured relative to the business-as-usual (or counterfactual) position, that is, the situation that would have existed had the policy not been implemented. If the cost of regulation is simply measured relative to the situation *x* years ago, then this will lead to an (inaccurate) measure of the total cost of regulation rather than the additional cost. This is one of the reasons why the emphasis of analysis should be on additional costs rather than on total costs.

Once the regulation is in place and becomes the new context within which those affected operate, it is very often difficult to separate the additional costs from the total. Business plans, investment decisions and corporate behaviour (all of which are in a state of constant evolution anyway) implicitly take into account the regulatory change such that it is no longer

---

BOX 3.1   EXAMPLE 3A: INTRODUCTION OF THE MINIMUM WAGE

The National Minimum Wage was introduced in the UK in 1999, in order to prevent excessively low pay and to create a level playing field for business. Its introduction resulted in an increase in labour costs in industries where significant proportions of the labour force had been receiving less than the new minimum – the latter is shown by the dotted line in Figure 3.1. In this example, the cost of the policy can be measured as B−A, that is, the *ex post* labour costs minus the *ex ante* labour costs adjusted for inflation (shown by the dashed line). This assumes that the labour costs would have remain unchanged if the minimum wage had not been introduced. In reality, labour costs may have changed without the policy (for example, there may have been increased costs resulting from employment tribunals that have been avoided by the policy) leading to a significantly different counterfactual. It may therefore be more accurate to measure the cost as B−C.

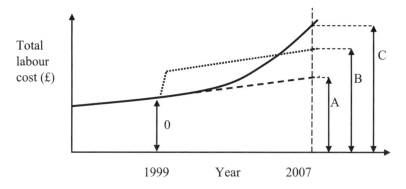

Figure 3.1   Measuring the cost of the minimum wage

possible to discern what the counterfactual (and thus the additional costs) might have been. This is especially true when:

1. there is a long lead-in time (corporate memories tend to be short);
2. compliance with a new standard is bundled with a range of other process or efficiency improvements in a given product or technology and/or fits well in natural investment cycles;

3. the contextual environment changes in some material fashion, such as competitive dynamics, corporate mergers and consolidation, step changes in consumer preferences and expectations or external price shocks.

The assessment of planned or actual policy impacts on businesses depends on the ability to anticipate (*ex ante*) or recall (*ex post*) the responses of business to the legislation, compared to their actions in the absence of the legislation. The counterfactual description is important in both *ex ante* and *ex post* assessments. Comparability requires that the baseline assumptions are the same in both cases. In the case of EU environmental policies, *ex ante* assessments are essentially exercises in long-term planning, with most EU environmental legislation taking several years to devise, plus several more years to transcribe, and yet more time is needed to allow for adoption and adjustment. This creates uncertainty, as the economy and business environment continually develops (not least because of other policy drivers), requiring consideration not only of current market conditions and technological options but also emerging market conditions, technologies and related policy drivers. This uncertainty is clearly a potential source of variation in counterfactual descriptions between the *ex ante* and *ex post* costs.

Various methods exist to construct the counterfactual or baseline scenario, including (OECD 1997 p 97):

1. Trend extrapolation – a simple approach to constructing a policy baseline is to assume that trends visible prior to the policy change would have continued unchanged if the policy measure had not been implemented.
2. Econometric methods – econometric models may be estimated which, for example, link pollution levels to various economic variables (such as the level of gross national product), and which include a dummy variable for the date of introduction of the policy measure. The model can then be used to make a counterfactual prediction of what would have happened to pollution levels if everything else had remained unchanged, except that the policy had not been introduced.
3. Linear programming techniques can be used to indicate how the decisions of firms might change in response to different constraints and incentives; the problem with these techniques is that they assume some form of optimal decision making, which may in practice be unrealistic.
4. 'Judgemental' methods can be used to describe the baseline in the absence of policy. However, one problem with definitions of the baseline scenario constructed purely on the basis of judgement is that the outcome of the evaluation study will depend critically on the judgements made; there may easily be scope for doubts about the

realism of such a baseline. What can be done depends partly on the availability of suitable data. In turn, data availability depends partly on the institutional setting of the evaluation. Issues of commercial confidentiality may obstruct access to some of the key data needed.

BOX 3.2   EXAMPLE 3B: ESTABLISHING A BASELINE FOR THE WATER FRAMEWORK DIRECTIVE

The Water Framework Directive (2000/60/EC) (WFD) is a wide-ranging and ambitious piece of environmental legislation that is currently being implemented in the European Union. Its overall objective is to bring about the effective co-ordination of water environment policy and regulation across Europe in order to:

1. prevent deterioration and enhance the status of aquatic ecosystems, including groundwater;
2. promote sustainable water use;
3. reduce pollution;
4. contribute to the mitigation of floods and droughts.

One of the requirements of the WFD is that long-term forecasts of water supply and demand are undertaken at a river basin district level. This includes forecasts of what supply and demand would be without the WFD, that is, the business as usual (BAU) or counterfactual scenario. In their guidelines on constructing BAU scenarios, the European Commission (2003 p146) highlighted three key tasks: assessing current trends; projecting changes; and integrating 'critical uncertainties' (see Table 3.4).

In order to aid its implementation of the WFD, the Scottish Executive commissioned a study to construct BAU forecasts for water use in Scotland. These were required to 'provide a policy-off counterfactual against which a programme of WFD sanctioned intervention measures can be judged for their cost-effectiveness' (Moran *et al.* 2007). This study identified the main sectors in terms of volumetric water use: domestic demand; agriculture; electricity generation; industry and commerce; and aquaculture. Each sector was disaggregated into components, and where appropriate, micro-components of water use. For example, in the sector of domestic demand, one component is personal washing. This can be disaggregated into the micro-components: bath; shower; power shower; hand basin.

Several techniques were used to forecast demand for each sector in 2015: For domestic demand, electricity generation and industry and commerce, trend extrapolation and judgemental techniques were used; in agriculture, linear programming was used. Trend extrapolation was used widely, and has the advantage that it is a relatively quick and simple technique. However, caution must be exercised when extrapolating, as 'the past is not necessarily a good indicator of the future' (European Commission 2003 p149), particularly in the medium to long term. In order to inform the analysis, judgemental techniques, based on expert advice, policy documents and so on were employed. These were particularly important for the electricity generation sector, which was (and is) undergoing a series of politically-driven (and therefore uncertain) step changes.

There is no clear-cut methodology that can assess the 'without policy' counterfactual. Essentially each case study must proceed to estimate it as best it can in order to arrive at the best possible assessment. However, frameworks such as those provided in the European Commission's WFD guidance can help to reduce some of the inevitable uncertainty.

Table 3.4   Key tasks in constructing BAU forecasts

Task	Output	Example: Domestic water supply in Scotland
Task 1: Assess current trends in trend variables, including physical parameters and socio-economic drivers	Short-term projections of trend variables based on existing trends	Assess trends in total population, number of households, per capita water consumption, leakage rates, etc.
Task 2: Project certain changes in water policy variables	Longer-term projections of variables incorporating changes in current trends	Predicting the effects of Scottish Water's investment programme on, e.g., leakage rates
Task 3: Integrate changes in 'critical uncertainties' and derive one or several realistic business-as-usual scenarios	Build several BAU scenarios	Develop scenarios based on (a) continued state ownership and (b) privatisation of Scottish Water

3.4   SCOPE

The cost of a regulation can vary considerably depending on where the boundaries are drawn, that is, which costs are included and excluded from the calculation (see Table 2.6). Limiting the calculation to the financial costs of those directly affected means that wider social and environmental costs and benefits to health, quality of life, third parties and industrial productivity and innovation are not accounted for. Table 3.5 lists the typical cost categories involved in environmental regulation and indicates whether or not they are routinely included in RIA cost calculations.

The total compliance costs arising from the activities involved in meeting regulatory requirements can be divided into two categories:

1.   The policy costs resulting from meeting the regulation, that is, costs directly attributable to the policy goal (for example, the costs of installing and maintaining flue gas desulphurisation equipment in a coal-fired power station).
2.   The administrative costs of complying with regulations, that is, costs associated with familiarisation, record keeping and reporting (for example, the costs of interpreting the Large Combustion Plant Directive (LCPD), evaluating the technical options, learning about the chosen equipment, monitoring and recording equipment performance and reporting to the regulator).

Policy costs include investment as well as operational costs. The first category relates to the capital costs of purchasing and modifying plant and equipment to ensure compliance. These can be annualised by applying a specific interest rate and depreciation period. Operational costs are the costs associated with the on-going requirement to maintain compliance (for example, materials, energy, labour). Policy costs can be relatively easily identified when only one known technological solution is (and will be) available, which is simply added to the existing production process with little or no effect on the wider operation of the plant or on the product. These are so called 'end-of-pipe' measures, and in general they will always create additional (marginal) costs.

There is a general trend in regulatory intervention away from inflexible command-and-control compliance (for example, defining what 'end-of-pipe' technology is to be applied) to more flexible, incentive-based models. This trend has occurred as economic theory suggests that giving firms such flexibility leads to lower overall compliance costs for society. The consequence of this trend however is that, where many solutions are available, it may be hard to predict which of these will actually be chosen by businesses.

Table 3.5   A taxonomy of costs of environmental regulation

Cost category	Counted in RIA?
DIRECT COSTS	
Private Sector Compliance Expenditures	
Capital	Yes
Operating and maintenance	Yes
Public Sector Compliance Expenditures	
Capital	Yes
Operating and maintenance	Yes
Government Administration of Environmental Statutes and Regulations	
Monitoring	Rarely
Enforcement	Rarely
Other Direct Costs (including negative costs)	
Legal and other transactional	Sometimes
Shifted management focus	No
Disrupted production	No
Waiting time	Sometimes
Intermedia pollutant effects	Sometimes
Other natural resource effects	Sometimes
Changes in maintenance requirements of other equipment	Sometimes
Worker health	Sometimes
Stimulation of innovation in clean technologies	No
INDIRECT COSTS	
General Equilibrium Effects	
Product substitution	No
Discouraged investment	No
Retarded innovation	No
Transition costs	
Unemployment	Sometimes
Plant closures	Sometimes

Source: Adapted by Harrington *et al.* (1999) from Jaffe *et al.* (1995).

This is especially the case with changes in processes, which often go together with re-engineering of (part of) the production process or simply changes in management. This can result in costs that are close or equal to zero. In addition, firms may incur administrative costs as a result of, for example, monitoring and reporting requirements. It has been estimated that 'on average, administrative costs are thought to be around 30% of the total costs of regulation' (Better Regulation Task Force 2005 p 13). Administrative costs for the authorities (for example, for monitoring and enforcement) are usually not considered to be compliance costs, as they are not paid directly by the affected business. Differences in the interpretation and calculation of these cost categories can in principle result in substantial differences in cost estimates.

3.4.1   Direct and indirect costs

Environmental legislation can lead to marginal or structural changes in many economic parameters. Some companies will see their market opportunities shrink, and employment may be reduced as a result of compliance costs being passed on in product prices. Quantifying such 'indirect' impacts of measures can either be done by estimating the foregone profits, by applying macro-economic modelling (but with the risk of losing sight of individual technologies) or by estimating welfare effects of the economic changes induced by the application of the (new) technology. It is sometimes argued that these indirect (or secondary) effects should be considered as 'costs' of the environmental legislation (see Table 2.6). However, from a methodological point of view this is problematic. First of all, the negative impacts are often compensated for by positive impacts elsewhere: some companies will lose, but other companies (the 'greener' competitors and the suppliers of environmental technology) may experience increases in turnover, profit and employment. Moreover, an assessment of these indirect effects often requires modelling of the (inter)national economy (for example using a General Equilibrium Model), or at least many assumptions and scenarios regarding economic behaviour that may invoke controversy. It is up to the decision makers to decide if, and to what extent, they want to analyse the complex web of economic responses to an environmental policy measure. In any case, when analysing differences between cost estimates, the possible impact of indirect costs having been included or excluded should be taken into account.

3.5   APPROACHES AND METHODS

A variety of methods can be used to gather data and calculate costs, such as surveys and audits, modelling and extrapolation. In order for the costs to be comparable, the methods used to calculate the *ex ante* and *ex post* costs should be as similar as possible, for example, they should use the same discount rates.

The most common way to make *ex ante* estimates of environmental costs that arise from the implementation of (stricter) regulation is to carry out technological-economic cost assessments. Basically, a cost engineer estimates the costs of an installation or a process change (by using a blueprint or certain physical parameters) that enables the required reduction of emissions. Sometimes this is done for individual facilities, but in most cases a modelling approach is followed: the population of polluters is classified (for example, by size, emissions, energy use, annual throughput), and a few 'model installations' are defined (here the word 'installation' is used, but it may also refer to a technology, a vehicle, a source of pollution, an enterprise and so on). For these 'model installations', investment and operational costs are estimated. Normally, this estimate can be based on empirical evidence (of a comparable installation that already exists). Here, a potential bias enters the cost equation, as these engineering estimates are normally derived from data on pilot plants or 'first applications'. By using engineering parameters (such as scale, volume, surface, length of wiring, piping), an individual estimate can be extrapolated to other scales, providing some differentiation of 'model installations'. By matching it with 'population' data, estimates for a whole sector affected can be made. In other words, we move from unit costs to total costs. Hartman *et al.* (1997) point out that a weakness of the engineering approach is the tendency to overestimate costs. One of the reasons is that in this approach, no allowances are normally made for technological and efficiency developments, leading to lower unit costs.

Finally, regarding the quality of the estimates, it seems obvious that detailed, rigorous *ex ante* assessments (where substantial investment has been made to understand costs and cost uncertainty) will provide a firmer foundation on which to base cost estimates than rapid policy screening tools, such as initial regulatory impact assessments. It would not be surprising to find that a detailed *ex post* assessment produces results that differ from those of a rapid *ex ante* assessment – different levels of resources having been deployed in the estimation process.

3.5.1   Availability and Reliability of Cost Data: Ex Ante Data

Limited data availability and reliability may be an important cause of gaps and inconsistencies in compliance cost estimates. Industry itself will usually have more information than the regulator (information asymmetry, see Hammitt 2000), and may have an interest in keeping some information secret or in revealing flawed data. Misspecification may thus arise as a result of bias introduced by specific stakeholder groups overstating the costs of adaptation (deliberately as a negotiating ploy, or inadvertently as a result of overly conservative project costing policies). This bias may relate to the frequency with which a group of operators is regulated and their perceived need to defend their interests. An underlying weakness in empirical approaches which rely on data from the regulated industry is therefore the inevitable bias towards technical descriptions which imply greater costs. This needs careful management using independent third-party estimates where available, or careful examination of pilot or 'typical' plants chosen as the basis for cost estimation.

Nevertheless, involvement of business is clearly helpful if credible estimates are to be presented. Suppliers of technologies can also be useful sources of cost data. Suppliers may however be overly optimistic about their technologies or be tempted to underestimate cost figures to 'open the market', and may not be able to give concrete data on installation costs.

Furthermore, engagement through stakeholder representatives on studies helps to build confidence and encourage the release of information. Use of experienced consultants with a track record in the regulated industry and capable of understanding the finer points of operational detail is also important to gain the trust of business. This can be backed up with legal requirements on consultants to observe strict confidentiality requirements. To the extent that businesses are already subject to environmental regulation, regulators will have some leverage to encourage businesses to participate and to release necessary data.

3.5.2 Availability and Reliability of Cost Data: Ex Post Data

Eurostat, in co-operation with the OECD, collects some information on the costs of environmental management in the EU. The collected data are highly aggregated (total sectoral expenditures on air, water, waste), making it impossible to assess the costs of individual pieces of legislation in the EU. However, statistical offices in Member States often collect more detailed data, which sometimes enable comparisons of *ex ante* and *ex post* costs on the level of Directives. This is for instance true for the Dutch Statistical Office (CBS), that collects data on environmental investment expenditure in industry, agriculture and transport. It also surveys the environmental services sector (so-called 'specialised producers' which specialise in wastewater collection and processing). However, it does not collect data for all sectors and types of legislation. Normally a distinction is made between expenditures per domain (water, air, soil, waste, noise, nature protection, research and administrative costs). In most EU countries, comparable data collection systems are in place, but the level of detail and the way data are collected and treated often differ. Subsidy registers (including agricultural) can sometimes also be a useful source of information.

3.6 CONCLUSIONS

Existing studies suggest that *ex ante* costs tend to be overestimated relative to *ex post*, to a greater or lesser extent. However, there are several notable exceptions to this, which demonstrate that *ex ante* costs are not inevitably overestimated. Discrepancies between the *ex ante* and *ex post* cost estimates can be the result of systematic or random errors. Systematic errors can lead to *ex ante* overestimation (through strategic behaviour by regulatees, asymmetric correction of errors, or the adoption of static assumptions) or underestimation (through strategic behaviour by regulators or cost turbulence). Random errors (associated with post-estimate changes in the regulation, uncertainty or compliance issues) can lead to both underestimation and overestimation.

The following eleven chapters will shed further light on the process of estimating regulatory costs by outlining a series of case studies of EU and UK regulation.

NOTE

1. When projects consist of a menu of options, there is a tendency to select the options that have been (inadvertently) underestimated.

Appendix 3.1 Summary of existing ex ante/ex post comparisons

Authors/Title	Country	Brief description	Ex ante estimate compared to ex post estimate	Findings
US Congress Office of Technology Assessment (1995)	USA	US Government analysis of 8 Occupational Health and Safety Administration (OSHA) regulations.	+	Inaccuracies due to: compliance issues; conservative assumptions about technology and misjudgement of industries' ability to adjust; measurement errors.
Goodstein and Hodges (1997)	USA	Independent meta study of 12 environmental protection regulations in the USA.	+	Emission reduction costs were overestimated due to underestimating innovation, static assumptions, lack of (industry) data. However, *ex ante* remediation costs were underestimated.
Burtraw *et al.* (1998)	USA	Modelling-based COBA of the 1990 Clean Air Act Amendments.	+?	'[C]ompliance costs have fallen significantly compared to prior expectations' (p 397) because of the trading scheme approach. '[T]he flexibility the program gives firms to find least-cost ways to reduce emissions' (p 399)
James jr (1998)	USA	*Ex post* estimates of OSHA costs based on extrapolation from 25 case studies.	–?	'OSHA has an incentive to underestimate the full compliance cost of its proposed regulations in order to ensure that the proposed rules are finalized' (p 331).
Pickman (1998)	USA	Empirical study of the US manufacturing industries using pollution abatement and control expenditure (PACE) data.	+	Environmental expenditure estimates resulting from US environmental policy are based on current technology which may overstate policy's true costs. Existing evidence hows that *ex ante* cost estimates are greater than realised costs due to unexpected technological progress.

Study	Country	Description	Direction	Findings
Hahn (1999)	USA	Overview of the effect of economic models on policy development and the use of *ex ante* and *ex post* estimates to assess the compliance cost of environmental regulations.	+	In the cap-and-trade programme for the regulation of SO_2 emissions, *ex ante* costs were grossly overestimated because models failed to take into account new technology, the allocation of 3.5 million bonus allowances, the actual (much lower) set price of the allowances, and the falling price of low-sulphur coal.
Harrington et. al (1999)	Mainly USA	Independent meta study of 25 Agency *ex ante* estimates (includes 6 of the 8 US Congress Office of Technology Assessment (1995) case studies).	+ 0	Reasons for overestimation: underestimating innovation; baseline and compliance issues; post-estimate changes in the regulation; asymmetric correction of errors; using maxima rather than means. Also suggests potential reasons for underestimation: cost turbulence and selection bias. Distinguishes between total costs and unit costs. Findings may be due in part to preponderance of economic incentive-based rules (which encourage innovation).
Stockholm Environment Institute (1999) (published as Haq et al. 2001)	EU/USA	5 detailed case studies comparing outturn and *industry ex ante* costs.	+ (industry) +/0 (regulator)	*Ex ante* and *ex post* often not comparable. Implementation strategy often differs from that proposed in initial legislation. Technical advances, innovation and economies of scale are difficult to predict and often underestimated. Industry more likely to overestimate than regulator, but different parts of industry can react in different ways. *Ex post* costs are sometimes absorbed by industry rather than passed on as price increases, making them difficult to calculate (p 39).
Ellerman *et al.* (2000)	USA	Detailed analysis of the US acid rain program, especially the 1990 Clean Air Act Amendments. Comparison of 6 *ex ante* estimates with the	0	'[T]he actual costs of compliance with Phase I have been on the low side of what was expected and . . . the earlier estimates, by both government and industry, were reasonable predictions of the cost of compliance in Phase I' (p 235).

Appendix 3.1 (continued)

Authors/Title	Country	Brief description	Ex ante estimate compared to ex post estimate	Findings
		authors' bottom-up, cost engineering *ex post* costs.		
Hammitt (2000)	USA	Comparison of CFC control costs based on the marginal cost revealed by the CFC tradeable permits scheme.	+	Underestimating innovation: 'EPA was an acknowledged proponent of CFC controls and the Regulatory Impact Assessment (RIA) was clearly intended to support the proposed consumption limits' (p 295).
Housley (2001)	UK	Survey of the costs of implementing the Pollution Prevention and Control Regulations 2000.	–?	Lack of detail in the RIA makes the *ex ante/ex post* comparison difficult. However, respondents indicated that the new (PPC) procedures were more expensive, while the RIA did not predict any 'significant new burden' for existing regulatees.
Anderson and Sherwood (2002)	USA	Direct comparison of *ex ante* and *ex post* costs for the 1990 Clean Air Amendments in the US.	+	The general pattern that is revealed indicates that all *ex ante* estimates tended to exceed actual price impacts, with the EPA estimates exceeding actual prices by the smallest amount.
Bailey *et al.* (2002)	EU/USA	Review article.	+	Interprets 'compliance as a negotiated process' (p 249). Overestimates due mainly to: lobbying exaggeration by industry during pre-implementation then innovation post-implementation.
McMahon (2002)	UK	Discussion of the use of Compliance Cost Assessments	?	The study highlights major differences between water companies' and OFWAT's assessment of costs of

Study	Country	Description		Comments
		and cost estimates in the OFWAT-regulated water sector.		complying with environmental regulation. Possible reasons: different assumptions regarding future efficiency savings; gaming/strategic behaviour; genuine lack of knowledge of future efficiencies and actual costs.
Thompson *et al.* (2002)	USA	Modelling of *ex post* costs and cost-effectiveness of the 1984 introduction of airbag rules.	0?	While the study 'did not uncover large errors in cost estimation' (p810) it concluded that 'the original analysis was biased in favour of mandatory airbags due to overly optimistic benefit estimates' (p810).
British Coatings Federation Ltd (2003)	UK	Industry survey of compliance costs arising from chemical labelling legislation.	0+?	Findings indicate *ex ante* costs either accurate or overestimated; however the study is inconclusive due to differences in the way the *ex ante* and *ex post* costs were calculated.
Dowlatabadi (2003)	Mainly USA	Meta study of the costs of climate policy. Based largely on the work of, amongst others, Harrington *et al.* 1999 and Burtraw *et al.* 1998.	+	Argues that the two main challenges in cost estimation are defining the boundary and the baseline (i.e. counterfactual).
Ellerman (2003)	USA	*Ex post* analysis of sulphur dioxide emissions trading; also provides comparison with *ex ante* estimates for the same policy measures.	+	Most of the disparity results from changes in the regulations, uncertainty and the underestimation of innovation.
Gaze *et al.* (2003)	UK	Questionnaire survey of butchers' (regulatees) and Local Authorities (implementing body) to assess the *ex post* cost of implementing Food Safety Regulations.	?	This study found that regulatees often failed to account for the cost of their time when assessing the actual cost of implementing Hazard Analysis and Critical Control Point (HACCP).

Appendix 3.1 (continued)

Authors/Title	Country	Brief description	*Ex ante* estimate compared to *ex post* estimate	Findings
Griffith *et al.* (2003)	UK	Survey and audit of butchers to assess compliance with Food Safety Regulations.	+?	'Whilst the areas of perceived increased cost from implementing HACCP were similar to previous findings, the magnitude of the perceived increases was lower than in a previous study' (p 21).
Harrington (2003)	USA	Comparison of the costs of the Clean Air and Clean Water Acts using US Bureau of Census data.	+	Overestimated due to: underestimating innovation; inaccurate baseline data; relaxation of the regulations.
International Chemical Secretariat (ICS) (2004)	EU/USA	Critique of cost estimation, based largely on previous studies (SEI 1999, Goodstein and Hodges 1997 and Harrington *et al.* 1999). Written in support of the EU Registration, Evaluation, and Authorisation of Chemicals (REACH) regulation.	+	'·industry organisations systematically inflate costs estimates to combat new regulations; – regulators and environmental economists generally overestimate costs because they underestimate the innovation potential within industry' (p 15). (Note: has the same case studies as SEI 1999 and Haq *et al.* 2001.)
OECD (2004)	Denmark	Refers to a review of the *ex ante* estimates (of administrative costs) made by the Danish Business Test Panels.	0	'The review found that the Danish BTPs estimated the realised administrative burdens of new business regulations with a margin of error ranging between 40 and 60% on average. This was viewed as acceptable in light of the inevitable complexity and uncertainties involved in *ex ante* evaluation' (p 33).

Source	Country	Description	Estimate	Comments
Watkiss et al. (2004)	UK	Review of the Air Quality Strategy, focusing on electricity generation and road transport	+ (−)	It is suggested that the ex post costs are much higher than ex ante estimates because 'legislation itself acts as a spur to research and innovation. However, we also have found some cases where ex ante costs were underestimated' (p xii).
Wilkes (2004)	UK	Polemical critique of RIAs, drawing on Goodstein and Hodges (1997) and Harrington et al. (1999) plus other evidence.	+	Argues that overestimation is largely as the result of strategic behaviour on the part of the regulatees, and a lack of understanding of the potential economic benefits of regulation.
Doble (2005)	UK	An evaluation of Government energy efficiency policies.	?	No specific analysis on ex ante/ex post cost estimates, but a variety of conclusions on a wide range (30+) of policies.
Friends of the Earth (2005)	UK	Pro-regulation critique of the effects of corporate lobbying on government legislation.	+	The report argues that business lobby groups tend to exaggerate the costs of environmental regulation for reasons of strategic interest.
OMB (2005)	USA	Review of 14 studies of environmental protection and car safety regulations.	?	Those studies with actual ex post cost estimates are already covered; the others (mainly transport safety) focus on ex post assessment of compliance and benefits, rather than cost.
Risk Solutions (2005)	UK	Government-commissioned impact evaluation of the COMAH regulations.	−	Discrepancies were due to baseline and compliance issues, and the asymmetric correction of (ex post) errors.
Sherrington and Moran (2007)	UK	Comparison of the ex ante and ex post costs of the congestion charging scheme in London.	0 (+)	The ex ante total cost of the scheme was accurate (within 25% of the costs); however the ex post compliance costs turned out to be lower than predicted due to baseline/compliance issues (greater reduction in traffic than expected) and innovation.

Notes: + indicates that the ex ante/estimate is overestimated relative to the ex post estimate; 0 = accurate; − = underestimated; ? indicates high degree of uncertainty.

REFERENCES

ADAS (2005) *Study on the Impacts of Regulation on Agriculture: A Supporting Document for Partners for Success – a Farm Regulation and Charging Strategy*, London: Defra.

Anderson, J.F. and Sherwood, T. (2002) Comparison of EPA and Other Estimates of Mobile Source Rule Costs to Actual Price Changes, paper presented at the *SAE Government Industry Meeting*, Washington, D.C. May 2002.

Bailey, P.D., Haq, G. and Gouldson, A. (2002) Mind the Gap! Comparing *Ex ante* and *Ex post* Assessments of the Costs of Complying with Environmental Regulation, *European Environment*, 12(5), 245–256.

Better Regulation Task Force (2005) *Regulation: Less is More*, London: Cabinet Office.

British Coatings Federation Ltd (2003) *BCF CHIP 3 Compliance Costs Survey*, Leatherhead: British Coatings Federation Ltd.

Burtraw, D., Krupnick, A., Mansur, E., Austin, D. and Farell, D. (1998) Costs and Benefits of Reducing Air Pollutants Related to Acid Rain, *Contemporary Economic Policy*, 16(4), 379–400.

Colatore, C. and Caswell, J.A. (2000) The cost of HACCP implementation in the seafood industry: A case study of breaded fish, in, L. Unnevehr (ed.), *The economics of HACCP. Costs and benefits*, St Paul, MN: Eagan Press, pp. 45–79.

Doble, M. (2005) *Evaluation of the Government's Energy Efficiency Policies and Programmes: A Report for Defra as Part of the Climate Change Programme Review*, Didcot: AEA Technology.

Dowlatabadi, H. (2003) *What Do We Know About Climate Policy Costs and How Can We Learn More?* ENV/EPOC/GSP(2003)11/FINAL, OECD Environment Directorate Working Party on Global and Structural Policies, Paris: OECD.

Ellerman, A. (2003), *Ex-post Evaluation of Tradable Permits: The U.S. SO₂ Cap-and-Trade Program*, Massachusetts: Massachusetts Institute of Technology. http://tisiphone.mit.edu/RePEc/mee/wpaper/2003-003.pdf, accessed 7 April 2008.

Ellerman, A.D., Joskow, P.L., Schmalensee, R., Monterro, J.-P. and Bailey, E.M. (2000) *Markets for Clean Air: The U. S. Acid Rain Program*, Cambridge, UK: Cambridge University Press.

European Commission (2003) *Common Implementation Strategy for the Water Framework Directive (2000/60/EC) Guidance Document No 1: Economics and the Environment – The Implementation Challenge of the Water Framework Directive, Produced by Working Group 2.6 – WATECO*, Luxembourg: Office for Official Publications of the European Communities.

Friends of the Earth (2005) *Hidden Voices: The CBI, Corporate Lobbying and Sustainability*, London: Friends of the Earth.

Gaze, R., Everitt, M., Goode, J., Allchurch, E. and Chappell, A. (2003) *Evaluation of the Butchers' Licensing Initiative in England*, Chipping Campden: CCFRA Technology Limited, http://www.food.gov.uk/multimedia/pdfs/ CCFRAbutcher seval. pdf, accessed 7 April 2008.

GHK (2006) *Costs of Compliance Case Study: Packaging and Packaging Waste Directive 94/62/EC*, Final Report to DG Environment, European Commission, March. http://ec.europa.eu/environment/enveco/ex_post/pdf/packaging.pdf, accessed 14 April 2008.

Goodstein, E. and Hodges, H. (1997) Polluted data, *The American Prospect*, 8(35). www.prospect.org/cs/articles?articleId=4757, accessed 5 April 2008.

Griffith, C.J., Hayburn, G. and Clayton, D. (2003) *An Evaluation of the Butchers' Licensing Initiative in England: Final Report*, Cardiff: Food Research and Consultancy Unit (FRCU). www.Food.gov.uk/multimedia/pdfs/butcherseral. pdf,accessed 14 April 2008.

Hahn, R.W. (1999) *The Impact of Economics on Environmental Policy*, Working Paper 99-04, Washington D.C. AEI-Brookings Joint Center for Regulatory Studies.

Hammitt, J.K. (2000) Are the Costs of Proposed Environmental Regulations Overestimated? Evidence from the CF Phaseout, *Environmental and Resource Economics*, 16(3), 281–301.

Haq, G., Bailey, P.D., Chadwick, M.J., Forrester, J., Kuylenstierna, J., Leach, G., Villagrasa, D., Fergusson, M., Skinner, I. and Oberthur, S. (2001) Determining the Costs to Industry of Environmental Regulation, *European Environment*, 11, 125–39.

Harrington, W. (2003) *Regulating Industrial Water Pollution in the United States*, Resources for the Future Discussion Paper 03-03, Washington D.C.: Resources for the Future.

Harrington, W., Morgenstern, R.D. and Nelson, P. (1999) *On the Accuracy of Regulatory Cost Estimates*, Washington D.C.: Resources for the Future. http://www.rff.org/Documents/RFF-DP-99-18.pdf, accessed 14 April 2008.

Hartman, R.S., Wheeler D. and Singh, M. (1997), The Cost of Air Pollution Abatement, *Applied Economics*, 29 (6), 759–74.

Housley, I. (2001) *Review of the PPC Application Process*, Fairford: CTC Environmental.

International Chemical Secretariat (ICS) (2004) *Cry Wolf: Predicted Costs by Industry in the Face of New Regulation*. http://assets.panda.org/downloads/crywolF040b.pdf, accessed 14 April 2008.

Jaffe, Adam B., Peterson, S.R. Portney, P.R. and Stavins, R.N. (1995) Environmental Regulation and the Competitiveness of U.S. Manufacturing: What Does the Evidence Tell Us? *Journal of Economic Literature*, XXXIII (March), 132–63.

James jr, H.S. (1998) Estimating OSHA Compliance Costs, *Policy Sciences – Special Issue on Regulatory Budgeting*, 31, 321–41.

Jantzen, J. (1989) *Costs of Environmental Management, 1988–2010, 3 policy scenarios*, Report for the Ministry of VROM, 25 May, The Hague: VROM.

McMahon, P. (2002) Cost of Compliance Assessments and the Water Industry in England and Wales, *European Environment*, 12(5), 257–68.

Moran, D, MacLeod, M., McVittie, A., Lago, M. and Oglethorpe, D. (2007) Dynamics of Water Use in Scotland, *Water and Environment Journal*, 21 (4), 241–51.

OECD (1997), *Evaluating Economic Instruments for Environmental Policies*, Paris: OECD

OECD (2004) *Regulatory Performance: Ex post Evaluation of Regulatory Tools and Institutions (Draft Report by the Secretariat)*, Paris: OECD.

OMB (2005) *Draft Report to Congress on the Costs and Benefits of Federal Regulation*, Washington D.C.: Office of Management and Budget.

Oosterhuis, F. (ed.) (2006) *Ex-post Estimates of Costs to Business of EU Environmental Legislation* Final Report to DG Environment, Amsterdam: IVM. http://ec.europa.eu/environment/enveco/others/policy/pdf/2007_final_report_conclution.pdf, accessed 5 April 2008.

Pickman, H.A. (1998), The Effect of Environmental Regulation on Environmental Innovation, *Business Strategy and the Environment*, 7(4), 223–33.

Risk Solutions (2005) *Impact Evaluation of the Control of Major Accident Hazards (COMAH) Regulations 1999*, London: Risk Solutions.

RIVM (2000) *Techno 2000: Modellering van de daling van eenheidskosten van technologieën in de tijd* (modelling change in the unit costs of technologies over time), Rapportnummer 773008003, April, Bilthoven: RIVM.

Romano, D., Cavicchi, A., Rocchi, B. and Stefani, G. (2005) Exploring Costs and Benefits of Compliance with HACCP Regulation in the European Meat and Dairy Sectors *Acta Agricultura Scandinavica Section C*, 2, 52–9

Sherrington, C. and Moran, D. (2007) The Accuracy of Regulatory Cost Estimates: A Study of the London Congestion Charging Scheme, *European Environment*, 17, 106–123.

Stockholm Environment Institute (1999) *Costs and Strategies Presented by Industry During the Negotiation of Environmental Regulations*, Stockholm: Stockholm Environment Institute.

Thompson, K.M., Segui-Gomez, M. and Graham, J.D. (2002) Validating Benefit and Cost Estimates: The Case of Airbag Regulation, *Risk Analysis*, 22(4), 803–11.

US Congress Office of Technology Assessment (1995) *Gauging Control Technology and Regulatory Impacts in Occupational Safety and Health: An Appraisal of OSHA's Analytic Approach*, Washington D.C.: US Government Printing Office.

VROM (1989), *National Environmental Policy Plan for the Netherlands*, 25 May, The Hague: VROM.

Watkiss, P., Baggot, S., Bush, T., Cross, S., Goodwin, J., Holland, M., Hurley, F., Hunt, A., Jones, G., Kollamthodi, S., Murells, T., Stedman, J. and Vincent, K. (2004) *An Evaluation of the Air Quality Strategy: Final Report to Defra, December 2004*, Didcot: AEA Technology.

Wilkes, A. (2004) *Regulatory Impact Assessments: Memorandum of Evidence for the Environmental Audit Committee's Pre-Budget 2004 Inquiry*, London: House of Commons Library.

PART II

Case studies

Air quality and energy

4. Assessment of the Air Quality Strategy for the UK: road transport sector

Winston Harrington and Richard D. Morgenstern

This review examines the evaluation, presented in *An Evaluation of the Air Quality Strategy* (AEA 2004a) (hereinafter EAQS) of transport-related air quality policies implemented in the UK since 1990. The relevant material is contained in Chapter 2 of the EAQS. What we find in that chapter are estimates of actual benefits and costs of these policies in 2001, projections of benefits and costs out to 2020, and comparisons of benefits and costs. In addition, the chapter contains a comparison of cost estimates made prior to the implementation of the policies, with estimates of actual costs.

In this brief commentary on the EAQS report, we will first review the methodology of *ex ante/ex post* cost comparisons, and then discuss the particular comparison produced in the EAQS.

4.1 METHODOLOGY

Probably the two most important reasons for completing an *ex post* analysis of a regulation or other public intervention are the following:

1. To evaluate the quality of the analysis supporting the regulation (that is, the Regulatory Impact Assessment – RIA – process).
2. To evaluate the performance of the regulation itself.

These two are obviously related but are not the same. The first reason is a response to concerns about the quality of RIAs, and in particular to concerns that the estimates of benefits and (especially) costs are biased in one way or another. The second is obviously even more important, inasmuch as it is about judging the policy, rather than the analysis of it. Operationally, the main difference is that an *ex ante* analysis is required for the first, but not for the second.

It is apparent that the EAQS is concerned with both the quality of the rules and the quality of the analysis of the rules, but the former seems to get most of the attention. In this regard it is useful to contrast the contents of the EAQS with the previous literature on cost estimation, in particular our review of *ex ante/ex post* cost comparisons (Harrington *et al.* 2000b), which is exclusively focused on the quality of the RIAs. Two of our findings are of particular interest in this context.

First, potentially important categories of costs exist that are not easy to measure and are rarely measured, either in *ex ante* or *ex post* studies. In particular, expenditures are not the same as costs, even though estimation of abatement expenditures is often a useful way of measuring the most important costs of environmental regulation. However, if there are costs that do not involve market transactions, or even if there are market costs that appear in unexpected places, a focus on abatement expenditures will overlook them. Among motor vehicle policies, examples of such costs are not difficult to find. Bresnahan and Yao (1985) show that the early efforts to reduce new vehicle emissions (in the 1970s) caused 'drivability' problems that adversely affected motorist's enjoyment of the vehicles. Eventually these problems were evident in anomalously low used car prices for vehicles of the affected model years. (This was a transitional problem and soon manufacturers figured out how to reduce emissions without unduly affecting vehicle performance.) A second example can be found in vehicle inspection and maintenance programs (I/M). The draft regulatory impact analysis (RIA) prepared by the USEPA (1992) for the Enhanced I/M program failed to include the value of motorist waiting times at the inspection stations. Waiting costs, which were shown by Harrington *et al.* (2000a) to be one of the largest components of the cost of I/M policies, were included in the final RIA.

Second, we found that it is potentially misleading to make a regulatory cost comparison without also considering the 'performance' comparison (in this case, the emission reductions). It turned out that measuring performance is very important if one is to put the cost estimate in the proper context. Among the cases we examined, one of the most important reasons that costs were overestimated was that regulatory effectiveness was overestimated as well. Having measures of both cost and performance meant that we could factor the total cost estimate into two components: performance (emission reductions) and unit cost (cost per unit emissions reduced). This factoring can bring great insight to the important question of why costs were overestimated. In our sample of studies, for example, the most frequent outcome was that total costs were overestimated and unit costs were estimated without any obvious bias, thus shifting the attention away from cost estimation issues to the reasons for incomplete implementation.

Of course, in Europe in general and in the United Kingdom in particular, results might be different. Our sample was dominated by the studies from the United States, where more opportunities may have arisen for differences to appear between a regulation as issued and the regulation as implemented. Still, it cannot be assumed *a priori* that such differences will not exist.

A possibly more important reason for being concerned about the actual emission reductions arises because of the potential for redundancy, synergy and even competition among the numerous fuel and equipment regulations that make up the regulatory strategy. Where *ex ante* studies have been prepared, they must make assumptions about how the various pieces of the strategy will fit together. In the retrospective study, it may be impossible to determine which of several regulations (or technologies) are accounting for the estimated *ex post* emission reductions, but it may at least be possible to compare the sum of emission reductions from those regulations *ex ante* and *ex post*. In such situations it is particularly important for *ex post* studies to examine whether the anticipated emission reductions have been realized.

By these lights, the EAQS transport study is both less and more than an *ex ante/ex post* comparison. It is less because it does not contain the *ex ante/ex post* comparison of emission reductions. It is more because it adds an *ex post* benefit-cost comparison not found in other comparisons. This is a potentially valuable addition, because it increases the prospect of adding the comparison of *ex post* and *ex ante* benefits to the typical analysis. As the EAQS points out:

> Note that because scientific understanding of risks to health from air pollution has developed enormously in recent years, an assessment now of the benefits to health of the same ambient pollution would be different, in important respects, from a corresponding assessment several years ago. These changes contribute to differences between *ex post* and *ex ante* estimates of the benefits of policy changes. (footnote 16 p. 6)

In principle, it would be possible to extend the factoring of the *ex ante/ex post* comparison into total effects (again, aggregate emission reductions) and unit benefits. Indeed, the 'ideal' *ex post* analysis would combine the *ex ante/ex post* comparison and the benefit-cost analysis (BCA) and would consist of a comparison of *ex ante* and *ex post* BCAs. In practice, however, the *ex post* benefit calculation is much more difficult than it is in the case of costs (which is itself no walk in the park), and that is why no such analysis has yet been produced.

As in the cost case, total benefits can be thought of as the product of regulatory performance (emission reductions) and the value of the performance unit – as long as the value is constant. But on the cost side it is the emission reductions that lead directly to costs, and even though unit or marginal costs may not be constant from one location to another, estimating total costs is an adding-up of the product of emission reductions and unit costs at each location. On the benefit side we have this same adding-up process, but there is no direct link between emission reductions and benefits. To value the health benefits of emission reductions, for example, one needs to link the emission reductions to changes in ambient air quality, the air quality improvements to reductions in human exposure, the exposure reductions to changes in health outcomes, and finally the health outcomes must be valued. Each of these steps requires a sophisticated modeling exercise, which means that producing a benefit study of a regulation is often quite costly. Although all those steps are required to complete the *ex ante* study, repeating them for the *ex post* study may be prohibitively costly. Unless the *ex post* study can bring to bear other empirical studies, made for other purposes, it is possible that an *ex post* benefit study will consist only of an updated assessment of the performance of the emission regulation, to which are applied the information used in the *ex ante* study to link emission changes to monetary changes in health outcomes.

Also, if there is more recent information that can update the links in an *ex post* benefit study, it is likely to be less decisive than are *ex post* costs, which most observers are tempted to regard as 'actual' costs, even though they are an estimate, though obviously a better one than the *ex ante* estimates. Few are similarly tempted on the benefit side, where, for example, a new epidemiological study can update and revise prior estimates of dose–response functions, but they are unlikely to be regarded as 'actuals'. The difference in attitude is reflected in the EAQS, for whereas *ex post* costs are repeatedly referred to as 'actual costs', the *ex post* benefits are never referred to as 'actual benefits', but are accepted to be highly uncertain and are subjected to a sensitivity analysis.

4.2   THE EAQS COMPARISON

The EAQS contains survey estimates of regulatory costs made before and after the regulation was implemented. Necessarily, the authors limited their attention to the 2001 *ex post* analysis and to the policies that could have produced significant emission reductions by that date. Those policies are as follows:

New Vehicle Policies

1. Euro I technology (mandatory from 1993 for most vehicles)
2. Euro II technology (mandatory from 1996 for passenger cars and 1998 for commercial vehicles)
3. Euro III technology (mandatory from 2000 for passenger cars and 2001 for commercial vehicles)
4. Euro IV technology (mandatory from 2005 for passenger cars and 2006 for commercial vehicles).

Fuel Policies

1. Unleaded petrol, first implemented by differential petrol taxes and made mandatory for new vehicles after 1988; leaded fuel phased out altogether in 1999
2. Low sulphur (500 ppm) diesel fuel, mandatory after 1 October 1996
3. Reductions in sulphur and benzene content of diesel fuel and petrol (2000)
4. Ultra-low sulphur (ULS) diesel fuel and petrol (both to 50 ppm), due to be implemented in 2005 but actually implemented in 2001 by the use of differential taxes.

In a separate report (AEA Technology 2004b) the study team also analyzes a set of 'local measures', behavioral or nonstructural policies that can be designed specifically for and applied to a particular local area. The local measures chosen were examined for the city of Sheffield, so that they could be compared with one another. Evidently, however, the analysis is hypothetical and contains no *ex ante/ex post* comparison of actual policies. Therefore we omit it from further consideration.

4.2.1 Vehicle Standards

It was impossible for the authors of the EAQS to rely on existing documents for the comparison of vehicle costs. For Euro I technology there was no RIA providing an estimate of *ex ante* costs, while for Euro II technology the authors were unable to find an existing *ex post* study. Although an *ex ante* Euro I estimate could not be found, the authors substituted other information from both European and American sources. The former included industry estimates of £400–£600 per vehicle for catalytic converter technology reported by the Stockholm Environment Institute (SEI 1999) and an estimate of £350 per vehicle in a report (not cited in the EAQS) commissioned by the UK government. EAQS also mentioned that a prominent manufacturer sold converters to the industry for less than £50 per unit, but that did not include other components of the emission control system (ECS) or the cost of installation. These Euro I estimates were really not very conclusive.

RIAs for Euro II–IV showed estimates of £250–£500 for Euro II cars, £210–£295 for Euro III cars and £210–£590 for Euro IV cars. There has been no *ex post* evaluation of the cost of these technologies. However, if the estimates are accurate and the costs were passed on to the consumer, the cumulative cost would have produced cost increases of 10 to 20 per cent between 1990 and 2004. The EAQS analyzed new car prices and found the increase in real prices to fall midway between the cumulative low and cumulative high costs of the Euro II standards between 1996 and 1999, after which new car prices declined by 15 per cent or more between 1999 and 2001, at which point the data series stops. No one is suggesting that tighter emission standards actually lower prices, for many other things are going on, but it does suggest that they are not important determinants of vehicle prices, and that they are lower than one would predict from the *ex ante* estimates.

The American estimates were of the cost of actual California state emission regulations. Cackette (1998) found estimates prepared by industry and the California Air Resources Board (CARB) of the cost of California low-emission vehicle (LEV) regulations from the early 1990s. Industry estimates ($877 per vehicle) greatly exceed CARB estimates ($174 per vehicle), with the latter being a little higher than actual data from 1998. For ultra-low-emission vehicles (ULEV), Cackette found estimates by individual firms. The GM estimate of this rule was 'up to' $1000 per vehicle, while the estimate submitted by Honda was only $300. CARB's estimate was $250. Cackette's study apparently did not report an *ex post* estimate. In addition, Anderson and Sherwood (2002) produced a comprehensive analysis of the cost of federal fuel and vehicle regulations in the US. They developed the cumulative technology approach later used in the EAQS and, applying it to US vehicle regulations, they found that between 1994 and 2001, EPA estimates of vehicle costs were close overestimates of the costs as revealed in actual vehicle price increases, while industry estimates were much higher and much less accurate.

4.2.2 Fuel Standards

The EAQS analysis of fuel standards is less extensive. For unleaded petrol, no *ex ante* study was found, but the authors cite an *ex post* cost estimate of £0.0042 per liter from the Competition Commission (1990). The report found two *ex ante* studies for the 2000 and 2005 fuel quality limits, a UK

RIA and a study by the oil industry association CONCAWE. Surprisingly, the CONCAWE *ex ante* estimate is much lower than the RIA estimate for both regulations: 90 per cent lower for the 2000 limits and 40 per cent lower for the 2005 limits. Needless to say, this is almost unheard of. In the event, it appears that both 2005 estimates were overestimates, for when the tax differential was implemented in 2001, it led immediately to compliance with the 2005 limits.

The EAQS, citing a study by Ecotec and GHK (2002), cautions that British refineries may be postponing investments in sulphur abatement. Evidently this postponement is made possible by Britain's having moved first relative to the rest of the EU; the tax differential has apparently attracted all the low-cost ULS fuel to the UK. Once all of the EU requires ULS fuels, movement up the supply curve will require refineries through-out Europe to install additional abatement equipment to produce sufficient quantities of compliant fuel. Besides these studies, the best source of *ex ante/ex post* comparisons of the cost of fuel regulations is found in Anderson and Sherwood (2002), which gives estimates of all US fuel control rules since 1990. Unfortunately, there is not much overlap between these rules and the UK rules except for limits on sulphur, for which good estimates already exist. By 1990, lead had already been removed from US gasoline. In addition, US policy makers had other concerns, including limits on fuel volatility and requiring oxygenates, that are not mentioned in the list of policies analyzed in this report.

4.3   BENEFITS AND QUANTIFICATION OF EMISSION REDUCTIONS

As noted above, the EAQS acknowledges that the 'best practice' dose–response functions connecting ambient air quality to health outcomes are likely to be very different today from what they were 10 or 15 years ago. But that is only one link in the chain that connects the regulation to the real-ization of monetized benefits. Most likely, the same could be said for other links in the chain. Thus, there have been revisions to the thinking regarding the value of statistical life (VSL) and the value of a life year (VOLY) used in the EAQS, as well as periodic revision and updating of meteorological models predicting air quality from spatial emission patterns and weather conditions.

Perhaps surprisingly, the same considerations apply to the estimation of emissions and changes in emissions from regulations. Neither the EAQS nor the Anderson–Sherwood paper (2002) appear to examine actual emis-sion reductions produced by the regulations they analyze. The EAQS does acknowledge that emission reductions can differ from *ex ante* forecasts, if indirectly, and apparently incorporates the most important differences in the analysis. On page 10 we find:

> The use of the latest emission factors demonstrates that the effects of policies on NO_x emissions are complex. A large proportion of the improvements seen are from the introduction of Euro I technology to petrol vehicles (around a 30% improvement relative to the 'no abatement'). However, the updated emission factors indicate that Euro I emission standards were detrimental for NO_x emissions from heavy diesel vehicles. This spreads the reductions of NO_x reductions more evenly over Euro I to IV standards. The analysis here predicts that the total reductions of successive technical standards are a 30% reduction for Euro I, increasing to 40% with the addition of Euro II, 60% with the addition of Euro III and 70–80% with the addition of Euro IV, relative to the 'no abatement' scenario.

The paragraph indicates that there was at least one surprise that followed implementation of the standards, and it came to light after emission inventories were updated. This statement illustrates the importance of emission inventories to the estimation of both current and future emissions. An emission inventory is usually constructed by combining results from an emission factor model (which predicts emission rates for various vehicle types under a variety of operating conditions) and a vehicle fleet model (which predicts vehicle ownership and use by type of vehicle, given socioeconomic conditions). Like all emission inventories, a mobile source inventory is based on a mix of measured data and model results, with the latter presumably based on measured data. However, vehicle emission inventories are much closer to the model end of things than, say, an inventory of electric utility emissions is. Utility boilers are large stationary sources, and the largest of them are now equipped with continuous emission monitors (CEMs). Total emissions, as well as their spatial and temporal distribution, can be estimated with great precision. So can emission rates, of course, since electricity production is known even more accurately than the emissions are. (Of course, while existing emissions can be measured with unusual precision, the effects of policies must still be based partly on modeled results, because they are measured against a no-policy counterfactual.)

CEM technology does not yet exist for motor vehicles, and even if it were available it would only be possible or economical to equip and monitor a small sample of all vehicles in the fleet. As a result emission data on typical vehicles in real-world operating situations is quite limited. There is good emission test data on new cars, but as discussed above, it can be inaccurate if actual driving patterns and air conditioner use do not match test conditions. For vehicles in use, emissions tend to increase with age, and estimation of those emissions must rely on emission test results from a sample of vehicles recruited from vehicles at large, remote sensing of vehicle emissions, or vehicle inspection and maintenance (I/M) programs that periodically test all vehicles. In each case there are concerns about the selection characteristics of the sample, that is, whether the vehicles sampled faithfully represent the vehicles in use, as well as the relationship between the emission data and the real-world performance of vehicles. In the US at least, vehicle emission inventories have periodically undergone drastic change as new empirical studies have revealed serious problems in the underlying emission models, although the model has been stable in the last few years. It would be somewhat surprising if the British experience was much different.

From the standpoint of evaluating previous analyses, it would have been useful if the EAQS had explicitly compared the *ex post* emission and benefit estimates not only to the 'no policy' counterfactual but also to the *ex ante* predicted emissions and benefits, at least where there were RIAs, and to factor the change in estimated benefits into component parts.

4.4   CONCLUSIONS

The EAQS authors' survey of the cost estimates led them to several conclusions. First, industry sources seriously and consistently overestimate the costs of vehicle regulations, and they also have been overly pessimistic about technological innovation. Second, official estimates produced by regulators in both Europe and the US also tend to be overestimates, but are much closer to actual costs. Third, the authors do not report on how the *ex post* emission reductions of the successive Euro technologies were determined, or indeed whether they were different from the *ex ante* estimates. Fourth, the benefits of the clean air strategy appear to exceed the costs by a wide margin, although it is not clear whether the same is true for each policy considered separately. Subject to the reservations expressed above and in the body of the report, we agree.

REFERENCES

AEA Technology (2004a) *An Evaluation of the Air Quality Strategy*, Report prepared for DEFRA. London: Defra.

AEA Technology (2004b) *An Evaluation of the Air Quality Strategy Additional Analysis: Local Road Transport Measures*, Report prepared for DEFRA. London: Defra.

Anderson, J. F. and T. Sherwood (2002) Comparison of EPA and Other Estimates of Mobile Source Rule Costs to Actual Price Changes, paper presented at the *SAE Government Industry Meeting*, Washington, DC, May 2002.

Bresnahan, Timothy and Dennis Yao (1985) The Nonpecuniary Costs of Automobile Emission Standards, *RAND Journal of Economics*, 16, 437–455.

Cackette, Tom (1998) The Costs of Emission Controls, presentation at *MIT Workshop on New Vehicle Technology*, MIT, June.

Competition Commission (1990) *The Petrol Industry*, www.competition-commis sion.org.uk/rep_pub/reports/1990/fulltext/265c3.pdf, accessed 14 April 2008.

Ecotec and GHK (2002) *A Study to Evaluate Cost Estimates of Specific Measures Associated with the National Air Quality Strategy,* Report no. C1966, commissioned by DEFRA. London: Defra.

Harrington, Winston, Amy Ando and Virginia D. McConnell (2000a) Are Vehicle Emission Inspection Programs Living Up to Expectations? *Transportation Research* Part D, 5(3),153–172.

Harrington, Winston, Richard D. Morgenstern and Peter Nelson (2000b) On the Accuracy of Regulatory Cost Estimates, *Journal of Policy Analysis and Management*, 19(3), 297–322.

SEI (1999) *Costs and Strategies Presented by Industry During the Negotiation of Environmental Regulations,* The Stockholm Environment Institute for the Swedish Ministry of the Environment, http://www.sei.se/dload/seiy/ministry.pdf, accessed 14 April 2008.

USEPA (1992) *I/M Costs, Benefits and Impacts.* Ann Arbor, MI: Office of Mobile Sources (November).

5. Assessment of the Air Quality Strategy for the UK: electricity generating sector

Winston Harrington and Richard D. Morgenstern

This chapter reviews the electricity-generating sector analyses presented in chapter 3 of *An Evaluation of the Air Quality Strategy* (AEA 2004). The focus is on the benefits and costs of the air quality policies in 2001, with projections to 2010. Methodological issues surrounding the calculation of emission reductions attributable to air quality policies, as well as the accuracy of the *ex ante* cost estimates developed for these policies are considered. Specific reference is made to the following sections of the Evaluation:

- Section 3.2: Policies in the Electricity Supply Industry and Emission Reductions;
- Section 3.3: Emission Reductions and Air Quality Benefits;[1]
- Section 3.5: Economic Costs of the Policies;
- Section 3.7: Conclusions and Lessons for Future Policy.

The Evaluation recognizes the contribution of both energy and environmental policies to improved air quality and it attempts to disentangle the specific role played by each. Evidence is presented on the tendency for overestimation of regulatory costs by the Environment Agency. Overall, the Evaluation presents a reasonably well-balanced treatment of the issues, although questions can be raised about the strength of the case presented on the relative importance of environmental policies, as well as the extent of overestimation of regulatory costs.

5.1 POLICIES IN THE ELECTRICITY SUPPLY INDUSTRY AND EMISSION REDUCTIONS

Section 3.2 of the Evaluation describes the major policy initiatives introduced since 1990, with a focus on the very dramatic changes in the UK fuel mix, as well as the changes in fuel quality, improved generation efficiency and the requirements for higher levels of pollution abatement equipment. Three types of policies are considered:

1. Energy policies, including electricity liberalization, introduction of gas in the electricity supply industry, and renewables policy;
2. European emissions and air quality policies (for example, the UNECE Sulphur Protocol, the Large Combustion Plant Directive, the Sulphur Content of Liquid Fuels Directive);
3. National environmental or emissions policy (Integrated Pollution Control (IPC) implementation and the introduction of technology or techniques).

A key challenge for the analysis is to distinguish between, on the one hand, the rather dramatic changes in energy policies, including electricity privatization and liberalization, increased gas use, and the introduction of the Renewables Policy (Non-Fossil Fuel Obligation – NFFO) and, on the other hand, the adoption of specific measures to limit emissions and improve air quality, including the IPC initiatives.

As the authors argue, the 'dash for gas' was driven primarily by the economic attractiveness of natural gas plants (low capital costs, quick build times). It was also aided by air pollution policies that required expensive abatement equipment on new coal plants and increasing pressure to reduce emissions from existing coal plants (UK Sulphur Strategy and IPC). Without the dash for gas, other actions would have had to be taken to meet the international commitments agreed under the UNECE Sulphur Protocol, which would have imposed additional costs on the electricity supply industry.

There is also a link between air quality policy and renewables. Although the NFFO was not specifically introduced to improve air quality, one of the primary aims was to address air pollution and other environmental externalities from conventional facilities. As the authors note, the 'convergences' between energy and air quality policies which have led to the observed emission reductions in the electricity supply industry (ESI) make it difficult to allocate emissions improvements accurately among the various policies. The approach adopted was to assess individual measures and then assign these to specific policies. Where more than one policy was involved, the authors presented ranges, reflecting the minimum and maximum benefits they believed could be attributed to individual policies. Arguably, this is a plausible approach. At the same time, a great deal of judgment is involved in the allocation of individual measures to specific policies. Thus, it is extremely difficult to distinguish the baseline or 'no abatement' scenario from the specific measures designed to limit emissions and improve air quality.

The authors identify two specific challenges in developing the 'no abatement' scenario:

1. The 1990 start date of the evaluation coincided with a time of major changes in the electricity supply industry, including market liberalization, the dash for gas and others;
2. In the absence of those energy policies, there would probably have been some changes in both the cost of generating electricity as well as the demand. However, as the authors note, the magnitude of these changes is highly uncertain.

The 'no abatement' scenario actually adopted for the evaluation was based on the actual electricity demand scenario observed over the evaluation period, projected to 2010 (that is, no gas in the fuel mix and no price effects). Between 1990 and 2001, this translated into a demand growth of about 16–17 per cent, and proportionate increases of SO_2, NO_x, and PM10 emissions. The authors have also undertaken a limited number of sensitivity analyses around the 'no abatement' scenario, including:

1. Adoption of the efficiency improvements that have been achieved since 1990, although still with 'no gas' and no price effects;
2. Adoption of alternative assumptions about nuclear, for example, no nuclear growth after 1990.

The basic approach for analyzing the effects of new policies is to first consider all the air quality benefits in the electricity supply industry since 1990 relative to the 'no abatement' scenario, regardless of why they occurred, and then consider the likely contribution of individual initiatives, including air pollution. As the authors note, however, this represents a 'pragmatic' approach, the results of which should be seen as 'indicative'.

In quantitative terms, the authors estimate that 53 per cent of the reduction in SO_2 is attributable to increased gas use, and another 4 per cent is attributable to the oil-fined power station closure – both of which are assigned to a 'combination of policies'. For NO_x and PM10 reductions, 59 per cent and 49 per cent, respectively, are attributable to a 'combination of policies'. Overall, the authors' calculations lead to the following attributions of emission reductions to air pollution policy:

1. 38–100 per cent of the SO_2 emission reductions;
2. 34–100 per cent of the NO_x reductions;
3. 46–100 per cent of the PM10 emission reductions.

Of course, all policy analyses of this type are inherently speculative, since it is not possible to know with precision what would have happened if a different set of policies had been chosen or if no new policy had been implemented at all. To produce *ex ante* estimates, both the 'with' and 'without' scenarios must be modeled. To produce *ex post* estimates, one must determine the actual outcome empirically and compare it to a hypothetical baseline based on the status quo ante. In other words, policy analyses of this type are arbitrary to some degree, whether they are *ex ante* or *ex post* in nature.

An alternative to the authors' assumption that key energy policies do not belong in the baseline would involve developing some scenarios which do incorporate such policies in the baseline. One could then compare the observed emission levels with these results as a means of establishing the magnitude of the improvements that could be attributed to the air quality policies.

Interestingly, similar difficulties in defining the relevant baseline were encountered in the retrospective analyses of costs and benefits of the US Clean Air Act conducted by the US Environmental Protection Agency (US Environmental Protection Agency 1997; see also Krupnick and Morgenstern 2002). In that analysis, an even more extreme choice was made – namely, to attribute to the Act all progress in air quality occurring since the passage of the Act. In the UK Evaluation, there has been at least some attempt to distinguish the fairly dramatic energy policy developments from the changes in air quality policies. However, it is clear that other modeling choices are plausible and, quite possibly, more defensible. If, for example, the liberalization of the electricity supply industry, the dash for gas and the oil station closure were all included in the baseline, 49 per cent or more of the emission reductions (depending on the specific pollutant) would have been attributed to the changes in energy policy. This would have reduced the contribution of air quality initiatives. Instead, the approach adopted by the authors assigns considerably larger reductions to the air quality policies.

5.2   ECONOMIC COSTS OF THE POLICIES (EVALUATION SECTION 3.5)

The comparison of *ex ante* and *ex post* costs is based on analyses of specific policies:

1.   UNECE Protocols;
2.   Renewable Policy;

3. Integrated Pollution Control;
4. National Emissions Ceiling Directive and the Gothenberg Protocol;
5. Large Combustion Plant Directive.

5.2.1 UNECE Protocols

A report prepared for the Swedish Ministry of the Environment (SEI 1999) is cited as the source of an *ex ante* estimate prepared by the industry group (Central Electric General Board) that generating costs would rise by up to 30 per cent (and prices by as much as 25 per cent) based on the assumption that flue gas desulphurization equipment would be fitted to generating plants to meet the UNECE Protocols. Without specific attribution, a non-industry source is cited as estimating cost increases of 2.5–5.0 per cent over a 15-year period. Further, the authors observe that by 1993, after liberalization was introduced but before significant gas generation capacity was in place, UK emissions of SO_2 had fallen by 36 per cent, a full 6 per cent more than required by the first UNECE Protocol.

Comparisons are also made with the German experience in complying with the first UNECE Sulphur Protocol. In that case, it is argued that the original government estimate was too low, but by only 25 per cent rather than the 100 per cent claimed by industry.

Taken together, does this information constitute credible evidence of over- or underestimates of costs? The first question to ask is whose *ex ante* estimates are being compared to the observed *ex post* information. Different types of institutions conduct *ex ante* analyses of the costs of environmental regulations: regulated firms, other industry sources (such as trade associations or consultants), government regulators, government authorities not involved in preparing the regulation, environmental groups and environmental think tanks. Based on data from the US, there is ample evidence to support the notion that industry estimates (whether from firms or trade associations) tend to overstate costs. It would not be terribly surprising if such a conclusion held for other nations, thus casting doubts on at least some of the cost estimates of the UNECE Protocols (Goodstein and Hodges 1997; Harrington *et al.* 2000; US Office of Management and Budget 2005). While it is important to distinguish *ex ante* estimates developed by regulated industries from those developed by institutions with a more plausible claim to objectivity, such as government agencies or independent observers in universities or think tanks, the more interesting question is whether *ex ante* analyses by the latter are also systematically biased. Based on the evidence presented in the Evaluation, the case for bias in estimates generated by government or independent observers is much less clear. Arguably, credible evidence is presented on government cost underestimation in Germany. In the UK, however, the evidence is not particularly strong. The fact that there was over-compliance with the UNECE Protocol in 1993, in a system that did not provide for banking of early reductions, at a time of liberalization of the electricity supply industry (and before significant gas generation capacity was in place) suggests that the marginal costs of SO_2 reduction may not have been very high. Since no sources of *ex ante* government cost estimates are cited, it is difficult to make the case that the government forecasts should be considered either over- or underestimates in this instance.

One often asked question is whether the *ex ante* cost estimates developed by regulated industries are so predictably biased that one could apply some generalized correction factor. The answer, of course, is that neither the nature nor the extent of the bias are so predictable (however, see Table 15.3). In the US, where there is more extensive information involving *ex ante–ex post* comparisons, there are reported cases of both under- and overestimation of costs. The only plausible approach to dealing with such estimates is to examine them on a case-by-case basis. In that regard, analysts should demand full transparency of the data and assumptions used and then scrutinize them carefully to assess their overall quality. Frequently, of course, there are good reasons why *ex ante* estimates from industry or other sources may differ from *ex post* observations. Before a regulation is adopted, information about response options and costs may be asymmetrically distributed. That is, potentially regulated parties generally have better information about alternatives for meeting requirements than regulatory agencies and advocacy groups. At the same time, how-ever, industry cost estimates may be too high if firms do not fully anticipate cost-saving measures they may discover once resources are directed to compliance. Delays in regulatory implementation can also affect costs (Harrington *et al.* 2000).

5.2.2   Renewables

This subsection presents information on the experiences with the Non-Fossil Fuel Obligation (NFFO), which was introduced in 1990 and required electricity suppliers to obtain specified amounts of non-fossil generating capacity. Utilities were permitted to pass on to consumers cost increases for added capacity in renewable technologies. As the authors note, it might be possible to assess whether the *ex ante* estimates of these cost increases were in close agreement with what the utility actually had to pay for renewable generating capacity, although this would require more detailed analyses than the authors of this study were able to carry out. In the absence of such analyses, the authors make a number of observations: 1) that the NFFO has been increasingly oversubscribed; and 2) that the price of renewables has declined dramatically from 7p/kWh in the first two orders to 2.7p/kWh in the fifth order. They also present information showing that the percentage of the awarded capacity that has actually been deployed in the latest rounds has fallen dramatically when compared to the initial rounds, although there is no indication that anything more than normal construction lead times account for these declines.

Does this information constitute evidence of over- or underestimation of costs? By itself, the fact that the NFFOs were oversubscribed might indicate that the government overestimated the cost of producing electric power via renewables. However, since the electricity supply industry also faced renewable obligation orders requiring adoption of specified levels of renewables, the oversubscription may not be so surprising. The fact that bid prices have declined so dramatically is certainly consistent with the notion of *ex ante* overestimates. However, since no *ex ante* time path of costs was presented, and since the stringency of the renewable obligation orders has increased over time, this is not particularly convincing evidence either. In sum, the evidence presented on biases in renewables cost estimates generated by the government is not strong enough to support a clear conclusion either way.

5.2.3 Integrated Pollution Control (IPC)

A number of early studies are cited on the costs of flue gas desulphurization (FGD), some by industry and some by independent analysts. Consistent with the experiences in the US, Germany and elsewhere, they indicate a dramatic decline in per ton SO_2 abatement costs over time (Watzold 2004 and Burtraw and Palmer 2004). At the same time, the authors present conflicting views about the future. At one point, they indicate that per ton abatement costs may rise as future load factors decline. At another point, they indicate that coal use rose from 2000 to 2001 as gas prices increased. For NO_x, the authors indicate that there is a general trend toward cost reductions from earlier to later studies. They also note that the scale of the cost reduction is relatively small compared to other pollutants.

A stronger argument for overestimation of costs applies in the case of low sulphur coal. The authors cite studies which find that costs are now lower than predicted, including an Entec (2000) study finding that the cost of using 1 per cent sulphur coal had fallen from an estimated £250/tonne SO_2 removed to a current value of zero. Such a finding would clearly support a conclusion of cost overestimation. The key caveat is that forecasts of coal price differentials according to sulphur content involve a number of highly specialized issues, including detailed assumptions about world coal markets. That said, an overestimate is an overestimate. However, the source of the error is also relevant in making a broader finding about the accuracy of cost estimates prepared before a regulation is issued.

5.2.4   National Emissions Ceiling Directive and the Gothenberg Protocol

This section reports what seems like a fairly gross overestimate of abatement costs by a team at the International Institute of Applied Systems Analysis (IIASA) involving overestimates by a factor of 2–10. As the authors explain, however, there are actually two opposing errors at work here. On the one hand, IIASA overestimated baseline SO_2 emissions, largely because they underestimated the amount of gas in use. On the other hand, IIASA underestimated the cost of FGD, principally because they overestimated the load factors for the coal-fired plants. On balance there appears to be a large cost overestimate in this case. However, the fact that the overestimate can be linked back to the underestimate of gas use only highlights the difficulties, noted earlier, of disentangling the large changes in energy policy occurring over the period from those occurring in environmental policy.

5.2.5   Large Combustion Plant Directive

This section does not present significant new information on the issue of *ex ante–ex post* cost comparisons. Overall, it further highlights the difficulties of disentangling the effects of energy and environmental policies. The principal conclusion drawn by the authors from Evaluation Section 3.5 regarding *ex ante–ex post* cost comparisons is that the strongest case for cost overestimation is in the area of IPC. This tendency has also been observed in the US and elsewhere. Yet, as noted, the fact that a good portion of the overestimation derives from a miscalculation of low sulphur coal prices tends to undermine the overall point that environmental agencies overestimate costs.

5.3   CONCLUSIONS AND LESSONS FOR FUTURE POLICY

Evaluation Section 3.7 highlights the fact that both energy and environmental policies implemented in the ESI have contributed to recent air quality improvements in the UK and reiterates the early findings on the attribution of emission reductions to the different policies. As noted, a case can be made that different baseline assumptions would produce quite different results in terms of the portion of the reductions attributable to environmental policy. The authors also observe that the coincidence of major energy liberalization and the increased stringency of air regulations is unlikely to be repeated in the future. In fact, the authors note the potential for a reversal of the trends back toward greater coal use should gas become more expensive, as has already started to happen (coal use increased in 2000 and 2001).

Regarding the *ex ante–ex post* cost comparisons, the authors go a bit further in this section than in earlier text in arguing that *ex ante* estimates are too high. In the opinion of this reviewer, the authors overstate the case somewhat, given the weak evidence on this issue. Of the various measures examined, overestimates are principally evident in the case of IPC and, as noted, the major reason for this is the mis-estimation of low sulphur coal premiums in international markets.

Overall, the report presents a reasonably balanced treatment of the contribution of environmental policies to improved air quality and a reasonably balanced analysis of the accuracy of regulatory cost estimates. At the same time, several instances have been noted where the authors have made specific assumptions or have drawn conclusions that tend to overstate the role of environmental policies and overstate the relatively soft evidence on cost overestimation. This is not to deny that such overestimation may have occurred, but simply to note that the evidence gathered in the Evaluation does not make a particularly strong case.

NOTE

1. Note: this review does not examine the calculation of benefits as discussed in section 3.3.

REFERENCES

AEA Technology (2004) *An Evaluation of the Air Quality Strategy*, Report to DEFRA. London: Defra.

Burtraw, Dallas and Karen Palmer (2004) SO_2 Cap-and-Trade Program in the United States: A 'Living Legend' of Market Effectiveness, in Winston Harrington, Richard D. Morgenstern and Thomas Sterner (eds), *Choosing Environmental Policy: Comparing Instruments and Outcomes in the United States and Europe*. Washington DC: Resources for the Future Press.

Entec (2000) *The Determination of the Implications of an Emission Reduction Strategy under the Revised Large Combustion Plant Directive*, Final report to DETR, May 2000. London: DETR.

Goodstein, E. and Hodges, H. (1997) Polluted data, *The American Prospect*, 8(35). www.prospect.org/as/articles? article Id=4.757, accessed 5 April 2008.

Harrington, Winston, Richard D. Morgenstern and Peter Nelson (2000) On the Accuracy of Regulatory Cost Estimates, *Journal of Policy Analysis and Management,* 19(32), 297–322.

Krupnick, Alan and Richard D. Morgenstern (2002) The Future of Benefit-Cost Analyses of the Clean Air Act, *Annual Review of Public Health,* 23, 427–448.

SEI (1999) *Costs and Strategies Presented by Industry During the Negotiation of Environmental Regulations,* The Stockholm Environment Institute for the Swedish Ministry of the Environment. http://www.sei.se/dload/seiy/ministry.pdf, accessed 14 April 2008.

US Environmental Protection Agency (1997) *The Benefits and Costs of the Clean Air Act: 1970 to 1990.* Washington, D.C.: Office of Air and Radiation/Office of Policy.

U.S. Office of Management and Budget (2005) *Report to Congress on the Costs and Benefits of Federal Regulation,* Washington D.C.: U.S. Government Printing Office.

Watzold, Frank (2004) SO_2 Emissions in Germany: Regulations to Fight Waldsterben, in Winston Harrington, Richard D. Morgenstern and Thomas Sterner (eds), *Choosing Environmental Policy: Comparing Instruments and Outcomes in the United States and Europe.* Washington D.C.: Resources for the Future Press.

6. The cost of complying with EU vehicle emission and fuel standards

Robin Vanner and Jochem Jantzen

This case study relates to EU vehicle emission and fuel standards for road transport. It focuses on *ex ante* and *ex post* costs estimated for the Netherlands in the period 1985–2001. The introduction of EU vehicle emission and fuel standards for road transport has led to a considerable reduction of emissions from road transport. This was achieved via the introduction of new technologies leading to additional costs. In general, early cost estimates (around 1985–1990) were later found to be overestimates by a factor of 2. This factor varied from 0.3 (that is, implementation was achieved at greater cost than anticipated) in the case of a switch to low-sulphur diesel, to a factor of 9 for the switch to unleaded petrol. The section on technological progress also shows that unit costs of environmental technologies have continued to decrease over a number of years at quite a high annual rate (around 10 per cent). If there is further refinement of the technology, as is assumed in many technological studies, it is likely that the cost decrease will continue. The results of the case study show that for *ex ante* cost assessments for the transport sector, the development of unit costs (due to technological developments and economies of scale) need to be taken into account.

6.1 INTRODUCTION

This case study aims to give an overview of *ex ante* and *ex post* assessments of the costs of applying environmental technologies in road transport. More specifically, the analysis focuses on the directives on emissions from motor vehicles, diesel engines, soot and so on (70/220) and lead content of petrol, quality of diesel and sulphur content (85/210). A number of studies were carried out in the Netherlands during the 1980s and 1990s on the costs of environmental measures. For the first National Environmental

Programme (VROM 1989) and *Concern for Tomorrow* (RIVM 1988), various scenario analyses were performed. At the same time the Central Bureau for Statistics (CBS) started to collect data on the costs of environmental policies. The basis for the case study is formed by time series of *ex ante* and *ex post* cost estimates in the Netherlands during the period 1985–2001:

1. The *ex ante* cost estimates were derived from a cost assessment for the second Netherlands National Environmental Programme (TME 1993).
2. The *ex post* costs estimations are based on CBS statistics (CBS environmental costs for transport on CBS Statline).

The reason for the focus on the Netherlands is not only that data is available, but also that the vehicle fleet is thought broadly to represent that of the rest of Western Europe. The data permits analysis of the Dutch transport sector, focusing on:

1. gasoline/LPG passenger and delivery vehicles (light duty vehicles);
2. diesel passenger and delivery vehicles (light duty vehicles);
3. diesel heavy duty vehicles;
4. cleaner gasoline and diesel fuels;
5. environmental inspection.

The case study aims to identify the additional costs due to the implementation of various parts of the EU legislation for the transport sector. In principle the Dutch legislation follows the EU standards. However, the introduction of cleaner transport has additionally been stimulated by means of differentiation in excise duties for unleaded gasoline and low sulphur diesel. This has led to a slightly faster implementation of EU standards than required under the EU directives.

The differences have been analysed by looking into the basic data used in the *ex ante* estimates (quantities, additional costs per unit), by statistical assessment and by paying specific attention to the influence of technological change (and economies of scale) on unit costs of environmental equipment.

6.2 METHODOLOGY

For both the *ex ante* and *ex post* studies that have been surveyed, costs are defined as 'environmental, compliance costs' (see chapter 3 of Oosterhuis

2006). This is a narrow definition of costs and directly links to additional costs due to environmental regulation.

Costs are estimated by multiplying unit costs of technology (for example the costs of a catalyst per vehicle excluding subsidies), share of new vehicles sold equipped with the technology and number of new vehicles sold per year. No effort has been made to estimate the influence of technological development on costs and efficiency of, for example, catalysts. It should be stated that, especially for diesel vehicles, little or no robust estimates of the costs of particle traps were available based on realisations in 1993. To make estimations and realisations comparable, the price level of both assessments needed to be adapted to 2002. This was done by applying the (harmonised) CPI (Consumer Price Index) (see CBS Statline 1995).

As only cost information was available, it is not clear if the expected environmental effects of the policy (emission reduction) have been realised as originally anticipated at the beginning of the 1990s. However, in general it can be said that the emission reduction in the transport sector has been in conformity with the projections.

6.3 RESULTS OF THE ANALYSIS

Table 6.1 summarises the results of the various analyses comparing the estimates for 2001 with the *ex post* cost estimates. The analysis behind these results now follows for a number of examples.

6.3.1 Gasoline and LPG Passenger and Light Duty Vehicles

The annual *ex ante* estimate, as shown in Figure 6.1, tends to be about twice as high as the annual costs estimated *ex post*. Also, the *ex post* costs show a slower and more gradual increase over the period 1985–1995, whereas in the *ex ante* estimation, it was thought that 'full implementation' would have been achieved by 1990. There are thought to be two reasons why the *ex ante* costs deviate from the *ex post* realisations:

1. The *ex ante* estimation used fixed unit costs throughout the time of implementation (for example, €771 per catalyst at price level of 1993) whereas CBS's *ex post* cost estimates used observed unit costs for catalytic converters, starting with the same (€771) in 1985 but reducing to about €230 by 2001 (that is, an *ex ante* overestimation in unit cost by a factor of 3.4).
2. Investments in catalytic converters for passenger cars were depreciated

Table 6.1   Summary of ex ante *and* ex post *estimates for measures to reduce emissions from road vehicles*

Case study item	Ex ante estimate € m	Ex post estimate € m	Cost ratio ex ante: ex post	Key drivers of difference
Catalytic converters for gasoline passenger cars	506	253	2.0	Resource efficiency and economies of scale
Modifications of diesel passenger cars	136	25	5.4	Integrated approach rather than add-on equipment
Modifications of diesel trucks	208	27	7.7	Integrated approach rather than add-on equipment, slower implementation
Unleaded gasoline	213	25	8.5	Unforeseen decrease in additional distribution and production costs for unleaded gasoline
Low-sulphur diesel	31	118	0.3	Lower sulphur content than anticipated and higher additional production costs
Vehicle inspection	30	81	0.4	Underestimation of (additional) inspection costs
Total transport	**1123**	**529**	**2.1**	**Technological development and economies of scale**

Source: CBS Statline (2005) and TME (1993).

in one year in TME's *ex ante* estimate, whereas in the CBS realisation, these investments were depreciated over a period of 9 years. This may explain why the costs of full implementation are reached in 1990 in the TME estimates (when exhaust limits became mandatory) and only in 1995 in the CBS realisation.

Therefore, the dominant reason for the overestimation of the costs for complying with emission reduction requirements for gasoline and LPG

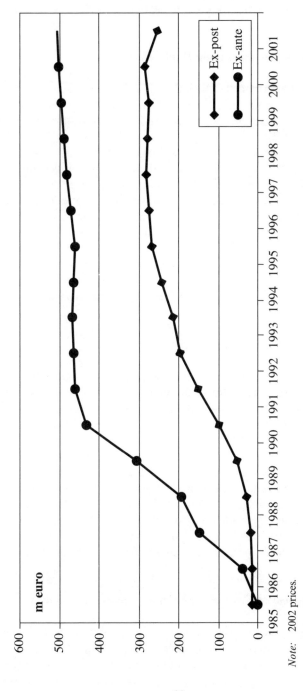

Note: 2002 prices.

Sources: *Ex ante* (estimated) TME (1993); *ex post* CBS Statline (2005).

Figure 6.1   *Comparison of* ex ante *and* ex post *annual cost estimates of catalytic converters and adaptation to LPG for passenger cabs and light duty vehicles*

vehicles is the decrease in unit costs for catalytic converters between 1985 and 2001.

6.3.2   Diesel Passenger and Light Duty Vehicles

Also, a comparison is made between the *ex ante* cost estimates of TME and the *ex post* realisation of CBS. The results of the analysis of costs of engine modifications for diesel passenger cars and diesel light duty vehicles are shown in Figure 6.2.

It can be seen that for smaller diesel vehicles, the *ex ante* estimate had been shown by 2001 to have overestimated the costs of implementation by a factor of 5. The assumptions behind the *ex ante* costs estimates were relatively conservative because little was known about the way that car producers would implement the stricter emission limits for diesels. Therefore, the *ex ante* costs were based on an oxy catalyst (€817 – €1588 per unit), but the producers of diesel engines found more integrated ways of improving the environmental performance of the engines, leading to a per unit investment of between €130 and €240 (that is, an *ex ante* overestimation in unit costs of a factor of about 6.5; see for example Touche Ross 1995, pp. 48–49).

6.3.3   Overview for the Road Transport Sector

Figures 6.3 and 6.4 show *ex ante* and *ex post* cost estimates for compliance with all emission reduction requirements for all road transport in the Netherlands. These figures suggest that *ex ante* estimates overestimated compliance costs by a factor of 2. The vehicle-specific case studies adopted here suggest that the main reason for this *ex ante* overestimation was an overestimation of unit costs of environmental equipment and measures. The *ex post* estimates suggest that unit costs often tend to decrease (for technological and efficiency reasons). This tendency was not factored into the *ex ante* cost estimates. This was particularly the case for the costs of complying with regulations concerning diesel vehicles. The automobile industry was able to supply complying cars at much lower costs (a factor of 6 or more for small diesel vehicles) than initially thought.[1]

6.3.4   Development of Costs of a Regulated Three-Way Catalyst

In 1995, a study was completed on the development of the unit costs of environmental technologies (Jantzen *et al.* 1995). One of the cases investigated was the case of the catalyst. Figure 6.5 shows the development of

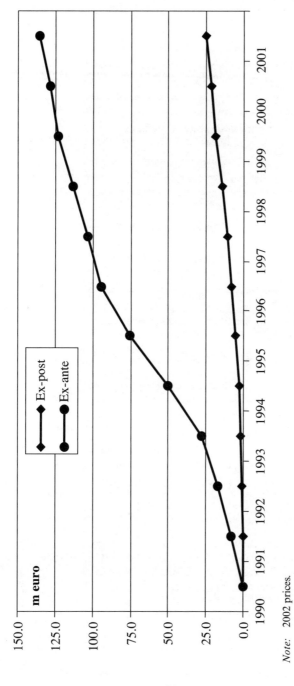

Note: 2002 prices.

Sources: *Ex ante* (estimated) TME (1993); *ex post* CBS Statline (2005).

Figure 6.2 Comparison of ex ante *and* ex post *annual cost estimates of engine modifications for diesel passenger cars and light duty vehicles*

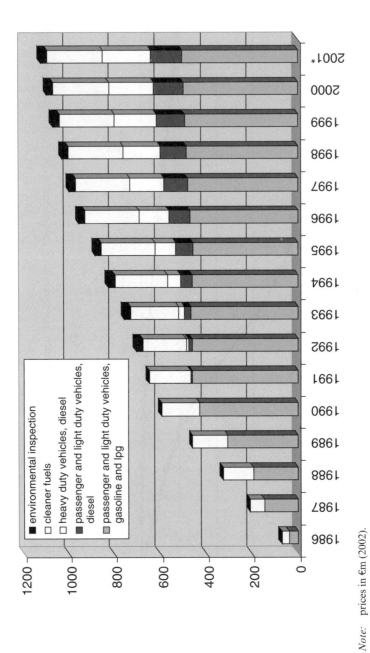

92

Note: prices in €m (2002).

Source: Estimate by TME (1993).

Figure 6.3 *Total ex ante estimate of annual environmental costs for road transport in the Netherlands, 1986 to 2001*

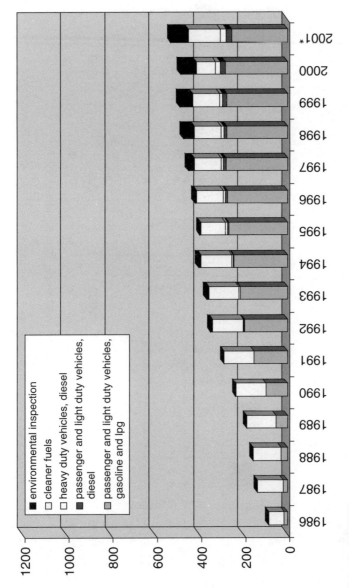

Note: Prices in €m (2002).

Source: Based on CBS Statline (2005).

Figure 6.4 Total ex post estimate of annual environmental costs for road transport, 1986 to 2001

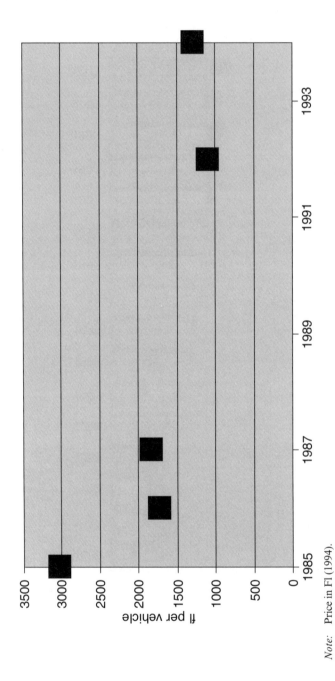

Note: Price in Fl (1994).

Sources: Jantzen et al. (1995) based on OECD (1986), Dietz (1991) and Touring Club der Schweiz (1994).

Figure 6.5   Development of the additional purchase costs of a regulated three-way catalyst, 1985–1994

the costs of three-way catalysts between 1985 and 1994. The observation for 1985 comes from Japan, the observations for 1986 and 1987 from the EU and the observations for 1992 and 1994 from the Netherlands.

In 1985 the costs of a regulated three-way catalyst were reported to be fl. 3043[2] in Japan (price level 1994). For the next two years, two observations from Europe showed costs of fl. 1750 and fl. 1850 per system. For 1992 and 1994, two observations for the Netherlands showed unit costs of fl. 1100 and fl. 1300 respectively. So in a nine-year period the costs dropped from over fl. 3000 to fl. 1300: an annual decrease of unit costs of about 9 per cent.

6.3.5 Development of Costs of a Catalytic Converter

The costs of the catalytic converter as part of the total regulated three-way catalyst system have also been investigated and are shown in Figure 6.6. Data for 1986 are from the US and for 1991–1994 from the Netherlands. This figure shows that the price of a catalytic converter has dropped significantly from fl. 634 in 1986 to fl. 261 in 1994, which represents an annual decrease in unit costs of 11.7 per cent.

6.4 CONCLUSIONS

In general, it is known that unit costs of environmental technologies have a tendency to decrease over time. RIVM and TME found from various case studies that the rate of cost decrease of environmental technologies (4 per cent – 31 per cent per year) is well above the average 'technological progress factor' (of 2 per cent) often used in macro-economic models. This finding is confirmed by this case study on transport. The studies performed by Honig *et al.* (2000) and Jantzen *et al.* (1995) indicate an annual rate of decrease of unit costs of around 10 per cent.

The results of the case study on road transport in the Netherlands show that *ex ante* estimates in general are a factor of 2 higher than the observed *ex post* costs. The section on technological progress also shows that unit costs of environmental technology have the tendency to decrease over time, with quite high annual changes (around 10 per cent). If technology is constantly refined, as is assumed in many technological studies, it can be assumed that this decrease in costs will continue. All empirical evidence points toward the same conclusion: in the automobile industry, production costs can drop quite significantly for new environmental technologies, and new introduced technologies rapidly become cheaper in use.

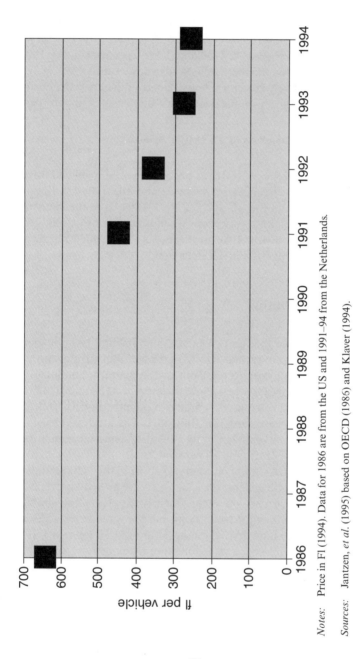

Notes: Price in Fl (1994). Data for 1986 are from the US and 1991–94 from the Netherlands.

Sources: Jantzen, *et al.* (1995) based on OECD (1986) and Klaver (1994).

Figure 6.6 Development of the additional purchase costs of a catalytic converter, 1986–1994

In considering the reason for the high *ex ante* estimates, it appears that either there was a lack of attention to 'normal innovations' (higher resource efficiency; economies of scale) or unforeseen developments leading to cheaper solutions (engine modification instead of particle traps and oxy catalysts for diesels). In some cases, the underlying assumptions about, for example, vehicle sales or the timing of implementation of certain pieces of legislation, explain part of the observed differences.

NOTES

1. It might be argued that the development of new or modified engines will have induced probably invisible research and development costs to the car industry, as the lifespan of current engine designs was shortened by the environmental requirements.
2. fl. = Dutch Guilder, 1 € = 2.20371 Dutch Guilders (Official Fixed Conversion Rate).

REFERENCES

CBS Statline (2005) *Milieukosten van het verkeer, 1990–2001* (Environmental costs of transport 1990–2001). All items selected (investments, operational costs etc), 1995.

Dietz, E.J. (1991) Milieukosten van het verkeer, 1989–1990, *Kwartaalbericht Milieustatistieken*.

Honig, E., A. Hanemaaijer, R. Engelen, A. Dekkers and R. Thomas (2000) *Techno 2000: Modellering van de daling van eenheidskosten van technologieën in de tijd*, report number 773008003, Bilthoven: RIVM.

Jantzen, J., H. Heijnes and P. van Duyse (1995) *Technische vooruitgang en milieukosten, aanzet tot methodiekontwikkeling* (Technological progress and environmental costs, initiative for methodological development), The Hague: TME.

Klaver, P. (1994) Voorverwarmde katalysator komt sneller in actie, *Auto en Motor Techniek*, 7/8, 38–39.

OECD (1986) *Enclair '86: energy and cleaner air: costs of reducing emissions: proceedings of the symposium, 28–30 October 1986, Taomina, Italy*. Rome: ENEA/OECD.

Oosterhuis, F. (ed.) (2006) *Ex post estimates of costs to business of EU environmental legislation: final report*. Amsterdam: IVM.

RIVM (1988) *Concern for tomorrow: environmental outlook 1985–2010*, Bilthoven: RIVM.

TME (1993) *Estimation of environmental costs for NEO-II*, internal document, Brussels: TME.

Touche Ross (1995) *A cost-effectiveness study on the various measures that are likely to reduce pollutant emissions from road vehicles for the year 2010: final report to the CEC, DG III*. London: Touche Ross.

Touring Club der Schweiz (1994) *10 Jahre Katalysatorautos*, Emmen, Switzerland: TCS.

VROM (1989) *Choose or lose: first National Environmental Plan for the Netherlands*, Leidschendam: VROM.

7. The Large Combustion Plants Directive

Cécile Des Abbayes and Robin Vanner

This chapter focuses on the implementation of the Large Combustion Plant Directive (LCPD) 88/609/EEC and the respective national regulations in the UK, Germany and the Netherlands. The comparison of *ex ante* and *ex post* cost estimates focuses on the reduction of SO_2 emissions in the power sector. It should be noted that the 88/609/EEC Directive is no longer in force as it was revised in 2001. However, since the revised Directive is still in the process of implementation,[1] no *ex post* costs are available, so this chapter considers only the 1988 Directive.

The UK's *ex ante* cost estimates made by the industry proved to be between six and ten times higher than the *ex post* costs. This is thought to be due to the unscheduled privatisation of the electricity sector, and the fact that the new private companies took advantage of the flexibility given in the UK's National Plan to innovate and develop a new technology using gas.

Germany and the Netherlands issued a more command-and-control type of regulation, requiring flue gas desulphurisation (FGD) retrofitting or closure of all power plants. In Germany, *ex ante* estimates provided by the industry were twice as high as the German Environment Agency's (Umweltbundesamt or UBA), because industry lacked experience in retrofitting technologies, and perhaps hoped that the prospect of high costs would lead to the legislation being changed or abandoned. UBA's estimates, based on technology providers' estimates and made early before the actual implementation of legislation, were broadly in line with the *ex post* costs. In the Netherlands, the government's *ex ante* estimates were 1.5 times higher in 1990, due to an *ex ante* assessment based on non-representative data.

7.1 INTRODUCTION

The Large Combustion Plant Directive (LCPD) 88/609/EEC applies to combustion plants with a rated thermal output $\geq$ 50 MWth irrespective of the type of fuel used. It provides two mechanisms:

1. For existing plants (for which permission was granted before 1 July 1987), it sets national emission ceilings for emissions of sulphur dioxide (SO_2) and nitrogen oxides (NO_X). Member States are required to draw up appropriate programmes and timetables for the progressive reduction of total annual emissions of SO_2, NO_X and dust.
2. For new plants, it sets emission limit values (ELV) for SO_2, NO_X and dust for individual installations based on Best Available Technology not Entailing Excessive Costs (BATNEEC).

This chapter also considers the implementation of two other pieces of regulation which pre-date but are very similar to the LCPD. They both take a more command-and-control approach and therefore provide less flexibility than was permitted within the LCPD:

1. The German GFA-VO Ordinance of 1983, which sets emission limits for both new and existing large (>50MW) combustion plants. After the LCPD came into force, the 1983 GFA-VO was adjudged to comply with its requirements. The Directive did not therefore require specific transposition into German law. As reported in Eames (2001), the GFA-VO was a classic piece of command-and-control legislation, setting uniform emissions limits and upgrading timetables for existing plants, which were required to meet the new plant SO_2 standards by the end of June 1988 and at the latest by 1 April 1993. New plants were required to comply with an SO_2 limit of 400 mg/m³ (or 650 mg/m³ of SO_2 for plants using high-sulphur coal). In addition, new plants were required to achieve an 85 per cent rate of desulphurisation.
2. The Dutch 1987 Bees WLV was also a command-and-control type regulation and shared many of its standards with the German legislation. It set uniform emissions limits (for SO_2, NO_X and dust) and provided timetables for existing plants. As in Germany, new plants were required to comply with an SO_2 emissions limit of 400mg/m³ and achieve an 85 per cent rate of desulphurisation. The LCP Directive was transposed into Dutch law by an amendment to the Bees WLV in 1991. The Bees was in general stricter than the LCPD, so only minor modifications were required.

7.2   THE COST-ESTIMATE STUDIES

Although the scope of the LCPD includes SO_2, NO_X and dust emissions from large combustion plants in a number of economic sectors (power generation, refineries, industrial boilers and so on), the data found in the literature and used in this chapter focus on the electricity sector, and mainly on SO_2 emissions reductions. Eames (2001) provides a good context for this, with a number of more specific cost-assessment studies providing more specific data. The quality and robustness of the cost estimates vary greatly according to the data found in the literature.

1. For the UK, *ex ante* and *ex post* qualitative assumptions about the increase of electricity generation costs due to desulphurisation equipment were found to be comparable in Haq *et al.* (1999) and Milieu Ltd *et al.* (2004). Quantitative *ex ante* and *ex post* estimates of FGD unit costs were also found and confirmed by an industry expert.
2. For Germany, the comparison between industry's and the UBA's *ex ante* estimates is reported in Haq *et al.* (1999), and confirmed by personal communication with the author of the UBA's estimates. Regarding the comparison between the UBA's *ex ante* estimates and *ex post* costs, a table providing cost elements for investment and operation costs for FGD equipment was found in Haq *et al.* (1999). There is no information available on the methodology used to assess *ex ante* costs. *Ex post* costs data are based on a survey of the German Power Plant Association (VDEW) of 1988, considered reliable by the UBA.
3. The most robust data found was for the Netherlands, provided by TME, where *ex ante* cost estimates made by the Ministry of the Environment (VROM) can be compared to statistical data gathered by the Central Bureau of Statistics (CBS).

The differences in the quality and the nature (electricity generation costs, investment costs in FGD, direct environmental costs to business and so on) of the cost data found, as well as the differences in baseline scenarios (legislations similar in their purpose but different in their content, different contexts for the electricity industry in the studied Member States and so on) do not allow comparisons between the *ex post* costs of the UK, Germany and the Netherlands to be made.

Monetary data found in the literature was in pounds sterling in 1978 and 1989, and in Deutschmarks in 1993. These were converted into year 2005 euros, taking inflation into account, using the following formula:

$A' = e \times A \times (1 + i) \wedge (2005 - \text{'initial year'})$

Where:

A': amount in 2005 euros

e: exchange rate between initial currency ('initial year' prices) and euros (2005 prices)

A: amount in initial currency, initial year prices

i: country inflation up to 2005.

7.2.1   The Country Case Studies

The United Kingdom
Background information on the UK's implementation of the 1988 LCPD
can be found in Eames (2001), mainly focusing on SO_2 emissions reductions
in the electricity sector. He reports the situation in the early to mid-1980s
as follows:

> At the time . . . the UK electricity industry, in the form of the Central Electricity
> Generating Board (CEGB), was operating within a technological paradigm
> committed to building large nuclear and coal-fired plants . . . .. Compliance with
> the LCPD was expected to require the retrofitting of Flue Gas Desulphurisation
> (FGD) to some 12GW of plant (approximately 17% of the UK's total generat-
> ing capacity). (Eames 2001 p 35)

But shortly after the LCP Directive was finally agreed in 1988, the British
government announced its intention to privatise the UK electricity industry. The CEGB's non-nuclear generating capacity was split between two
new companies, National Power and PowerGen.

The UK's national emissions reduction plan (1990) required emissions
reductions that were slightly stricter than those set out in the LCPD. These
were distributed as annual reduction targets by geographical area (England
and Wales, Scotland and Northern Ireland) and by sector (power sector,
refineries and other industries). For the power sector, the plan required a
combination of complementary measures aiming at reducing SO_2 emissions; this included:

1. Retrofitting 8GW of FGD equipment
2 Construction of some new low-emitting plants
3 Use of low-sulphur coal in existing plants.

Each power plant was allocated a fixed BATNEEC limit and a (stricter)
quota allocation, the sum of the quotas of all of the plants within a given
sector being equal to the annual limit set in the national plan. There was
more flexibility for PowerGen and National Power in England and Wales,
as they were assigned specific emissions "bubbles", to be distributed
between their plants. Each plant could exchange quotas with another of the
company's plants, as long as both its BATNEEC limit and the company's
bubble were not exceeded. This enabled PowerGen and National Power to
allocate emissions reductions measures between plants in a cost-effective
way.

Germany

Eames (2001) reports that the ambitious standards of the GFA-VO ordinance of 1983 meant that all large German combustion plants were required to fit FGD equipment by April 1993 or close down. The sector was initially opposed to the GFA-VO Ordinance. Some of the arguments presented at the time were as follows:

1. The necessary abatement technology was untested (Eames 2001).
2. The proposed limit of 400 mg SO_2/m^3 and the timetable for its introduction were considered to be impractical, as the installation of denitrification and desulphurisation systems were required to be developed by German suppliers (Milieu Ltd *et al.* 2004).
3. The proposed legislation would damage the German coal industry (Eames 2001).
4. The proposed legislation would lead to a loss of international competitiveness due to electricity price rises (Haq *et al.* 1999).
5. There was no clear scientific evidence to show that SO_2 emissions were actually responsible for forest damage (Eames 2001).

The Netherlands

Eames (2001) presents the following background to the implementation of the 1987 Bees. This required the use of FGD for new plants and made retrofitting FGD or closure eventually inevitable for existing plants. In 1990, a Covenant between the Government and the electricity sector (which was presented to the Commission as the Dutch National Emissions Reduction Plan required by the LCPD) was adopted. Since the 1987 Bees was not very flexible, negotiation mainly centred upon the degree of flexibility to be provided to the plant operators regarding the desulphurisation technologies to be used. Finally, the Covenant established SO_2 emission ceilings for the electricity sector as a whole, whilst no new SO_2 emission limits were specified at plant level.

For SO_2 emissions reductions, the Dutch National Emissions Reduction Plan specified:

1. the closure of five coal-fired plants with no SO_2 abatement equipment
2. the planned closure of a further plant in 1999/2000
3. the building of two new coal-fuelled plants
4. the retrofitting with FGD equipment of all remaining coal-fired plants by the year 2000
5. greater than 90 per cent desulphurisation rates to be achieved with plants equipped with FGD
6. additional abatement to be achieved through the use of low-sulphur coal

7. additional measures to ensure fewer malfunctions of abatement equipment.

7.3 RESULTS

The LCP Directive was adopted in a context where many EU countries had already decided to implement measures to reduce acidifying emissions, either by signing a voluntary international agreement (for example, the First UNECE Protocol on the Reduction of Sulphur Emissions and their Transboundary Fluxes), or implementing national legislation. Some other EU Directives also influenced the context of LCPD implementation. So it is difficult to identify costs related specifically to the LCPD compared to costs due to other regulations implemented in a given country.

Also, the varied national contexts prior to the implementation of the LCPD, the differences between the chosen policy options (flexible implementation in the UK for existing plants versus strict command-and-control legislation in Germany and the Netherlands), the various emissions limits and timetables and so on, make comparisons between countries impossible.

7.3.1 National Cost Estimates

United Kingdom
In the case of the UK, *ex ante* and *ex post* costs for electricity generation related to SO_2 emission reduction in the electricity supply industry were compared. Haq *et al.* (1999) report that the Central Electricity Generating Board (CEGB) estimated in 1979 that operating costs for equipment controlling sulphur emissions would increase the cost of electricity generated at the power station by about 25 per cent to 30 per cent. Milieu Ltd *et al.* (2004) report that a recent analysis of costs for the UK after adoption of the UNECE Protocols on acidification and the 1988 LCPD found that costs increased by only 2.5 per cent to 5 per cent over a 15-year period.

Regarding the unit costs of retrofitting FGD, Haq *et al.* (1999) report that the CEGB estimated in 1978 that the installation of FGD units would cost 539 €/kW installed (2005 prices). In 1993 and 1994, Drax and Ratcliffe power stations were retrofitted with FGD at costs of €318 and €241 per kW respectively (2005 prices). Therefore, *ex ante* electricity generation costs provided by industry were notably higher than *ex post* costs, and FGD unit costs estimated in 1978 were higher than the costs experienced in 1993 and 1994.

Table 7.1   Costs of retro fitting FGD (€/kW)

	Capacity of generating plant (MWth)			
	300	**700**	**1100**	**1500**
UBA (*Ex ante*)	73 €	58 €	49 €	47 €
VB (*Ex post*)	93 €	73 €	61 €	57 €
ex ante/ex post	*0.8*	*0.8*	*0.8*	*0.8*

Note: The *ex post* estimates are based on a survey of the German electricity industry, and are considered reliable by the UBA.

Source: Haq *et al.* (1999).

Germany

Haq *et al.* (1999) report that the industry's *ex ante* cost estimates for installing and operating FGD were approximately twice those estimated by the Umweltbundesamt (UBA) officials. The UBA's *ex ante* estimates for end-of-pipe equipment investment costs were later shown to be broadly in line with *ex post* estimates (about 80 per cent of *ex post* costs, see Table 7.1).

The Netherlands

The cost estimates available are the annual additional financial requirement for SO_2, NO_x and dust emission reductions from power stations from 1990 to 2004. The *ex ante* cost estimates were made by the Dutch Ministry of the Environment (VROM), while the *ex post* costs were surveyed by the Dutch Central Bureau of Statistics. As can be seen from Figure 7.1, the *ex ante* estimates were higher than the *ex post* costs: from one and a half times higher in 1990, to twice as high in 2004.

7.3.2   The Distribution of Costs

This section explores whether the various emission reduction targets were met in the UK, Germany and the Netherlands and how the costs were distributed among the actors.

The United Kingdom

Eames (2001) reported that by the mid-1990s, the requirements of the LCPD were achieved with remarkable ease. Compliance with the LCPD was originally expected to require the retrofitting of FGD to some 12GW of plant. By the time the UK National Plan was published in December 1990, it was thought that, if done in combination with other measures, only

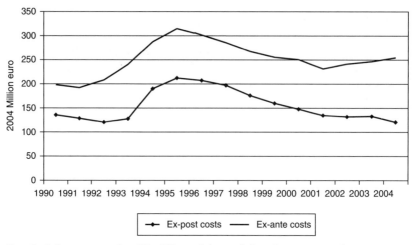

Note: Includes costs to reduce SO_2, NO_x, and dust emissions from power stations.

Source: TME Jochem Jantzen (2005).

Figure 7.1   Ex ante *and* ex post *for air protection in the power sector in the Netherlands, 1990–2004*

8GW of plant would need to be retrofitted. However, by the mid-1990s the industrial context had changed completely, mainly because of the privatisation and introduction of competition into the UK electricity supply industry. This led the new private companies (PowerGen and National Power) to respond as follows:

1. Plans to build new large coal-fired plants were abandoned in the face of high capital costs and anticipated difficulties in obtaining planning consents.
2. Many coal-fired plants closed between 1990 and 1995 and many of the remaining coal-fired plants were switched from base-load to peak-time generation and switched to imports of lower sulphur coal where necessary.
3. Both new and existing operators invested in a new technology, Combined Cycle Gas Turbine (CCGT) plants. These not only had low generation costs but also posed much less risk to the operator as the price of electricity became tied to the wholesale price of gas. In addition, CCGT plants offered investors shorter lead times and fewer planning risks.
4. The output of existing nuclear plants was increased.

In the event, only 6GW of coal-fired plant were actually retrofitted with FGD and the UK met its LCPD SO$_2$ emission reduction targets with ease.

In the UK, the anticipated *ex ante* increase in electricity generation costs due to SO$_2$ emissions reductions proved to be much higher than the *ex post* costs estimates. A number of factors explain this result:

1. A dynamic market structure after the privatisation of the electricity supply industry, which led new private companies to seek cost-effective measures to comply with the LCPD.
2. A flexible emissions abatement plan in some areas in the form of company bubbles, which made space for innovative measures.
3. The possibility of introducing new technologies (because of a phasing out of long-term coal contracts) including the development of Combined Cycle Gas Turbine (CCGT) plants. This was in part permitted by the lifting of an EU-wide restriction on the use of gas for base-load peak power generation.
4. To a lesser extent, the decrease in the unit costs of fitting FGD and the increase in nuclear output.

Germany
Eames (2001) reported that, apart from a few exceptions, retrofitting was completed between mid-1987 and mid-1988. In North Rhine-Westphalia, 30 power stations with a total capacity of approximately 62GWth (roughly 75 per cent of the total 82.5GWth) were retrofitted with FGD systems. In the former West Germany as a whole, more than 70 power stations with a total capacity of 109.8GWth (again roughly 75 per cent of the total 145 GWth) were retrofitted with FGD. Only a few of the electricity industry's large combustion plants were closed, or had their capacity reduced as a consequence of the new limits. Of these, most would have done so in any case due to their age.

7.3.3   High *ex post* costs

Germany
Industry's *ex ante* cost estimates were higher than *ex post* costs, in spite of the fact that the 'real' costs were particularly high in Germany as many studies report: the emissions reductions could have been carried out more cheaply by some form of trading. For example, Milieu Ltd *et al.* (2004) report that some LCPs could have reduced their SO$_2$ emissions less, while other LCPs (for whom emission reduction was less costly) could have reduced their emissions still further.

German electricity generators were constrained by long-term domestic coal contracts, thereby ruling out switching fuels or generating technologies as an abatement strategy, and further reducing the scope for cost-effectiveness gains (Eames 2001). In addition,

> At the time the GFA-VO was enacted, knowledge of desulphurisation technologies was fairly limited, being mainly restricted to the use of additive techniques and wet flue-gas scrubbing (in Japan). Furthermore in order to meet the GFA-VO . . . deadline, operators had to plan, construct and commission FGD facilities much more quickly than would normally have been the case

and in parallel with their licence application. As a result many experienced difficulties.

> Furthermore, as all German plants had to be retrofitted at the same time, FGD suppliers were overburdened. This led to a loss of quality and the subsequent need for additional repair work. It also resulted in a failure to optimise the operation of the FGD systems across the entire fleet of power stations, as there was no opportunity to learn from earlier mistakes, such as equipment faults, that might otherwise have been avoided. (Eames, 2001)

The fact that industry's estimated costs were twice as high as the UBA's for SO_2 emissions reduction is believed to be due to UBA's lack of experience with end-of-pipe technologies and perhaps a hope that these high estimates would lead to the regulation on LCPs being abandoned. When these *ex ante* estimates are compared to *ex post* costs, it appears that the UBA's estimates were in fact underestimates, but were close to the 'real' *ex post* costs (about 80 per cent of *ex post* costs). According to Schärer (1993), who performed the UBA's *ex ante* estimates, they were close to the *ex post* costs because they were based on interviews with technology providers. These providers had no more experience with desulphurisation end-of-pipe technologies than industry, but had submitted several tenders for building desulphurisation plants, so had worked quite extensively on cost estimates. This, added to the fact that these technologies were implemented in a very short time, and that, consequently, technology prices did not evolve much, explains why the UBA's *ex ante* estimates were so close to their *ex post* costs.

The Netherlands

The Dutch National Emissions Reduction Plan presented in the Covenant made between the government and the power sector in 1990 was applied as scheduled and the Netherlands met its emissions reductions requirements. The *ex post* cost, as monitored by CBS, shows that the pattern of annual financial requirement predicted *ex ante* was broadly correct (see Figure 7.1). However, the actual annual financial requirement turned out to be considerably lower than estimated *ex ante*. This overestimation was relatively small in 1990 (46 per cent) but had increased to 110 per cent by 2004.

The peak in total financial requirement was observed in 1995, which corresponds to the deadline for implementing the standards and therefore the latest time for capital investment. It is notable that the actual *ex post* costs decreased by 43 per cent after this. Although it is not possible to be certain about the reason for this, some interviews with the actors involved suggest that it was due to an optimisation of operations. It was reported that the main cost driver (the use of coal) remained more-or-less stable (a decrease of only 7 per cent) during this period. This would indicate that it was the more efficient than anticipated operation of FGD-fitted plants which provided costs savings of about 35 per cent.

The overestimation of *ex ante* costs is believed to be because these estimates were made in the late 1980s, on the basis of data for the very first small-scale applications of desulphurisation and denitrification technologies, that is, emerging technologies that improved in the following years.

7.4   CONCLUSIONS

In the case of the UK, *ex ante* costs provided by industry (electricity generation costs) were found to be between six and ten times higher than *ex post* costs. This major difference is explained by the fact that the context of the UK's electricity supply industry changed radically between the time the *ex ante* estimates were made and the time the *ex post* costs were assessed. The main change influencing the costs was the use of natural gas for power generation through a new technology, the Combined Cycle Gas Turbine (CCGT), causing the number of coal-fired plants needing FGD retrofitting to decrease. This technological innovation was facilitated by the flexibility of the LCPD, which left Member States free to choose the way they would comply with the national ceilings set up for existing plants, and the privatisation of the UK's electricity industry. The situation in the electricity market was therefore very different once the LCPD came to be implemented. Indeed, it is worth speculating that the targets as set out in the Directive might have been achieved without any regulation. It is clear, however, that the *ex ante* estimates provided by pre-privatised industry did not include the technology changes and fuel-switching (coal to gas), and this influenced the fact that the *ex ante* cost estimates were higher than the *ex post* costs (for electricity generation costs).

For Germany and the Netherlands, the GFA-VO of 1983 and the Bees WLV of 1987 were command-and-control regulations, requiring major investment in end-of-pipe equipment for desulphurisation and denitrification. In Germany, industry *ex ante* estimates were twice as high as the German Environment Agency (UBA)'s estimates. This difference is believed to be because they did not have much experience with end-of-pipe technologies and perhaps hoped that these high estimates would lead to the regulation on LCPs being abandoned. In Germany and in the Netherlands, official *ex ante* estimates (made by the UBA and the Dutch Ministry of the Environment – VROM) were respectively 80 per cent and 150 per cent of the 1990 *ex post* costs.

Mr Schärer from UBA (1993) considered that the *ex ante* estimates were close to the *ex post* costs because they were based on interviews with technology providers who had already submitted several tenders for building desulphurisation plants, so had worked quite extensively on cost estimates. This, added to the fact that these technologies were implemented in a very short time and that consequently technology prices did not have time to change much, explains why the *ex ante* estimates were so close to the *ex post* costs.

In the Netherlands, the overestimation of *ex ante* cost estimates is believed to be because these estimates were made in the late 1980s, on the basis of data on first small-scale applications of desulphurisation and denitrification technologies, that is, emerging technologies that improved in subsequent years.

The following insights emerge from this case study:

1. The UK's example shows that it will not necessarily be operators in their present form which will implement a regulation. If flexibility is provided within a regulation a quite different response from that expected might emerge.
2. The German case study gives an example where industry's opposition to a given regulation and lack of experience of retrofitting technologies led to an overestimation of *ex ante* costs. The UBA's *ex ante* estimates, which were close to the *ex post* costs, were based on data from technology providers.
3. In the Netherlands, the VROM's overestimated *ex ante* costs are believed to be due to an *ex ante* assessment based on emerging technologies which had little operational data. In the event, operators found operating efficiencies that reduced costs by perhaps 35 per cent.

NOTE

1. According to the Directive, Member States (MSs) must achieve significant emission reductions by 1 January 2008 at the latest, by means of a national plan or adopting an Emission Limit Value approach. The national emission reductions plans (for MSs who chose this option for their existing plants) were, at the time of writing, still under discussion between MSs and the Commission.

REFERENCES

CBS (2005), Statline-website, http://statline.cbs.nl/statweb/

Eames, M. (2001), The Large Combustion Plant Directive (88/609/EEC): an effective instrument for pollution abatement? In Glachant, M. (ed.) *Implementing European Environmental Policy: The Impacts of Directives in Member States.* Cheltenham: Edward Elgar.

Haq, G., Forrester, J., Kuylenstierna, J., Leach, G. and Bailey, P. (1999), *Costs and Strategies Presented by Industry during the Negotiation of Environmental Regulations.* Stockholm: Stockholm Environment Institute.

Milieu Ltd, the Danish Environmental Research Institute and the Centre for Clean Air Policy (2004), *Assessment of the Effectiveness of European Air Quality Policies and Measures*, a project carried out for DG ENV. Brussels: Milieu Ltd.

MNP (2005), *Milieubalans 2005* (Environmental Balance 2006), Bilthoven: MNP.

RIVM (2004), *Databases MONNIE: databases with cost-estimates for the MONNIE environmental costing model of RIVM.* Bilthoven: RIVM.

Schärer, B. (1993), Technologies to clean up power plants: experience with a DM 21 billion FGD and SCR retrofit programme in Germany, *Staub-Reinhaltung der Luft*, 53, 87–92.

TME/Jochem Jantzen, (2005), *Achtergrond-document: Actualisatie Milieukosten voor de Milieubalans 2005* (Background document: Updating Environmental Costs for the Environmental Balance 2005), for the MNP (Environmental and Nature Planning Agency of the Netherlands), Nootdorp: MNP.

VROM (1989), *National Environmental Policy Plan*, The Hague: VROM.

Industrial processes and products

8. The Control of Major Accident Hazards (COMAH) Regulations 1999 (UK)

Manuel Lago

Studies undertaken during the implementation of the COMAH regulations in the UK provide a perfect opportunity to compare *ex ante* and *ex post* assessments of the total costs of the regulations. Minor adjustments had to be made to compare the initial Regulatory Impact Assessment (RIA) of the regulations, carried out in 1998, with a detailed impact evaluation of the COMAH regulations undertaken by Risk Solutions in 2005.

A comparative analysis of both studies shows that the costs incurred by industry exceeded the *ex ante* predictions by a significant margin. This may be due to changes in the scope and status of COMAH during implementation and the interaction with other related or overlapping health and safety regulations introduced at the same time. Under these circumstances, an *ex ante* assessment can prove inaccurate, as there would be a risk of overestimating (or double counting) the total costs if some of the costs had previously been assessed under the appraisal of other regulations or, as this case study suggests, a risk of underestimating if these costs were fully ignored for the same reason. This raises the question of which cost categories should be included in such analyses and how they could be assessed, in order to improve the accuracy of the estimates.

8.1 INTRODUCTION

The Control of Major Accident Hazards Regulations 1999 (COMAH) came into force on 1 April 1999. They implement Council Directive 96/82/EC, known as the Seveso II Directive in Great Britain, and replace the Control of Industrial Major Accident Hazards Regulations 1984 (CIMAH).

The main aim of the COMAH regulations is to prevent or mitigate the effects of those major accidents involving dangerous substances which can cause serious damage or harm to people and/or the environment. The regulations are enforced by the following bodies: The Health and Safety Executive (HSE) and the Environment Agency (EA) in England and Wales; and the HSE and the Scottish Environment Protection Agency (SEPA) in Scotland (collectively known as the COMAH Competent Authority). Land-use planning aspects of the Seveso II Directive have been implemented through separate legislation, and Northern Ireland implemented all aspects of the Directive through its own legislation. COMAH regulations apply where the presence of dangerous substances at establishments exceeds set qualifying quantities. There are two levels of regulatory control: the lower level requires notification, a major accident prevention policy and land-use planning and inspection; the upper level requires, in addition, a safety report, emergency plans and provision of information to the public.

8.2   *EX ANTE* VERSUS *EX POST* COST ESTIMATED COMPARISON

The COMAH Competent Authority commissioned Risk Solutions to carry out an impact evaluation of the COMAH regulations (Risk Solutions, 2005). The specific aims of the project were to:

- estimate the full range of costs and benefits of the regulations
- identify additional work that might be required to establish further the impact of the COMAH safety report regime
- compare actual experience with the predictions of costs and benefits presented in the Regulatory Impact Assessment (RIA) that was carried out prior to the introduction of the regulations in 1999 and investigate industry claims about the underestimation of the cost of COMAH in the RIA.

The method developed by Risk Solutions combined a review of existing data with an in-depth survey of establishments subject to the regulations, in order to estimate the full range of associated costs and benefits.

This study provides a perfect opportunity to compare *ex ante* estimates of the direct costs to COMAH, as reflected in the original RIA (see HSE, 1998), with an *ex post* assessment of the actual costs. Table 8.1 shows the different cost categories that were analysed in both studies. The *ex post* study looked exclusively at compliance costs to business, and the associated costs to the competent authorities were therefore not estimated. An important cost element that was not considered in the RIA was the cost to industry of plant modifications.

Table 8.1 Taxonomy of the cost benefits undertaken for the COMAH regulations

Cost category	Counted in RIA? *Ex ante* cost estimates	Counted in Risks Solutions report? *Ex post* cost estimates
Familiarisation and notification (including training and initial analysis)	Yes	Yes
Preparation of Major Accident Prevention Policy (MAPP) (lower tier) or Safety Report (top tier)	Yes	Yes
Provision of information to members of the public (top tier)	Yes	Yes
Emergency planning and testing	Yes	Yes
Modifications to plant	No	Yes
HSE policy development and implementation	Yes	na
Competent Authority enforcement	Yes	na
HSE facility for public examination of safety reports	Yes	na
EA/SEPA facility for public examination of safety reports	Yes	na
Cost savings	No	Yes

8.3 METHODOLOGY

For comparability purposes, we follow the criteria of Harrington *et al.* (1999) for the comparison of *ex ante/ex post* analyses of individual regulations. These criteria label an *ex ante* analysis as 'accurate' if the *ex post* estimated costs fall within the error bounds of the *ex ante* analysis or if they are between 25 per cent higher and 25 per cent lower than an *ex ante* estimate.

In order to compare both analyses, some minor adjustments have to be made. First, it is necessary for the basic assumptions for the estimation of the costs to be the same (that is, assumptions used in the RIA about the total number of companies affected by the regulations). Second, prices are adjusted and compared on the basis of their net present values. Table 8.2 illustrates this comparison.

This comparative analysis confirms that the costs incurred by industry exceed the RIA predictions by a significant margin. Following the criteria of Harrington *et al.*, this may be for the following reasons:

Table 8.2   Comparison of ex ante *and* ex post *cost estimates*

Costs category	Mean total net present (NPVs) values analysis across all establishments			
	RIA values £m, 98/99 prices	*Ex post* study values £m, 98/99 prices[a]	% difference	Comment
Familiarisation and analysis (including notification)	4	111	2675	Inaccurate: Underestimated
Preparation of safety reports	17	79	365	Inaccurate: Underestimated
Preparation of MAPPs	55	33	−40	Inaccurate: Overestimated
Provision of information to the public	2	4	100	Inaccurate: Underestimated
Emergency planning	20	36	80	Inaccurate: Underestimated
Plant modifications	–	84		Not quantified in RIA
Quantifiable ongoing benefits	–	−0.1		Not quantified in RIA
Total costs of COMAH	*98*	*347 (263)*	*254 (168)*	*Inaccurate: Underestimated*
Total savings from major accidents reductions	−27	−72	167	Inaccurate: Underestimated
Total net costs of COMAH	*71*	*275*	*287*	*Inaccurate: Underestimated*

Notes:
a.   Using RIA assumptions.
b.   In brackets, total costs of COMAH excluding plant modifications and ongoing benefits categories.

1.   Errors of estimation

   a.   The validity and accuracy of the assumptions made to develop the RIA, which produced a significant underestimation of the unit costs compared with those of the Risk Solutions analysis. Examples: the total number of incumbents has proven to be smaller than previously assessed, especially amongst lower tier incumbents.

   b.   The RIA failed to identify important categories of costs of compliance with the regulations (for example, no consideration of the costs of plant modifications or changes to practices that might be required as a result of any assessment carried out under the regulations), and also failed to consider the full range of the costs (for example, the wider costs of familiarisation, including staff training).

2. The *ex post* study was developed from costs reported by industry. As such, affected companies may have reported an overestimation of the costs for two main reasons: firstly, to justify their claim that the costs were hugely underestimated in the original RIA; and secondly, to influence the imminent implementation process of amendments to the COMAH regulations.

3. Operators may have over-complied with the regulations. As such, compliance costs with the regulations may have been raised beyond any *ex ante* assessment expectations.

8.4 DISCUSSION

The estimation of the costs of compliance is full of uncertainties and often relies on a large number of assumptions, implying that the estimates found would generally be subject to large errors. These errors can come from a failure in characterising the universe of firms and agents likely to be affected by the regulations, as well as the cost-effectiveness of the compliance technologies employed (Harrington *et al.*, 1999). This may affect both the assessment of the *ex ante* and also the *ex post* estimates of compliance costs with regulations.

In this sense, the post-consultation RIA of the COMAH regulations highlighted the uncertainties surrounding the estimates arising from their reliance on a large number of assumptions (HSE, 1998). For example, many of these assumptions were built on the previous regulatory structure (mainly the CIMAH regulations). Undoubtedly, this could be another reason for the huge disparities between the *ex ante* and the *ex post* cost estimates, because in practice the COMAH regulations took a significantly different approach in some respects from that of the previous regulatory regime, CIMAH. This especially concerned the scope and application of the regulations and the preparation of safety datasheets.[1] In consequence, and regarding the development of safety reports, it became evident that some companies did not have the necessary in-house expertise to complete these reports and had to rely on expensive (and not previously accounted for) consultancy work. Also, some companies had to do further work on their reports after an initial assessment by the Competent Authority, substantially increasing the costs of compliance with the regulations.

The uncertainty associated with the estimation of the cost of compliance can also affect *ex post* analyses. The Risk Solutions study combined a review of existing data with an in-depth survey of establishments subject to the regulations, in order to estimate the full range of associated costs with COMAH. This survey consisted of five case study visits and 20 telephone surveys. The study tried to ensure that the sample chosen was representative of the range of establishments affected by the COMAH regulations. However, the accuracy of the cost estimates relied very heavily on the assumption that this small sample was representative of all the affected firms and, as a consequence, the reported costs may be highly dependent on any possible strategic bias in the responses.

Also, errors of estimation could be associated, to an extent, with the difficulty in identifying and segregating those costs resulting exclusively from compliance with COMAH from those additional costs (or parallel costs) that could arise as a consequence of increased compliance with other health and safety at work or environmental legislation.

The duty to identify, assess and manage hazards and risks already exists in other health and safety regulations that apply to most operators in the UK (for example, Chemical Hazard Information Packaging for Supply (CHIP3) regulations, the Health and Safety at Work Act and so on). Under these circumstances, the implementation of COMAH could have made duty holders aware of their non-compliance status with these regulations and, as a consequence, to report 'all the associated compliance costs' as COMAH costs, even if some of those costs should have already been incurred in complying with other regulations. This could represent a feasible explanation for the overestimation of the *ex post* estimates of COMAH.

The previous section illustrates the huge discrepancies in the cost estimates between the RIA and the Risk Solutions study. Following this discussion, the reasons for the discrepancies could be:

1. The RIA estimates were clearly underestimated in comparison with the *ex post* assessment because the analysis did not include plant modification costs; also, some other cost categories were scaled down, on the basis of avoiding the risk of double counting, as many of the costs could relate to measures that should already have been taken into account and costed under other regulations.
2. The Risk Solutions analysis, influenced by industries' own views on the regulations, stressed the importance of taking full account of all the associated costs and in doing so, probably overestimated the total costs of COMAH.

The Risk Solutions study complements an earlier study undertaken by Entec UK Ltd in 2002 (Entec, 2003), which was commissioned by the HSE's Hazardous Installations Directorate (HID) to evaluate the impact on new entrants of the COMAH safety report regime. The Entec study surveyed a larger number of operators and analysed costs by sector and separately by COMAH level (new top tier sites, existing top tier sites, lower tier sites). The report reached broadly similar conclusions to the Risk Solutions study, with substantially lower than predicted costs for lower tier sites and substantially higher than predicted costs for both new entrant and existing top tier sites. There was considerable variability in costs: for example, the sector analysis of top tier sites identified that one sector (potable spirits) had substantially lower writing and analysis costs, perhaps due to the restricted range of hazards on site, but substantial change costs. The explosives sector had similar analysis and writing costs but low change costs, perhaps because the sector has always been heavily regulated.[2] Finally, the potential for significant bias in small samples was noted, with an operator in one sector identifying costs very substantially above the average for that sector (Entec, 2003).

Alternatively, the new Regulatory Impact Assessment for the amendments to COMAH regulations recognised that COMAH could act as a catalyst to operators for the identification of areas where improvements could also be necessary to comply with other regulations (HSE, 2005). By acknowledging that COMAH could have triggered these additional measures, the RIA presents estimates of the overall costs of COMAH under two scenarios: one including the costs of additional safety measures in general, and the other excluding them. Table 8.3 illustrates the extent of these costs. Total costs excluding control costs are around £30 million, and including them, around £76m. The lower and upper bound estimates draw a better picture of the overall impact of the regulations to affected businesses. This is an attempt to differentiate those costs that may be borne exclusively as a result of compliance with COMAH from those that may also include other overlapping health and safety regulations introduced at the same time.

8.5 CONCLUSIONS

This case study proves that a degree of uncertainty in the *ex ante* assessment of the cost of compliance can be found because of changes in the scope and status of the regulations, especially in relation to the interaction with other related or overlapping regulations introduced at the same time. Under these circumstances, the *ex ante* assessment can prove inaccurate, as

Table 8.3   Total costs of COMAH regulations to businesses for all new and upgraded sites

Risk category	RIA mean total costs values £m, 98/99 prices (NPVs over a ten-year period, 3.5% discount rate)			
	Businesses entering COMAH at lower tier	Businesses entering COMAH at top tier	Businesses moving from lower to top tier	Total for all businesses
Analysis	1.2	1.2	4.8	7.1
Writing	1.1	1.3	5.5	7.8
Notification	0.3	–	–	0.3
Information	–	0.3	1.5	1.8
Emergency planning and testing	–	0.6	3.1	3.8
Competent Authority charges	3.0	1.0	2.7	6.7
Costs recovered by other authorities	–	0.3	1.6	1.9
Total scenario 1 (excluding control costs)	*5.5*	*4.7*	*19.1*	*29.4*
Control costs (additional safety measures)	21.0	6.8	18.8	46.6
Total for scenario 2 (including control costs)	*26.6*	*11.5*	*37.9*	*76.0*

Note: Costs should not be compared with those presented in Table 8.2, as these estimates only cover the impact to those businesses that will be affected by the amendments to the COMAH regulations.
1.   The RIA mean total.
2.   Discrepancies in figures are due to rounding errors.

Source: Modified from HSE (2005).

there would be a risk of overestimating (or double counting) the total costs if some of the costs had previously been assessed under the appraisal of other regulations or a risk of underestimation if these costs were fully ignored for the same reason. This raises the question of the cost categories to be included in such analyses and how they can be assessed in order to improve the accuracy of the estimates. In this respect, the RIA developed for the amendments in COMAH (see Table 8.3) is an example of good practice, as the development of different scenarios can be very useful for obtaining a better understanding of the overall costs that operators may face as a result of the regulations.

NOTES

1. Personal communication from A. Pompermaier; Economic Adviser's Unit, Health and Safety Executive, 2005.
2. Personal communication from A. Wilson, Major Hazards Control, Health and Safety Executive, 2006.

REFERENCES

Entec UK Ltd (2003) *Safety Report Regime: Evaluating the Impact of New Entrants to COMAH*. Research report 092. Prepared by Entec UK Ltd for the Health and Safety Executive in 2003. http://www.hse.gov.uk/research/rrhtm/rr 092.htm, accessed 22 April 2008.

Harrington, W., Morgenstern, R.D. and P. Nelson (1999) *On the Accuracy of Regulatory Cost Estimates*. Discussion paper 99–18. Washinton DC: Resources for the Future.

HSE (1998) *Implementation of SEVESO II Directive: Regulatory Impact Assessment*. Post-consultation Version. London: HSE.

HSE (2005) *Proposed Regulations to Implement Directive 2003/105/EC, Amending Council Directive 96/82/EC on the Control of Major Accident Hazards Involving Dangerous Substances (SEVESO II): Regulatory Impact Assessment*. http://www.hse.gov.uk/ria/chemical/comah.pdf, accessed 22 April 2008.

Risk Solutions (2005) *Impact Evaluation of the Control of Major Accident Hazard (COMAH) Regulations 1999*. Report to the COMAH Competent Authority. London: Risk Solutions.

9. *Ex post* estimates of costs to businesses in the context of BAT and IPPC

Peter Vercaemst, Erika Meynaerts, Diane Huybrechts and Robin Vanner

Directive 96/61/EC on Integrated Pollution Prevention and Control (IPPC) requires EU Member States to issue operating permits for large industrial installations. The Directive aims at further environmental improvements on the basis of what is affordable according to the Best Available Techniques (BAT) principle. By definition, economic assessment plays a central role, as the abatement techniques must take account of what is available under economically viable conditions.

At the moment, the availability of cost information and the number of in-depth economic analyses in the field of IPPC and BAT determination is relatively limited. The lack of cost data is partly explained by the reluctance of operators to provide real cost figures for reasons of confidentiality. The information from suppliers of environmental technology also needs to be treated with great caution when used to develop BAT reference documents, as they have the incentive to underestimate costs so that their technology is considered to be BAT. This case study compares the *ex post* economic evaluation to the *ex ante* assessment of BAT options for the ceramic industry in Belgium. The analysis reveals that the *ex ante* estimates of costs based on suppliers' information were quite realistic, but these suppliers seemed to be too optimistic on the *ex ante* estimates of emission reduction efficiencies.

9.1 POLICY BACKGROUND

The IPPC Directive introduced a framework requiring EU Member States to issue operating permits for industrial installations carrying out certain defined activities. These permits must contain conditions that are based on 'Best Available Technology' (BAT), in order to achieve a high level of protection of the environment as a whole. BAT are technologies and organisational measures that minimise the overall environmental impact and that are available at an acceptable cost (see Article 2 of the Directive).

A key feature of the IPPC Directive (Article 16) is to stimulate an intensive exchange of information on Best Available Techniques between EU Member States and the industries concerned. For the defined activities (as listed in Annex 1), the European IPPC Bureau organises this exchange of information and produces BAT reference documents (BREFs). Member States are required to take these BREFs into account when determining permit conditions for companies.

The IPPC Directive requires that, in addition to environmental benefits and technical practicability, economic viability is also taken into account when assessing any technique considered to be BAT. However, practical experience has shown that this economic evaluation is an arduous task for BREF writers, researchers and policy makers. Given that Member States are still in the process of implementing the IPPC Directive and a number of BREFs have yet to be finalised, literature on practical experiences of the application of BAT reference documents remains limited. There is also a scarcity of *ex post* studies assessing the real costs of implementing BAT, the efficiency in terms of environmental benefit per unit of investment or the impact that the policy has had on the viability of the industry.

Generally, to evaluate the economic feasibility of BAT options, an expert estimation is made of the cost drivers of the investment associated with the implementation of BAT options in a sector. The information on these estimated costs is then related to the environmental benefit obtained by implementing the BAT options in order to calculate their cost-effectiveness. Finally a judgement is made to ensure that implementing the BAT options does not weaken the viability of the sector to an unacceptable level (Vercaemst 2002). The approach is in line with the recent Reference document Economics and Cross-media Issues (European IPPC Bureau 2006).

9.2   THE CASE STUDY

The case study for the ceramic industry involves an assessment of BAT for Belgium which was used as an input for the European reference document for the ceramics industry (European IPPC Bureau 2007). In total, about 60 kilns are considered, which emit about 15 kt of SO_2. These plants produce bricks, roof tiles, vitrified clay pipes and expanded clay aggregates. As the sector is one of the most SO_x-polluting sectors in Belgium, the case study focuses on BAT options to reduce SO_x emissions. It is worth noting that the high SO_x emissions from the Belgian ceramic industry is not representative for the ceramics industry in the rest of the European Union.

9.3   METHODOLOGY

VITO's BAT report for the ceramic industry (Huybrechts *et al.* 1999) provides an overview of the *ex ante* assessment of costs and environmental
benefits of the various BAT options. The selection of BAT is based on a
socio-economic analysis of the industry, cost calculations of emission
reduction techniques, BAT reports from other countries, plant visits and
discussions with industry experts, suppliers, representatives of industry and
public authorities.

Ex post data on investments and operational costs are gathered by means
of surveys from plants that have invested in one of the BAT options. These
cost data are processed according to the guidelines of the reference document on Economics and Cross-Media Effects (European IPPC Bureau
2006). Finally, the *ex post* cost data gathered from the survey have been
used to recalculate the range of BAT options as used in the *ex ante* cost
assessment to see whether any difference between *ex ante* and *ex post* cost
estimates have led to the incorrect identification of BAT.

9.4   *EX ANTE* COST ESTIMATES OF BAT OPTIONS

The BAT analysis for the ceramic industry involved, among other things, a
detailed evaluation of the economic feasibility of the BAT options. The
focus of the analysis was on flue gas cleaning techniques. The process-
integrated techniques were assumed to have negligible investment costs.
Five flue gas cleaning techniques were selected that were technically suitable to reduce emissions of SO_2, SO_3, HF, HCl and dust emitted from the
ceramics industry:

1.   cascade counter flow adsorption unit with $CaCO_3$ as the adsorbent;
2.   cascade counter flow adsorption unit with Wülfragran (modified
     $CaCO_3$) as the adsorbent;
3.   wet flue gas cleaning with water followed by water treatment with
     $Ca(OH)_2$;
4.   wet flue gas cleaning with $CaCO_3$ as the adsorbent;
5.   dry flue gas cleaning with filter and $Ca(OH)_2$ as the adsorbent.

Figure 9.1 presents the assessed annual costs as a function of SO_2 emission in the untreated gases. Technical parameters and cost data for the five
techniques were derived from the responses of 11 suppliers. For the cost calculations, a depreciation period of 10 years and an interest rate of 5 per cent
were used.

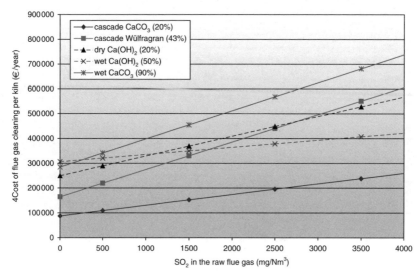

Figure 9.1   Annual cost for five flue gas cleaning techniques as a function
of SO_2 concentration in the untreated flue gases

Figure 9.1 shows that for all the flue gas cleaning techniques considered, the cost of flue gas cleaning increases with the concentration of SO_2 in the flue gases. This increase is caused mainly by an increase in the cost of adsorbent and waste disposal. Furthermore there are considerable cost differences between the various flue gas cleaning techniques. A cascade counter flow adsorption unit which uses $CaCO_3$ as the adsorbent is the least expensive flue gas cleaning technique as both the investment and operating costs for such a unit are relatively low compared to the other techniques. Wet flue gas cleaning which uses $CaCO_3$ as an adsorbent is the most expensive technique of the five as both the investment and operating costs are relatively high.

9.4.1   Economic Feasibility Evaluation of BAT Options

In VITO's report of the *ex ante* estimated cost of BAT (Huybrechts *et al.* 1999) the cost data of the five flue gas cleaning techniques were used both to determine the most cost-effective reduction technique(s) and to evaluate the effect of the different scenarios (that is, implementation of techniques) on the viability of the sector.

In order to calculate cost-effectiveness, firstly the removed HF, SO_2, SO_3 and HCl emissions were converted to SO_2 equivalents on the basis of the acidification potential. Next, the annual costs of flue gas cleaning

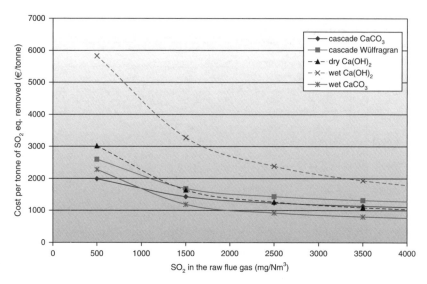

*Figure 9.2   Cost-effectiveness of the various flue gas cleaning techniques
            for removal of acid emissions as a function of SO$_2$
            concentration in the untreated flue gases*

were divided by the number of SO$_2$ equivalents removed. The cost per
unit of SO$_2$ equivalent removed by flue gas cleaning is shown in
Figure 9.2.

If cost-effectiveness was the only factor in the selection of the flue gas
cleaning technique, wet cleaning with CaCO$_3$ as the adsorbent would be the
preferred technique for kilns with high SO$_2$ emissions (>1000 mg per Nm^3).
For kilns with lower SO$_2$ emissions, a cascade counter flow adsorption unit
with CaCO$_3$ as the adsorbent is the most cost-effective. Where process-
integrated measures are used in combination with flue gas cleaning, it was
assumed that process-integrated measures provide an additional SO$_2$ emission reduction of 10 per cent, without involving substantial costs.

The effect of the BAT options on the viability of the ceramic industry in
Belgium was also analysed. A distinction was made between three groups
based on their SO$_X$ emissions:

Group 1:   SO$_X$ emissions < 500 mg SO$_2$ per Nm^3
Group 2:   500 mg per Nm^3 <SO$_X$ emissions < 1800 mg SO$_2$ per Nm^3
Group 3:   1800 mg per Nm^3 <SO$_X$ emissions < 3300 mg SO$_2$ per Nm^3

Table 9.1 gives an overview of the investment and the annual cost of
the flue gas cleaning techniques for an average company in groups 1, 2 and

Table 9.1   *Investment and annual costs of flue gas cleaning techniques for an average company in groups 1, 2 and 3 as a percentage of the annual turnover*

	Group 1	Group 2	Group 3
Cascade CaCO$_3$			
Investment	4%	5%	8%
Annual cost	2%	3%	7%
Cascade Wülfragran			
Investment	12%	14%	23%
Annual cost	3%	6%	17%
Wet Ca(OH)$_2$			
Investment	10%	11%	19%
Annual cost	5%	7%	13%
Wet CaCO$_3$			
Investment	11%	13%	22%
Annual cost	5%	8%	21%
Dry Ca(OH)$_2$			
Investment	16%	18%	31%
Annual cost	5%	7%	16%

3 as a percentage of the annual turnover. There is no presently accepted reference point to benchmark the ratio of annual costs to annual turnover. Five per cent of annual turnover has been assumed to represent an affordable level of cost in this case. Therefore BAT options that require less than 5 per cent of annual turnover are considered potentially affordable and are subject to discussion with the regulator.

Using this assumption in combination with the calculations in Table 9.1, it can be concluded that companies in group 3 would face major difficulties if they were required to invest in even the least costly flue gas cleaning technique and that the most costly technique would jeopardise the viability of the companies in groups 2 and 3. However, companies of group 1 are thought to have sufficient economic strength to invest in a cascade counter flow adsorption unit with CaCO$_3$ as the adsorbent, but the additional emission reductions that the other techniques offer do not appear to justify the greater expense.

In their evaluation of BAT, Huybrechts *et al.* (1999) consider the lessons learnt in the implementation of flue gas cleaning techniques in other countries. Nevertheless, it should be recalled that the problem of high SO$_2$ emissions seen in the Belgium ceramic sector is not representative for the ceramic industry in Europe. In the Dutch ceramic industry, the implementation of flue gas cleaning techniques is limited, as SO$_2$ emissions are

*Table 9.2   ELV for the ceramic industry in Flanders for SO$_2$ and HF
(mg per Nm^3, 18% O$_2$)*

% S	1 Jan. 2004 to 31 Dec. 2009		From 1 Jan. 2010	
	SO$_x$	HF	SO$_x$	HF
x ≤ 0.25	500	5	500	5
0.25 < x ≤ 0.50	1000	10	500	5
0.50 < x ≤ 0.75	1500	15	500	5
x > 0.75	2000	15	500	5

relatively low. The Dutch industry's focus has been mainly on HF emissions. In the German ceramic industry, several companies have implemented a flue gas cleaning technique. The cascade counter flow adsorption unit with $CaCO_3$ or Wülfragran as the adsorbent is used in most cases, but two wet flue gas cleaning techniques have been fitted.

9.4.2   *Ex Ante* BAT Findings

The BAT analysis resulted in the selection of process-integrated measures combined with flue gas purification by $CaCO_3$ adsorption as BAT for the reduction of SO$_x$/HF emissions in the ceramic industry in Belgium. Based on this BAT conclusion, VITO's proposed emission limit values (ELV) were adopted for the ceramic industry in Flanders. In March 2003 the Flemish Government amended the existing permit legislation for the ceramic industry in Flanders based on the proposals in VITO's BAT report (Huybrechts *et al.* 1999) and the detailed analysis of the cost-effectiveness of different SO$_x$ emission reduction techniques described in Meynaerts and Vercaemst (2003).

From 1 January 2010, all installations have to apply the same ELV of 500 mg per Nm^3 for SO$_x$ and 5 mg per Nm^3 for HF. Although this new sectoral ELV was based on the analysis of BAT, it was decided to go beyond what is achievable with BAT in order to comply with Belgium's SO$_2$ emissions ceiling as set out in the framework of Directive 2001/81/8EC on national emission ceilings (NEC).[1] The NEC Directive requires that Belgium reduces the SO$_2$ emissions to 99 kt by 2010. The Flemish Region was allocated 65.8 kt of the Belgian emission ceiling. In order to comply with this, the Flemish Government required the ceramic industry in Flanders to reduce its SO$_2$ emissions by 11 kt and an overall target value was set at 5.5 kt. The emission limit values that apply from 1 January 2004 until 31 December 2009 were imposed to reduce the SO$_2$ emissions by 11 kt. The emission limit value of 500 mg per Nm^3 (from 1 January 2010) was imposed to realise the target value.

Based on the results of the cost-effectiveness analysis (Meynaerts and Vercaemst 2003), it is assumed that the emission limit values can be reached if kilns which use high-sulphur clay (≥ 0.5 per cent) fit wet flue gas cleaning. Although wet flue gas cleaning with $CaCO_3$ as the adsorbent was not considered to be BAT, it offers the most cost-effective option for removing acid emissions for kilns with SO_2 emissions of greater than 1500 mg/Nm^3. Kilns which use clay with a sulphur content of <0.5 per cent need to fit dry flue gas cleaning or cascade adsorption.

9.5   *EX POST* COSTS OF IMPLEMENTING BAT

In collaboration with the industry federation, technical data on the various implementation measures were collected and used as an input into the draft BREF Ceramics (now finalised as European IPPC Bureau 2007) and the review of the local BAT report (Huybrechts *et al.* 1999). For the purpose of this case study, additional more detailed economic data have been gathered via a number of surveys of individual plants.

In order to meet the new emission regulations, the Flemish ceramic industry has implemented the following emission reduction measures since 2003–2004:

1. Process-integrated measures involved the addition of low-sulphur and/or Ca-rich additives to sulphur-rich raw materials.
2. Flue gas cleaning techniques. Most plants installed a cascade counter flow adsorber. Two plants installed a dry flue gas cleaning technique with filters. Wet or semi-wet flue gas cleaning installations were not installed.

9.5.1   *Ex Post* Emission Reduction

Detailed emission reduction performances were reported for eight representative ceramic plants. The following reported reductions are a result of the combined effect of process-integrated measures and flue gas cleaning techniques:

1. For plants using high-sulphur clays, the percentage reduction in emission of SO_x due to the fitting of dry flue gas cleaning techniques[2] was lower than expected based on the suppliers' information, even when the dry flue gas cleaning techniques were used in combination with process-integrated measures.

2.   For plants using low-sulphur clays, SO_x emission reductions were higher than expected based on the suppliers' information.
3.   The emission reductions for HF and HCl were generally in line with what was expected based on the suppliers' information.
4.   Reductions in dust emissions were lower than expected based on the suppliers' information.

Two elements explain the generally lower than expected reduction efficiencies. On the one hand, *ex ante* data of the suppliers of the equipment were too optimistic, most likely due to limited experience with using these techniques in the ceramic sector. On the other hand, all installations considered were part of SMEs that have limited technical expertise to operate these technologies correctly.

9.5.2   Capital and Operating Costs

Ex post cost data for emission reduction measures were reported for six plants that use a combination of process-integrated measures and cascade-type bed adsorbers. These data have been processed according to the guide-lines of the BREF Economics and Cross-Media Effects report (European IPPC Bureau 2006). In common with the *ex ante* assessments, to calculate the annual investment cost, a discount rate of 5 per cent and a depreciation period of 10 years were assumed. The following conclusions can be drawn from the anaysis:

1.   Process-integrated measures – The *ex ante* assessment of costs assumed that the cost of process-integrated measures would be negligible. However, for several plants the implementation of the process-integrated measures required substantial investment costs, sometimes as high (or even higher) than the investment costs for installing the flue gas cleaning equipment.
2.   The capital costs for the cascade-type adsorbers were in line with the *ex ante* cost estimates (the difference between the average *ex post* investment cost for the six plants and the *ex ante* estimate was less than 10 per cent).
3.   The operational costs for the cascade-type adsorbers were at least 20 per cent lower than expected based on the *ex ante* cost estimates. Especially the adsorbent costs and the residue disposal costs were overestimated in the *ex ante* assessment of BAT options.
4.   The maintenance costs were found to have been underestimated in the *ex ante* cost estimates.

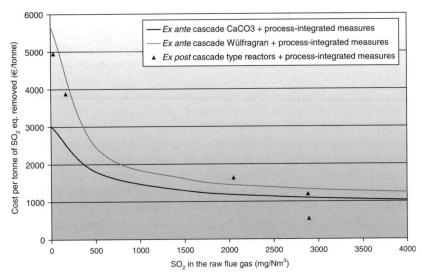

Figure 9.3   Comparison of ex ante *and* ex post *cost-effectiveness for plants using cascade type bed adsorbers and process-integrated measures*

9.6   COST-EFFECTIVENESS ANALYSIS

In Figure 9.3 the results of the *ex ante* analysis are compared with the results of the *ex post* analysis. For the *ex post* analysis, the combined cost-effectiveness of process-integrated measures and flue gas cleaning (by cascade-type bed adsorbers) is calculated. The comparison of *ex post* and *ex ante* data cannot be made for semi-wet cleaning techniques or dry cleaning techniques with filters as *ex post* data are not available.

Figure 9.3 suggests that the overall *ex ante* estimates of cost-effectiveness were quite realistic, despite the fact that the estimates of the underlying cost and efficiency data did not always agree. It would appear that the underestimations within *ex ante* cost were compensated by other overestimations. A close look at the data shows that adsorbent costs and residue disposal costs for cascade-type bed adsorbers were overestimated; by contrast, capital costs for process-integrated measures and maintenance costs and SO_x removal efficiencies of cascade-type bed adsorbers were underestimated (especially for high-sulphur clays).

9.6.1   The Distribution of Costs

The anonymous nature of the cost data does not permit a comparison of *ex post* costs with the financial status of the companies concerned. However, as an input for negotiations on the implementation of the NEC Directive, Van Biervliet (2005) assessed the financial strength of the most important industrial sectors in the Flemish region of Belgium. This analysis described the ceramics industry in Belgium as a relatively poorly performing sector. Furthermore, it is believed that the regulations which emerged as a result of the assessment of BAT were one of the key factors in the subsequent restructuring of the sector. It is also believed that a number of mostly family-owned companies ceased their activities as they were not able to make the necessary investments in flue gas treatment. Furthermore, a few plants were taken over by international players in the sector and there has been a clear tendency towards increases in scale.

9.7   CONCLUSIONS

By comparing the *ex ante* and the *ex post* data, it can be concluded that:

1. *Ex ante* estimates of emission reduction efficiencies based on suppliers' information were too optimistic (that is, *ex post* estimates showed them to be too high).
2. *Ex ante* estimates of costs based on suppliers' information were quite realistic for investments in cascade-type adsorbers (within a range of 20 per cent) but resulted in an overestimation of the operational costs of the cascade-type adsorbers.
3. The cost of process-integrated measures was underestimated in the *ex ante* estimates.
4. These overestimations and underestimations broadly cancel one another out, resulting in the *ex ante* cost estimates actually being in line with the reported *ex post* cost estimates.

This case study suggests that data from technology suppliers are useful to determine economic feasibility but should be used with care. Ideally, data from different sources (suppliers, operators, researchers and so on) should be analysed to arrive at a reliable range of cost figures.

NOTES

1. The NEC Directive imposes national emission ceilings (NECs) for four air pollutants that cause acidification and the formation of ground-level ozone: sulphur dioxide (SO_2), nitrogen oxides (NO_x), volatile organic compounds (VOCs) and ammonia (NH_3).
2. That is, cascade-type bed adsorbers or dry flue gas cleaning with filter.

REFERENCES

European IPPC Bureau (2006) *Reference Document on Economics and Cross-Media Effects*, available at http://eippcb.jrc_es/pages/FActivities.htm, accessed 16 April 2008.

European IPPC Bureau (2007) *Reference Document on Best Available Techniques in the Ceramic Manufacturing Industry*, available at http://eippcb.jrc_es/pages/FActivities.htm, accessed 16 April 2008.

Huybrechts, D., Vercaemst, P. and Dijkmans, R. (1999) *Beste Beschikbare Technieken voor de kleiverwerkende nijverheid (BAT for the ceramic industry)*, Gent: Academia Press.

Meynaerts, E. and Vercaemst, P. (2003) *Kosteneffectiviteitsstudie voor SO_2-reductie in de kleiverwerkende nijverheid (Cost effectiveness of SO_2 reduction in the ceramic industry)*, Boeretang, Belgium: VITO.

Van Biervliet, E.A. (2005) *Opstellen en uitwerken van een methodologie voor een intersectorale afweging van de haalbaarheid en kostenefficiëntie van mogelijke maatregelen voor de reductie van diverse polluentemissies naar de lucht*, Antwerp: Ecolas/VITO.

Vercaemst, P. (2002) *BAT:* When do Best Available Techniques become Barely Affordable Technology? Paper presented at workshop *Economic Consequences of the IPPC-Directive*, Brussels: European Commission.

10. The cost of reducing ozone depleting substances in the EU

Robin Vanner

The phasing out of ozone depleting substances (ODS) provides an early example of how the cost estimates provided by industry in response to proposed legislation can overestimate the costs which are later actually incurred. This case study has found that the ratio of *ex ante* to *ex post* costs (the comparison factor) can range from at least 1.4 at an overall macro level to 40 for individual case studies, and as high as 125 for administrative costs of compliance, although such results are complicated by a range of methodological drawbacks, not least the effect of inflation.

10.1 INTRODUCTION

This report considers the reasons for the differences between the industry's *ex ante* and *ex post* cost estimates, and whether they can be said to be the result of exaggeration by the industry or the expression of genuine uncertainty in the face of unknown future technological developments. The report also considers how these differences may have differed geographically between the USA and Europe, and within Europe and the EU. Finally consideration is given to the lessons which can be learnt from this case study and how it might be used in the process of informing future policy.

10.1.1 Policy Introduction

Under the auspices of the United Nations, the global community agreed to adopt the Vienna Convention to combat the threat of ozone depletion in 1985. The provisions for phasing out the production and use of ODS were laid down in the Montreal Protocol in 1987. As a result of subsequent incremental strengthening of the provisions, the Protocol now provides for the worldwide phase out of all major ODS: CFCs, halons, methyl chloroform (1,1,1 trichloroethane), carbon tetrachloride, partly halogenated CFCs (for example, hydrochlorofluorocarbons – HCFCs) and methyl bromide.

136

EU ozone policy dates as far back as 1978, but it was not until 1994 that major steps were taken towards a total phase out of the major ozone depleting substances (CFCs and halons). The existing EU policy relating to ODS consists mainly of two Regulations, one from 1994, Regulation 3093/94/EC, and one from 2000, Regulation 2037/00/EC. Whereas the first regulation aimed at reducing the production particularly of CFCs and halons within the EU, the latter aims at controlling both production and consumption of all ODS within the EU. Regulation 2037/00/EC was proposed in August 1998, agreed in June 2000, and came into force 1 October 2000; it contains new and faster phase-out schedules for HCFCs and methyl bromide, stricter regulations for the handling of ODS including new staff training schemes, mandatory recovery and destruction, and improved monitoring and licensing schemes.

10.2   INTRODUCTION TO THE LITERATURE

The predictions made by industry when faced with the prospect of having to phase out the use of ODS is a much-used example of when *ex ante* estimates turn out to be too high (see for example Cook 1996, SEI 1999, Naess 2001 and ICS 2004). However, due to the early nature of this case study, very limited actual quantitative *ex ante* estimates were made. The only available economy-wide *ex ante* estimates were made on behalf of the USA's Environmental Protection Agency (EPA) by the Rand Corporation (see for example Palmer *et al.* 1980), which have often been compared to their later reports, as well as a series of post-implementation progress reports written by the United Nations Environment Programme's (UNEP's) Technical and Economic Assessment Panel (TEAP) (for example, UNEP 1989, 1991a, b, 1994, 1995, 1997, 1998, 2002, 2003 and 2005). The UNEP reports express all cost figures in US dollars. This report therefore quotes all figures in US dollars as provided, and generates a cost comparison factor, *ex ante/ex post* cost estimates, to express the difference in estimates.

10.3   RESULTS

Any comparison of *ex ante* and *ex post* cost needs to be done with reference to a counterfactual reference scenario (that is, what would have happened if the legislation had not been implemented). ODS is a case study where the counterfactual can be assumed to have been the continued use of cheap CFCs at similar low prices. SEI (1999) reports that the sector's CFC patents had expired and therefore there was little available profit in CFCs.

However, extensive research of the literature has not found any suggestion that the industry had any intention or incentive to develop alternatives in the absence of a regulated phase out.

Table 10.1 shows that the ratio of *ex ante* to *ex post* costs (the comparison factor) can range from 1.4 at an overall macro level to 40 for individual case studies, and as high as 125 for administrative costs of compliance. Any such result is complicated by a range of methodological drawbacks, not least the effect of inflation. One way around these problems is to use a like-for-like material-based comparison, that is, *ex ante* and *ex post* estimates of how many times more expensive a substitute will be relative to the ODS it is designed to replace. Using this approach, the comparison of costs before implementation of the Montreal Protocol and a 1998 real-market cost differential for the substitution of CFC 11 and 12 with HFC 134a generates a comparison factor of 2.5. Further down the product chain for consumers, the *ex ante* estimates of prices of their products due to the Montreal protocol differed by a factor of about 1.25 (see Table 10.1).

10.4   ANALYSIS

10.4.1   Pre-implementation

Early on in the policy formulation process (in the late 1970s), the chemical industry which produced ODS were in opposition to phasing them out. This opposition was founded on the perceived high costs of a substitution away from ODS and the possible impact on jobs, although proper cost estimates were not provided at this stage (ICS 2004). This perception was largely based on the extensive application of CFCs and other ODS throughout the economy, and the capital equipment associated with their use. In the late 1980s, DuPont pointed out that 'in the United States alone, there is now more than US \$135 billion worth of installed equipment dependent on current CFC products' (reported in SEI 1999). The Association of European Chemical Companies argued in 1987 that regulating CFCs would cause 'very large' costs, leading to 'redesign and re-equipping of large sectors of vital industry . . ., smaller firms going out of business . . . and an effect on inflation and employment, nationally and internationally' (reported in SEI 1999). The sector also argued that 'Development of alternatives to CFCs having equivalent safety and thermodynamic properties is extremely unlikely' (quoted in UNEP, 1991a). In 1980, DuPont led the creation of the Alliance for Responsible CFC Policy (ARCFCP) with the stated aim of preventing, or at least mitigating, any further regulatory threat to the CFC business (Gabel 1995, p.330).

Table 10.1 Summary of ex ante and ex post costs estimates

Case study	Ex ante	Ex post	Cost ratio ex ante: ex post	Key driver of difference	Source
Macro cost estimates					
Total CFC phase-out in the US	50% @$3.55/kg (1988)	100% @$2.20/kg (1992)	>1.6	The 1988 RIA estimate was for a 50% phase out over 10 years; the 1992 estimate was for a 100% phase out over 4 years	Cook (1996, p.7)
Cost to consumers	20–25% (Reported in SEI 1999)	Little or no cost (UNEP 1995)	~1.25	Proportional increase in consumer product prices. Based on low ex ante estimate	
Social cost of reduction	50 %; $2.7 billion	100%: $1.9 billion	>1.4	In 1988, the EPA estimated that the social cost of a 50% reduction by 2000 would be $2.7 billion. Complete elimination was estimated to be 30% less than this by 1992	Hoerner (1996, p.50)
Case study cost estimates					
Costs of substitutes	10 times CFCs (Industry)	3–5 times CFCs	~2.5	Comparison of cost of HFC 134a relative to what it substituted for (CFC 11 or 12). Ex post costs as reported in 1988. Difference due to competition	SEI (1999, p.37)
Reporting and record keeping	$300 million (1988)	$2.4 million (1989)	125	Regulators moved the focus from the use sectors to producers and importers	Lee (1996, p.33)
Foam blowing plant – interim use of HCFC-22	Up to $2m	$50k	40	Regulator permitting interim use of HCFC-22 whilst developing hydrocarbons	Cook (1996, p.5)
Rate of cost reduction		$0.48/kg/yr	–	Median Cost of Multi-lateral Fund (MLF) funded projects	UNEP (2003, p.13)

139

The early *ex ante* costs estimated, which were produced with the co-operation of industry representatives (see for example Palmer *et al.* 1980), were later shown to have simultaneously underestimated the extent and the feasible rate of phase out, whilst overestimating the unit costs of substitution. As shown in Table 10.1 and reported in Cook (1996), in 1988 it was estimated that 'it would cost \$2.7 billion to halve U.S. CFC consumption within 10 years at an average cost of \$3.55 per kg reduced. Four years later, the RIA estimate for a total CFC phase-out by 2000 was \$3.8 billion' at a rate of \$2.20 per kg. A later 1993 estimate predicted that a total phase out could be feasibly accelerated to 1996 at an overall cost of \$6.4 billion (Cook 1996). This evolution in estimates needs to be seen in the context of the sector's relatively sudden change in its opposition to the Montreal Protocol during a period of technological development of substitutes leading up to the provision of data.

After its initial opposition to the Montreal Protocol, DuPont, which was leading in the race towards substitute development in the 1980s, was in 1986 first to support international controls (SEI 1999). Only one year after predicting economic chaos in the event of CFC restrictions, Pennwalt declared its intentions to acquire a leadership position in the substitute market (Cogan 1988). At this point the producer sector was divided, with the remaining opposing companies, reportedly mostly European, having by the end of the 1980s to accept the fate of CFCs and attempt to catch up and compete with the market leaders (SEI 1999). The cost of this situation to EU businesses is considered later in the section on distributional effects.

Behind this split was a technological divergence between DuPont and its mostly European competitors. DuPont invested in HCFC technology: a quick-to-develop substitute for CFCs with only 2–10 per cent of the environmental impact of CFCs. The European sector opted to spend longer developing HFCs, which provided a total ozone solution (Gabel 1995, p.337).

10.4.2   Post-implementation

During the implementation of the Protocol, a further division emerged between the producers and the diverse groups of users of ODS who maintained their opposition. 'Estimates sponsored by user industries remained higher during that period as these sectors remained sceptical of ODS controls' (SEI 1999). The work of UNEP's Technology and Economic Assessment Panel (TEAP) in the 1990s was focused on exploring specific examples of applications which did not have practicable substitutes. For example, ODS were thought to be essential for electronics manufacturing. The focus of the TEAP therefore evolved to consider the relative cost of enforcing the legislation for such applications. After making no reference to costs in its 1989 report, the TEAP was making numerous references to costs in its reports published in the later 1990s and early years of this century (for example, there were 79 cost references in UNEP 1998) as the regulator sought detailed economic analysis to justify any application for exception.

The outcome of this process was that by the middle of the 1990s, CFCs in medical metered-dose inhalers were the only significant ODS use accepted as being essential (UNEP 1998), and that virtually all of the global reductions in CFC use (50 per cent by 1995) had come at little or no cost to consumers (UNEP 1995). Refrigerator manufacturers were significant users of CFCs. Early hydrocarbon-based 'Greenfreeze' substitutes were less energy efficient and had a greater cost. However, by the end of the 1990s, Greenfreeze technology was as energy efficient as the ODS alternative and, if there was a cost differential, it was in favour of hydrocarbon Greenfreeze technology (UNEP 1997). By the late 1990s, hydrocarbon-based Greenfreeze technology was the dominant technology in the European refrigeration market (SEI 1999).

10.5 DISTRIBUTIONAL EFFECTS

10.5.1 Distributional Effects within the Production Chain

This case study not only demonstrates that the *ex ante* estimates provided by business were overestimates, it also shows that the businesses which helped generate the estimates would not have been the ones which ultimately paid any additional cost. From the literature, it is clear that the mandatory nature of the Montreal Protocol often provided a way for business to pass the costs on to the user sectors, and ultimately to the consumers. In addition to this, those companies which led in the development of CFC substitutes achieved a market rent so long as their competitors were in the process of catching up. These lead companies also opposed legislation, but only until they had managed to develop substitutes, after which they moved to encourage the regulations which they then gained from. The laggards were reported to be the European companies (SEI 1999), which therefore lost out due to their delay in innovation.

The *ex post* cost estimates showed that the phase out occurred at a much lower cost than the *ex ante* estimates had suggested, and in some cases was achieved with cost savings or efficiency benefits in other areas (see for example SEI 1999). This finding highlights a possible additional cost which would not have been captured by either the *ex ante* or *ex post* cost estimates.

Review of one part of any production process is likely to promote unexpected efficiencies as the wider process is captured by the review. It could be argued that if these sectors had not been required to phase out ODS, their efforts could have been somehow directed towards more targeted forms of innovation which might have provided more efficiencies than had actually occurred, and in turn provided other social goods in terms of jobs and growth. ODS legislation clearly provided social benefits in terms of environmental protection at a financial cost which was less than was originally considered socially acceptable. This may however have been achieved at an unacknowledged opportunity cost in terms of foregone efficiencies.

10.5.2   Geographical Distributional Effects

As already discussed, European producers of ODS developed totally ozone-safe HFCs whilst the US-owned DuPont developed partially ozone safe substitutes – HCFCs – more quickly (Gabel 1995, p.334). This led to European producers losing out whilst HFCs were in development. Naess (2001) examines a number of European country case studies to explore how the legislation was implemented differently. The key relevant outcomes from these country case studies are explored below.

Norway's role as an international frontrunner in terms of ozone policy has been facilitated by the lack of opposing interest groups within the country. Neither industry nor consumers have had particular incentives to oppose a phase out of the main ODS in Norway (Naess 2001). This is an example therefore where the regulator was not presented with negative *ex ante* predictions from its own industry, and was therefore free to follow relatively stringent regulations.

Naess (2001) explores the theory that Southern Member States often face a disproportionate share of compliance costs, as regulations can often reflect Northern problems and are adapted to Northern conditions. A lack of capacity and capability in these countries is thought to lead to difficulties or additional costs during implementation. 'This general trend seems to be valid also in terms of ozone policy where Southern states have scored rather low in terms of both implementation and enforcement' (Naess 2001):

> Spain has been one of the major ODS producers and consumers in the EU . . . Spain has phased out consumption of CFCs and halons domestically, but still produces CFCs for export to developing countries and for essential uses, which is allowed under the Montreal Protocol, but banned within the EU under the latest regulation 2037/00/EC.

> The most recent data for Italy from 1999 show that Italy is still producing CFCs for essential uses and export to developing countries, and that production has stabilised around 7 000 tons a year of CFCs.

Naess (2001) predicts that "many of the problems experienced in Southern Europe may occur also in the Central and Eastern European countries (CEECs), such as illegal trade and an implementation deficit, due to lacking administrative capacity and trained personnel". Naess (2001) then goes on to report that:

consumption had stabilised at a low level by the mid 1990s in the CEECs and international contributions from the Global Environment Facility and the Multilateral Fund of the Montreal Protocol of US$ 111 million was given to 11 countries in Eastern Europe (Belarus, Bulgaria, the Czech Republic, Hungary, Poland, the Russian Federation, Slovakia, Slovenia and Ukraine) but most CEECs had not fulfilled their obligations as set out in the latest Amendments to the Montreal Protocol, which suggest that potential problems persist due to administrative, legal or institutional failure to implement regulations properly.

10.6 CONCLUSIONS

This report has found that a comparison of *ex ante* and *ex post* cost estimates can produce a comparison factor from at least 1.4 at an overall macro level to 40 for individual case studies, and as high as 125 for administrative costs of compliance. The relatively modest overall figure of 1.4 is actually hiding a much greater failure to predict the implications of policy implementation. Analysis of the details of these *ex ante* cost estimates shows they simultaneously underestimated the extent and the feasible rate of phasing out the use of ODS, whilst overestimating the unit cost.

Analysis of the behaviour of the actors involved reveals that these major changes in costs estimates coincided with the leading company DuPont successfully developing HCFCs as a substitute for ODS, and therefore relaxing its opposition to the proposed legislation. DuPont achieved a market rent due to its innovation in anticipation of the legislation. This rent was maintained so long as its mostly European competitors were in the process of developing their alternatives, HFCs. A later negotiation to phase out HCFCs due to their continued partial ozone depleting nature was resisted by DuPont (Gabel 1995). It is useful to explore the reasons behind the industries' failure to predict correctly the costs of implementing legislation. The change in DuPont's position was perfectly reasonable in the context of its development of HCFCs. However, this technological development occurred notably ahead of its previous predictions. Furthermore, once competitive pressure was applied, its competitors swiftly followed and developed their own alternatives. This raises the question of whether these pessimistic *ex ante* estimates were the result of exaggeration by the industry or just conservative assumptions in the face of unknown prospects for future technological development.

The phasing out of ODS is a very complex and technical matter. Different groups within an organisation would have quite possibly generated very different cost estimates. Those responsible for the prospective development of the CFC substitutes would tend to be conservative in their assumptions about future developments to avoid promising to deliver innovations they were unsure of. Therefore, although explicit exaggeration by the industry cannot be ruled out, this is not an explanation which is required to explain the failure. The implementation of the Montreal Protocol was in many ways the first of its kind in phasing out a widely used substance from a modern economy. However, the chemical industry had previously always managed to develop new compounds to fulfil societal demands to generate profits. It would therefore be difficult to conclude that the failure to predict the costs of developing substitutes accurately was because the outcome was genuinely unforeseeable.

This case study has also shown that the industry did not lose out due to the Montreal Protocol as the costs were passed on through the product chain to the consumers. It was not of course in their interest to encourage legislation until they either had, or were confident about developing substitutes. From this analysis it therefore seems sensible to conclude that the failure to predict the true costs of implementing the phase out of ODS successfully was likely to be due to conservative assumptions by some within the industry in the face of uncertain future technological developments. This situation was in the context of there being no real incentive for senior managers to intervene until alternatives were known to be on the way.

Both industry and policy makers will have to some degree already learnt from the outcomes of this case study when considering more recent environmental legislation. Perhaps the most useful finding which has been made possible by the historical nature of the case study is the likely underlying dynamics and interests of the actors involved which led to the failure of the industry to predict implementation costs accurately. This conclusion suggests that policy makers need to consider *ex ante* cost estimates in the context of the incentives and interests of the actors who generate them. Formal review procedures of *ex ante* cost estimates might go some way to reduce the chances of overestimation. Peer review procedures within organisations and between companies in a given sector might highlight excessive conservatism in assumptions. However, if a sector's interest lies in talking down the prospects of innovation, it is likely that only detailed external reviews of company assumptions can critically challenge *ex ante* cost estimates.

REFERENCES

Cogan, D.G. (1988) *Stones in a Glass House*. Washington: Investor Responsibility Research Center.

Cook, E. (1996) Overview. In *Ozone Protection in the United States: Elements of Success,* edited by Elizabeth Cook. Washington, DC: World Resources Institute, 1–10.

Gabel, H.L. (1995) Environmental management as a competitive strategy: the case of CFCs. In *Principles of Environmental and Resource Economics*, edited by H. Folkmer, H. L. Gabel and G. H. Opschoor. Cheltenham, UK: Edward Elgar.

Hoerner, J.A. (1996) Taxing Pollution. In *Ozone Protection in the United States: Elements of Success*, edited by Elizabeth Cook. Washington, DC: World Resources Institute, 39–51.

ICS (2004) *Cry Wolf: Predicted Costs by Industry in the face of new regulations*, Report 6:04. Göteborg: International Chemical Secretariat.

Lee, D. (1996) Trading pollution. In *Ozone Protection in the United States: Elements of Success*, edited by Elizabeth Cook. Washington, DC: World Resources Institute, 31–38.

Naess, T. (2001) *The Effectiveness of the European Union (EU) Ozone Policy*, FNI Report 15/2001 The Fridtjof Nansen Institute. Lysakes, Norway: Fridtjof Nansen Institute.

Palmer, A.R., Mooz, W.E., Quinn, T.H. and Wolf, K.A. (1980) *Economic Implications of Regulating Chlorofluorocarbons Emissions from Non Aerosol Applications*, Report No. R-2524-EPA. Santa Monica, CA: Rand.

SEI (1999) *Costs and Strategies Presented by Industry during the Negotiation of Environmental Regulations Prepared for the Swedish Ministry of the Environment.* Stockholm: Stockholm Environment Institute.

UNEP (1989) *Montreal Protocol on Substances that Deplete the Ozone Layer: Economic Panel Report*. Nairobi, Kenya: UNEP.

UNEP (1991a) *Economic Assessment Report: Economic Options Committee.* Nairobi, Kenya: UNEP.

UNEP (1991b) *Assessment, Report of the Technology and Economic Assessment Panel*, Nairobi, Kenya: UNEP.

UNEP (1994) *Scientific Assessment of Ozone Depletion: 1994*, Report No. 37. Nairobi, Kenya: UNEP.

UNEP (1995) *Montreal Protocol on Substances that Deplete the Ozone Layer: 1994 Report of the Economics Options Committee.* Nairobi, Kenya: UNEP.

UNEP (1997) *Montreal Protocol on Substances that Deplete the Ozone Layer: Technology and Economic Assessment Panel, Volume II*. Nairobi, Kenya: UNEP.

UNEP (1998) *Montreal Protocol on Substances that Deplete the Ozone Layer: 1998 Report of the Technology and Economics Assessment Panel.* Nairobi, Kenya: UNEP.

UNEP (2002) *Montreal Protocol on Substances that Deplete the Ozone Layer: 2002 Report of the Technology and Economics Assessment Panel.* Nairobi, Kenya: UNEP.

UNEP (2003) *Montreal Protocol on Substances that Deplete the Ozone Layer: May 2003 Report of the Technology and Economics Assessment Panel: Progress report.* Nairobi, Kenya: UNEP.

UNEP (2005) *Montreal Protocol on Substances that Deplete the Ozone Layer: May 2005 Report of the Technology and Economics Assessment Panel: Progress report.* Nairobi, Kenya: UNEP.

Food and agriculture

11. Compliance costs of nitrates reduction policies in Denmark and the Netherlands

Onno Kuik and Robin Vanner

This case study examines the differences in *ex ante* and *ex post* cost estimates to farmers of implementing the EU Nitrates Directive. This Directive aims to protect European waters against pollution caused by nitrates from agricultural sources. Comparisons of *ex ante* and *ex post* estimates are available for Denmark and the Netherlands. The *ex ante* estimates of the private cost per kg nitrogen (N) reduced were found to be between 1.2 and 1.8 times greater than the *ex post* estimates; these lower than expected costs were due to improved fertiliser management. For Denmark, the major reasons for this difference were that the stricter requirements on the utilisation of the N content of animal manure turned out to be cheaper than expected at the time of the *ex ante* estimate. For the Netherlands, the major difference was that the expected costs for dairy farms to dispose of their surplus manure were much less than expected, largely due to better management of fertilisers at these farms.

11.1 POLICY

Because of environmental and health concerns over increasing nitrate concentrations in surface and ground waters in the EU's intensively farmed agricultural areas, in 1991 the Council of Ministers adopted a Directive on the protection of waters against pollution caused by nitrates from agricultural sources (the Nitrates Directive, 91/676/EEC). The Directive contains a number of provisions for the governments of Member States that include, among other things, the identification of Nitrate Vulnerable Zones (NVZs) and the establishment of Codes of Good Agricultural Practice whose standards were to become binding for farmers in NVZs. Its impacts were anticipated to be greatest for intensive livestock (pigs and poultry), followed by cattle (beef and dairy) enterprises and arable crops.

This chapter examines the implementation of the Nitrates Directive in Denmark and the Netherlands and analyses the private costs of compliance for farmers. Both countries have large livestock sectors and have experienced pollution from animal manure and fertilisers. They each implemented the provisions of the Nitrates Directive in their own way, based on country-specific circumstances and political preferences. It should be noted that the European Court of Justice ruled in 2003 that the Netherlands had not properly implemented the Directive. As a consequence of this ruling, the Netherlands had to change its policies. It is not however considered that this materially impacts on the findings of the case study as the discontinued policy had some real effects on agricultural production and pollution.

Since the mid-1980s, the Danish government has developed actions and strategies to reduce the leaching of nitrates from farmland. In 1998 the Danish Parliament enacted the Action Plan on the Aquatic Environment II, with the aim of further reducing nitrogen leaching so as to bring Denmark into compliance with the EU Nitrates Directive. The Action Plan contains a number of specific measures to be taken at the farm level.[1] They include:

1. Improved fodder utilisation and changes in feeding practice.
2. Implementation of stricter criteria governing livestock density.
3. Stricter requirements on utilisation of the nitrogen content of livestock manure.
4. The requirement to grow crops which reduce leaching of nitrates (catch crops) on 6 per cent of farmland.
5. Reducing the amount of added nitrogen (the nitrogen norm) by 10 per cent (for example, farmers may only apply nitrogen in amounts corresponding to 90 per cent of the economically optimal level).

The Netherlands has also developed policies in this area since the 1980s. In the first instance the policies were aimed at a more even geographical distribution of manure, on the timing and methods of application and on a reduction of its phosphorus content. Whilst the policies resulted in a reduction of local manure surpluses and of the phosphorus content of manure and phosphate leaching, they did little to reduce the total nitrogen input to agriculture or nitrate leaching. In response to the EU Nitrates Directive, the Netherlands government introduced new legislation in 1998 as part of the Fertilisers Act. The most important piece of legislation was the Mineral Accounting System (MINAS)[2] that obliged farmers to keep records of nutrient flows entering and leaving their farms. If the difference between inputs and outputs of nutrient flows exceeded certain 'loss norms', a levy had to be paid. The MINAS 'loss norms' depended on the type of cultivation (arable or grassland), and soil type (sand, clay or peat, or other) to take into account differences in leaching profiles.

11.2 METHODOLOGY

Ex ante and *ex post* estimates of compliance costs for farmers implementing the Nitrate Directive in Denmark and the Netherlands are derived from published sources. Jacobsen (2002, 2004) was used for Denmark and Hoop and Stolwijk (1999) and Eerdt *et al.* (2005a, 2005b) were used for the Netherlands. For both countries the *ex ante* cost estimates were produced in 1997/98 and the *ex post* estimates in 2002/3. Because the *ex ante* and *ex post* estimates of the costs of the Dutch policy are taken from different studies from different years, a consumer price index is used to correct the *ex ante* estimate for inflation to make both cost estimates comparable. As the *ex ante* and *ex post* estimates for the Danish policy were reported in the same study, it can be assumed that those estimates were already comparable. The cost-effectiveness of the measures under the policies (in Euro/kg nitrogen reduction) is computed by dividing total annual compliance costs (in Euro) by the (estimated) annual reduction in nitrates pollution (in kg nitrogen). There is a small difference between the measures of nitrates pollution in Denmark and the Netherlands, as the Danish studies estimated the leaching of nitrates whilst the Dutch studies measured the level of nitrogen surplus applied to farmland. However, it has been assumed that surpluses of nitrogen all lead to leaching (in kg nitrogen).

Before a comparison of *ex ante* and *ex post* estimates of cost-effectiveness is made, it is worth providing a simplified diagrammatic representation of how nitrates flow within the farming system.

Figure 11.1 shows the flow of nitrates within the farming system as referred to in the Danish and Netherlands case studies. At first sight it would appear that the system boundary should be physically defined and drawn around the boundary of the farm. However it is possible that nitrates can leach into the environment but remain within the farm boundary. The system boundary therefore needs to be drawn based on the economic interest of the farmer, where leached nitrates represent an externality. Within this system boundary:

1. Nitrates are introduced via feedstuffs which are fed to livestock, and are either retained within the livestock, which is sold as meat, captured within manure, or are leached into the environment.
2. The manure is sometimes put on to the land to promote the growth of crops. A further option is to add nitrate-based fertilisers in order to

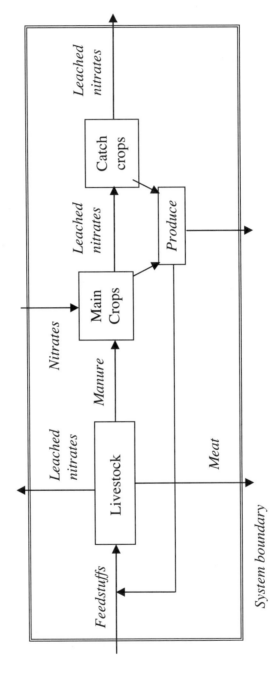

Figure 11.1   Representation of flows of nitrogen within the farming system

152

Table 11.1 Ex ante *and* ex post *estimates of the costs to farmers in Denmark*

	Ex ante (1998)			*Ex post* (2004)		
	Reduction of leaching (ton N)	Farm costs (€ m.y^{-1})	Cost-effect (€ kgN^{-1})	Reduction of leaching (ton N)	Farm costs (€ m.y^{-1})	Cost-effect (€ kgN^{-1})
Nitrogen in feedstuffs	2 400	0	0	3 800	5.8	1.5
Stocking density	300	4.1	13.7	140	1.5	10.7
Catch crops (6%)	3 000	20.3	6.8	3 000	6.4	2.1
Nitrogen norms	10 500	15.3	1.5	12 850	22.8	1.8
Utilisation of manure	10 600	27.2	2.6	10 110	6.7	0.7
Total	**26 800**	**66.9**	**2.5**	**29 900**	**43.1**	**1.4**

Source: Jacobsen (2002, 2004).

promote the growth of crops. In both cases the nitrates may be leached by water, and if not captured by so called 'catch crops', will leach into the environment.

3. The produce from the growing of crops is then either sold outside the farm or used to feed the livestock of the farm.

11.3 THE COSTS OF COMPLIANCE

11.3.1 Denmark

The *ex ante* study of Danish policy estimated the total annual reduction of nitrogen leaching from farms to be 26 800 tonnes of nitrogen. Most of this reduction was expected to be achieved by a lowering of the nitrogen norms for fertiliser application and an increased utilisation of nitrogen in animal manure. The farm measures were expected to cost €66.9 million per year. The average cost-effectiveness of the measures was expected to be €2.5 per avoided kg nitrogen leaching (see Table 11.1).

The *ex post* evaluation showed that the farm measures of the Action Plan had been successful in reaching their environmental target at less cost than expected. It was estimated that farm measures reduced nitrogen leaching by

29 900 tonnes per year at a total annual cost of €43.1 million. While some measures were more costly than anticipated in the *ex ante* assessment (reducing the nitrogen content in feedstuffs and the lowering of the nitrogen norms), these were offset by lower-than-expected costs for the reduction of the stocking density of livestock and, especially, the better utilisation of nitrogen in animal manure. The average cost-effectiveness of the farm-related measures was estimated at €1.4 kg N^{-1}, which is substantially less than was anticipated by the *ex ante* assessment (see Table 11.1).

11.3.2   The Netherlands

The *ex ante* study for the MINAS policy estimated total annual costs of MINAS of €174 million.[3] The cost estimate was made up of all costs related to the administration of the mineral flows and the storage, transportation and distribution of the surplus manure, and it accounted for cost savings on artificial fertiliser. The study did not report on the costs of specific measures or the total amount of nitrate leaching avoided because of MINAS, but it did present estimates of the reduction of nitrogen surplus per hectare for certain farm sectors (specialised dairy: 73 kg ha^{-1}, mixed intensive animals: 71 kg ha^{-1}, and arable: 13 kg ha^{-1}). On the basis of these changes in per hectare surpluses, total avoided nitrogen surplus (as a proxy to nitrate leaching) can be tentatively calculated as 87 000 tonnes of nitrogen.[4] The cost-effectiveness suggested by the *ex ante* study was therefore €2.0 kg. N^{-1} (see Table 11.2).

A summary of *ex post* estimates of MINAS by Eerdt *et al.* (2005a, 2005b) showed increasing additional costs to farmers because of the MINAS policy in the period 1998–2002. The *ex post* studies also estimated annual net costs of MINAS of €174 million (average net costs over the period 1998–2002). This estimate includes savings on fertiliser (€36 million) and other cost savings (including subsidies received) of €15 million. With respect to specific measures, the highest costs were for administration (52 per cent) and manure disposal (36 per cent). The annual reduction in nitrogen surplus because of the MINAS policies was estimated to be on average 100 000 tonnes of nitrogen over the 1998–2002 period. These numbers suggest a cost-effectiveness of the MINAS policy of €1.7 kg. N^{-1}.

A comparison of the *ex ante* and *ex post* estimates of compliance costs of the MINAS policy show that they are identical (€174 million), but that the *ex post* estimate of cost-effectiveness exceeds the *ex ante* estimate by approximately one-fifth (1.7:2.0) because of the larger amount of nitrogen surplus avoided (see Table 11.2). However, unlike the *ex post* studies, the *ex ante* study did not mention subsidies to farmers. If all of the €15m 'other' costs estimated in the *ex post* study were taken to represent subsidies, the

Table 11.2   Ex ante *and* ex post *estimates of costs to formers of MINAS in the Netherlands*

	Ex ante (1999)			Ex post (2005)		
	Reduction of nitrogen-deposition (ton N)	Farm costs (€ m.y⁻¹)	Cost-effect (€.kgN⁻¹)	Reduction of nitrogen deposition (ton N)	Farm costs (€ m.y⁻¹)	Cost-effect (€.kgN⁻¹)
Manure disposal		} 208			92	
Administrative					132	
Other					−15	
Cost savings		−33			−36	
Total	**87 000**[2]	**174**	**2.0**[2]	**100 000**[3]	**174**	**1.7**

Notes:
1. Prices are in Euros, converted to the 2004 price level by the Harmonised Consumer Price Index of Eurostat.
2. This figure is based on rather tentative costs estimates.
3. Average annual reduction over the period 1998–2002.

Source: Hoop and Stolwijk (1999), Eerdt *et al.* (2005a,b) and own computations.

ex post estimates of cost-effectiveness would equal 1.9 ((174 + 15)/100), very close to the 2.0 *ex ante* estimate.

11.4   COUNTRY COMPARISON

Table 11.3 represents a summary of the differences in *ex ante* and *ex post* estimates of compliance costs of measures to reduce nitrates pollution in Denmark and the Netherlands. In both countries, the *ex post* estimates of the cost-effectiveness of the measures are more favourable than the *ex ante* estimates. The ratio between the two estimates is between 1.2 and 1.8.

11.4.1   The Distribution of Costs

The cost estimates provided in all of these studies represent private costs to the farmers affected. If all farmers throughout Europe were to be faced with the same costs, some of these could be passed on to consumers, particularly in sectors such as dairy where there is limited competition from outside the EU. This issue was not explored in the case studies. The Dutch studies do however provide some information on the distribution of costs

Table 11.3 Comparison of the ex ante *and* ex post *estimates of the cost-effectiveness of nitrogen-reducing policies in Denmark and the Netherlands*

	Ex ante CE (€.kgN⁻¹)	*Ex post* CE (€.kgN⁻¹)	Ratio of *ex ante/ex post* CE
Denmark	2.5	1.4	1.8
Netherlands	2.0	1.7	1.2

Note: CE = cost-effectiveness.

between farm sectors and the differences between the *ex ante* and *ex post* studies. In the *ex ante* study, the major share of the costs (about two-thirds) falls upon the dairy sector, followed by the pig rearing sector (breeding and fattening). The study also predicted that the net effect on the income of the arable sector would be positive due to savings on mineral fertilisers.

However, the *ex post* Dutch study estimated that costs were low (possibly even with a saving) for dairy farmers but higher for intensive livestock (pigs and poultry) farmers. This was due to high manure disposal costs for the farmers using more intensive farming techniques, as reported in Westhoek *et al.* (2004). By contrast, dairy farmers managed to lower their nitrogen surplus by reducing the input of mineral fertilisers and feed concentrates and saved money. MINAS therefore had little to no effect on average farm income in the dairy sector. Westhoek *et al.* (2004) note that 'a considerable number of [dairy] farms even improved their farm income, probably because there was room for improvements in efficiency and it was MINAS that made the farmers aware of this' (Westhoek *et al.* 2004: 112).

The similarity of *ex ante* and *ex post* estimates of total compliance costs in the Netherlands seems to be coincidental, with the positives and negatives having cancelled one another out. It would appear that *ex ante* estimates for costs in the intensive livestock sector underestimated compliance costs, while those in the dairy sector overestimated these costs. However the *ex ante* study does not appear to include subsidies to farmers. If all of the costs described as 'other' estimated in the *ex post* study were to represent subsidies and this was removed from the *ex post* calculations to make them comparable with the *ex ante* calculations, the overall cost would no longer be so similar but the estimates of cost-effectiveness would become closer at 2.0 *ex ante* and 1.9 *ex post*.

11.5   CONCLUSIONS

The comparison of *ex ante* and *ex post* estimates in the Netherlands suggests that the *ex ante* estimate did not foresee the efficiency gains in the dairy sector that, through a more rational management of fertilisers, offset part of the *ex ante* expected costs. In contrast, the Dutch *ex ante* study seems to have underestimated costs for the intensive livestock sector. The Danish *ex ante* study overestimated the costs of certain farm measures such as better utilisation of nitrogen in animal manure and the requirement to grow catch crops, but underestimated the costs of certain other measures. In the aggregate, in both countries, the *ex ante* cost estimates (per kg nitrogen reduced) exceeded *ex post* estimates by a factor of between 1.2 and 1.8. It is worth noting that had the *ex ante* estimates from the Netherlands considered subsidies, then the *ex ante* and *ex post* estimates of the average cost of nitrogen reduction would probably have been the same.

NOTES

1. The Action Plan also contained measures to be carried out by the state, such as an increase in the area of wetlands and the promotion of organic agriculture (Jacobsen 2004).
2. Accompanying legal instruments included livestock quota, manure contracts, the livestock farm closure scheme and the Nitrate Projects Action Programme (Eerdt et al. 2005b).
3. The original study reported costs of NFL 318 million. This amount has been converted to Euro (divide by 2.20371) and adjusted for inflation (multiply by 1.202).
4. (1 048 234 ha grassland * 73 kg/ha) + (796 352 ha arable * 13 kg/ha) = 86 874 ton N.

REFERENCES

Eerdt, M.M. van, Born G.J. van den and Dam, J. van (2005a), *Environmental Costs and Benefits of the Dutch Manure Policy 1998–2003* (in Dutch), Bilthoven, Netherlands: Environmental Assessment Agency.

Eerdt, M.M. van, Grinsven, H. van, Willems, J. and Schotten, K. (2005b), A Review of Dutch Manure and Fertiliser Policy, Contributed Papers, *The 3rd International Nitrogen Conference*, New Jersey: Science Press USA Inc., 349.

Hoop, D.W. de and Stolwijk, H.J.J. (1999), *Economic Effects of Policy Proposals for Agriculture for 2002 and 2003* (in Dutch), LEI/CPB report 2.99.12, The Hague: Agricultural Economics Research Institute (LEI-DLO) and Netherlands Bureau for Economic Policy Analysis (CPB).

Jacobsen, B.H. (2002), Reducing Nitrogen Leaching in Denmark and the Netherlands: Administrative Regulation and Costs, Paper presented to the *Xth EAAE Conference* in Zaragoza, 2002.

Jacobsen, B.H. (2004), *Final Economic Evaluation of the Action Plan for the Aquatic Environment II* (In Danish with English summary), Rapport No. 169, Copenhagen: Fødevareøkonomisk Institut.

Westhoek, H., Berg, R. van den, Hoop, W. de and Kamp, A. van der (2004), Economic and Environmental Effects of the Manure Policy in the Netherlands: Synthesis of *Ex post* and *Ex ante* Evaluation, *Water Science and Technology*, 49 (3): 109–116.

12. The Groundwater Regulations 1998 (UK)

Michael MacLeod

This chapter examines the implementation of the EU Groundwater Directive in the UK, with emphasis on the response of the farming industry to the licensing of sheep dip disposal. The results indicate that the *ex post* costs are likely to be lower than anticipated because of compliance issues and post-implementation changes to the legislation; however the analysis does not take into account the wider effects of the regulations, such as increased incidence of parasites on sheep. The study highlights the difficulties involved in (a) predicting the response to regulation (and hence costs) for a rapidly changing sector and (b) applying the polluter pays principle in a situation where the polluter has limited potential to absorb or pass costs on.

12.1   BACKGROUND

The Groundwater Regulations 1998 'are an environmental protection measure which complete transposition of the Groundwater Directive (80/68/EEC) and provide enhanced protection for groundwater' (DETR 2001, p 1). They prohibit the disposal of designated substances that could pose a threat to groundwater quality and require the introduction of a system of disposal authorisation and monitoring. The regulations were introduced on 2 December 1998 and 1 January 1999 and are enforced by the Environment Agency (EA) in England and Wales and the Scottish Environment Protection Agency (SEPA) in Scotland. Table 12.1 shows the estimated compliance costs in the RIA (DETR 1998).

The RIA identified farming and petrol retailing as the two sectors likely to bear the highest costs arising from the regulations. For the farming sector, most of the costs are associated with the operation of a licensing scheme to ensure that the disposal of sheep dip (and, to a lesser extent, other pesticides) is carried out in ways that minimise the risk to groundwater quality. SEPA and the EA charge farmers fees so that they can recover the costs they incur in administering the licensing schemes in line with the

Table 12.1   Groundwater Regulations ex ante costs *estimates*

Sector	Annual costs (£m)	One-off costs (£)
All	5–17	32–120
Farming	4	17.4
Petrol retailing	Low	14.2

polluter pays principle, for example, SEPA recovered 88 per cent of the costs it incurred administering the Groundwater Regulations during 2003–04 through charging.[1] The main costs of the regulations for the petrol retailing sector arise from carrying out capital works (mainly storage tank renovation and replacement) on assets that are identified as posing a risk to groundwater. Most of these costs would be one-off and borne directly by the operators identified.

12.2   METHODOLOGY

The large variation in the cost estimates for all sectors makes a meaningful comparison of the *ex ante* and *ex post* costs difficult – if the *ex post* one-off costs were calculated to be £32m or £120m these results would, strictly speaking, validate the *ex ante* estimates. It is more useful, therefore, to examine a specific element of the regulations for which there are more accurately defined *ex ante* costs. The RIA contains detailed estimates for two of the main sectors affected: farming and petrol retailing. The *ex ante/ex post* comparison focuses on the farming sector as it is the sector bearing the highest costs.

12.3   FARMING AND THE GROUNDWATER REGULATIONS

The RIA identified the disposal of sheep dip as being the main cost for the farming sector arising from the Groundwater Regulations. Compliance costs for a typical farmer were estimated to be:

- Recurring costs per annum: £100
- Non-recurring costs: £85

This was based on the analysis of the four main options outlined in Table 12.2. Based on this analysis, the RIA predicted one-off costs of £17.4m and

Table 12.2 Cost of the four main options from the RIA (£)

	Option A1 (>90%): disposal to area of LOW vulnerability	Option A2 (<10%): disposal to area of HIGH vulnerability	Option B: Disposal by an approved waste contractor	Option C: Treatment of sheep by injectables
Application charge	85	85		
Additional prior investigation		50–1 000		
Sinking of a borehole		500–10 000		
Capital investment to meet requirements of authorisation		100–1 000		
Total one-off costs	**85**	**735–12 085**		
Annual subsistence costs payable to the Environment Agency to monitor compliance with authorisation	100	100		
Use of injectables on flock *three* times per year				1 000
Consignment to authorised waste disposer once a year (including in storage facilities)			1 123	
Total costs at the end of year one	**185**	**835–12 185**	**Up to 1 123**	**1 000**

annual costs of £4m for the farming community (see Table 12.1). However, the number of applications for authorisation to dispose of sheep dip was much lower than anticipated: by 2000, SEPA had received 2600 instead of the anticipated 10 000 and the Environment Agency in England and Wales had received 12 000 instead of 20 000 (Scottish Parliament Information Centre 2000). Data from Scotland indicates that the number of authorisations granted each year has continued to decline since the introduction of the regulations (see Figure 12.1). In order to determine the reasons for the shortfall and the cost implications, it was decided to contact SEPA and the Environment Agency and interview an independent expert in sheep dipping.

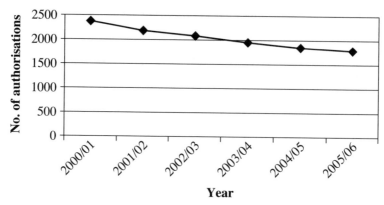

Source: Personal communication from Alex Pritchard, Senior Policy Officer (Groundwater) SEPA, 14 September 2005.

Figure 12.1   Authorisations to dispose of sheep dip in Scotland

12.4   RESULTS AND DISCUSSION

There are two main reasons why the *ex post* costs are likely to be significantly different from the *ex ante* cost estimates presented in the RIA:

- Farmers' behaviour has not turned out as predicted and applications for disposal authorisation have been much lower than anticipated.
- The unit costs of the regulations are less than initially proposed, as a result of fee reduction, waiving and cost sharing.

12.4.1   Responses to the Regulations

Farmers' responses to the regulations were more complex than predicted in the RIA, with many apparently adopting new strategies rather than continuing dipping as before (plus applying for authorisation). It has been suggested[2] that those who have not applied for authorisation are most likely to have adopted one of the following strategies:

1. Using pour-on treatments;
2. Hiring a contractor to carry out dipping;
3. Not treating their sheep for parasites.

It was considered unlikely that many farmers would shift to the use of an approved waste contractor to dispose of dip (option B in the RIA) or treatment by injectables (option C) due to their prohibitive cost. Increased production costs are particularly problematic in sectors such as sheep farming where, due to the small profit margins and industry structure, regulatees have limited scope for absorbing or passing on costs. However, the shift in practice is likely to have been the result of a combination of factors, rather than simply a cost-minimising response to the regulations. Farmers' decision making was also influenced by the improved efficiency of pour-on treatments, and by changing risk perceptions. The new regime made the use of ageing dipping equipment a less viable option, and there was also growing concern about the human health risks of dip, particularly organophosphates, during the 1990s. According to Alex Pritchard[3] 'There was a significant downward trend over the 3–4 years preceding the Regulations in the use of sheep dip chemicals due to concerns over health and due to the introduction of mandatory training for the purchase of both organophosphate and synthetic pyrethroid dips'.

In financial terms, the costs to the industry arising directly as a consequence of the regulations (that is, of obtaining authorisation to dispose of spent dip) were lower than predicted due to the low levels of application for authorisation. However, evaluating the financial cost of the unanticipated shift in practice is more difficult. We may assume for sheep farming overall that:

1. getting a contractor to carry out dipping is more expensive than the cost of dipping and authorisation;
2. the cost of pour on dips (which do not require disposal and authorisation) is less expensive than the cost of dipping and authorisation once the costs of the regulations are included;
3. for the industry as a whole, the increased cost of using contractors is not more than the cost savings achieved by using pour on dips;
4. farmers that don't use pour on dips, authorised dipping or contractors don't treat for parasites.

In that case, the *ex post* costs would be less than the *ex ante* estimate by an amount equal to or greater than the direct costs avoided by those farmers who decide to stop routine treatment for parasites. This is based on the assumption that farmers that choose to stop dipping are engaged in a profit-maximising control strategy. However, Milne (2004, p 103) notes that, in the absence of sufficient information, farmers often simply seek to avoid transaction costs and, in doing so, incur disease losses.

It should be noted that the RIA does not quantify some of the wider effects of the regulations, such as: raised awareness of the polluting potential of sheep dip; and increased incidence of parasites on sheep – increased scarring of fleeces indicates that the regulations may have led to fewer sheep being treated for parasites.[4] These can lead to costs and benefits. However, determining the relative magnitude of these costs and benefits requires considerable further work and was outwith the remit of this study.

12.4.2   Non-compliance

It is likely that the costs of disposal have been avoided by some farmers and contractors through the unauthorised disposal of spent dip. However, it is difficult to determine how much of the shortfall in applications (relative to *ex ante* predictions) is due to non-compliance. The regulations were introduced at a time when there was a significant downward trend in the use of sheep dipping chemicals for a variety of reasons (health concerns regarding dipping, the introduction of mandatory training, uptake of alternative treatments). SEPA[5] pointed to the dramatic reduction in sheep dip chemical sales (down by approximately 50 per cent in 1999) as evidence that the shortfall in authorisations reflected a genuine reduction in their usage, rather than mass non-compliance. The Environment Agency[6] noted the lack of reliable data regarding the shortfall, but indicated that anecdotal evidence suggested that 'avoidance and ignorance' had played a significant role.

12.4.3   Unit Costs

In addition to compliance patterns, the accuracy of the *ex ante* estimates also depends on the validity of the unit costs used in the RIA. The *ex ante* costs were based on the assumption that most farmers (that is, those in low vulnerability areas) would be charged an annual fee (referred to as the 'maintenance charge' or the 'subsistence fee') of £100 and a one-off fee (the "application charge") of £85. The actual unit costs for the UK as a whole from 1998 to the time of writing have turned out to be much lower than anticipated as a result of (a) fees being waived and (b) the authorisation of cost-sharing schemes. However, there are significant differences in the unit costs in England and Wales compared with Scotland (see Table 12.3).

Table 12.4 compares the *ex ante* charges used in the RIA with the average of the actual (*ex post*) charges, expressed in 1998 prices. The *ex post* one-off charge for England and Wales and Scotland is higher than the *ex ante* one-off charge. However, in England and Wales, the annual fee was waived for four years from 2000/01 to 2003/04 for 'small disposals not exceeding 5m^3 a day for more than 6 days/year' (Scottish Parliament Information Centre 2000, p 3). This was in response to concerns raised at the 'Agriculture Summit' in 2000 regarding the problems some farmers

Table 12.3   Charges for authorisation to dispose of sheep dip

Year	Annual charge (£): England and Wales	Annual charge (£): Scotland	One-off fee (£): England and Wales	One-off fee (£): Scotland
1998				
1999	0	0	–	–
2000	0	123	92	152
2001	0	127	94	157
2002	0	129	98	160
2003	0	132	103	162
2004	130	143	106	167
2005	134	166	110	172

Note: Dashes indicate that the data were unavailable.

Sources: SEPA Summary Charging Booklets
(http://www.sepa.org.uk/charging/booklets/index.htm); Environment Agency (2004, 2005);
DETR (2001); Scottish Parliament Information Centre (2000); personal communications
from N. Crane, EA, and A. Pritchard, SEPA.

Table 12.4   Comparison of RIA charges with average actual charges

	RIA (£)	Average actual charge (£) – England and Wales	Average actual charge (£) – Scotland
Annual charge (not including waived fees)	100	114 (1999–2005)	123 (1999–2005)
Annual charge (including waived fees)	NA	32 (1999–2005)	106 (1999–2005)
One-off charge	85	91 (2000–2005)	146 (2000–2005)

Note: 1998 prices.

were having in paying the fees. This waiver more than compensated for the higher than predicted one-off costs. The annual fee was only waived in Scotland for one year (1999/2000) as the Executive believed that any extended waiver 'would be a serious breach of the polluter pays principle' and that 'a waiver for sheep farmers would set a dangerous precedent for other industries' (Scottish Executive 2005). In addition, it was argued that the annual charge was 'considerably less than originally proposed during public consultation on the Groundwater Regulations' (Scottish Executive 2000). This means that both the one-off and annual *ex post* costs from 1998 to the present are higher than the *ex ante* costs in Scotland. However, extensive use was made of cost-sharing schemes in Scotland, where two or more farmers could apply for a single authorisation and pay one fee between them. By 2000, it was estimated that 300 such schemes had been authorised (Scottish Parliament Information Centre 2000, p 3). It should be noted that the charges in Scotland are applied per farm or crofting township, whereas in England charges are applied per disposal site – therefore the charges in Scotland may actually be lower per disposal as each farm or township may have several disposal sites.[7]

12.5 CONCLUSIONS

- Overall costs are likely to be overestimated because of compliance issues and post-implementation changes to the legislation.
- Overall unit costs are lower than predicted due to fee waiving and cost sharing.
- There is significant regional variation in the *ex post* unit costs between (a) Scotland and (b) England and Wales due to the extended period of fee waiving and lower charges in England and Wales.
- Farmers' responses have been influenced by a range of factors: the cost, perceived intrusion of the regulations; changing risk perceptions; innovation.
- The case study shows the difficulty of applying the polluter pays principle in practice - low authorisation rates may reflect the difficulty of applying the polluter pays principle in a situation where the polluter is not able to pass the costs on.
- The marked difference between the predicted response and the actual response of farmers raises doubts over the usefulness of the RIA small business 'litmus test', which 'did not think any farmer would seek to avoid applying for authorisation to dispose of spent sheep dip under these Regulations' (DETR 1998, p 6).
- The RIA does not quantify some of the wider effects of the regulations, such as raised awareness of the polluting potential of sheep dip and increased incidence of parasites on sheep. However, determining the relative magnitude of these costs and benefits requires further work and was outwith the remit of this study.

12.5.1 Lessons from the Case Study

This study illustrates why it is important to adopt dynamic rather than static assumptions when attempting to forecast for a rapidly changing sector (in this case dipping practices were undergoing significant change prior to, and during the implementation of the regulations). Trends need to be analysed so that the effects of temporal variation can be taken into account. Furthermore, realistic assumptions about compliance should be adopted, particularly amongst regulatees who are unable to absorb or pass on costs and have a strong incentive to adopt cost-minimising strategies. Finally, the results of any business impact or 'litmus tests' should be treated with caution, particularly when based on small samples providing non-anonymous responses on sensitive issues.

NOTES

1. www.sepa.org.uk/pdf/charging/costs_and_charges.pdf, accessed 22 April 2008.
2. Interview with C. Milne, Scottish Agricultural College, 11 August 2005.
3. Personal communication from Alex Pritchard, Senior Policy Officer (Groundwater) SEPA, 14 September 2005.
4. Interview with C. Milne, Scottish Agricultural College, 11 August 2005.
5. Personal communication from Alex Pritchard, Senior Policy Officer (Groundwater) SEPA, 14 September 2005.
6. Personal communication with N. Crane, Technical Advisor (Groundwater) Environment Agency, 17 October 2005.
7. Personal communication from Alex Pritchard, Senior Policy Officer (Groundwater) SEPA, 14 September 2005.

REFERENCES

DETR (1998) *Regulatory Impact Assessment: The Groundwater Regulations* (CCA 98/137). London: DETR.

DETR (2001) *Guidance on the Groundwater Regulations 1998.* London: DETR.

Environment Agency (2004) *Scheme of Charges in Respect of Discharges to Controlled Waters,* April.

Environment Agency (2005) *Scheme of Charges in Respect of Discharges to Controlled Waters 2005.*

Milne, C. (2004) *The Economic Modelling of Sheep Ectoparasite Control in Scotland,* PhD Thesis awarded by Scottish Agricultural College/University of Aberdeen.

Scottish Executive (2000) *Scottish Executive Written Answers S1O-2165,* www.scottish.parliament.uk/business/pqa/wa-00/wa0907.htm, accessed 22 April 2008.

Scottish Executive (2005) *Scottish Executive Water Environment FAQs,* www.scotland.gov.uk/Topics/Environment/Water/15561/3710, accessed 22 April 2008.

Scottish Parliament Information Centre (2000) *Research Note 00/87: Charges Made Under the Groundwater Regulation 1998.* Edinburgh: Scottish Parliament Information Centre.

13. The Welfare of Farmed Animal (England) (Amendment) Regulations 2003

Michael MacLeod

The implementation of regulations designed to improve the welfare of pigs is examined in this chapter. The evidence suggests that the *ex ante* costs are likely to have been overestimated, due primarily to baseline errors that are the inevitable result of not attempting to account for temporal variation in an industry undergoing rapid change. It is important to adopt dynamic rather than static assumptions, particularly: (a) when attempting to forecast for a rapidly changing sector; and (b) when there is a significant time gap between the *ex ante* estimation and the implementation of the measures. The findings also highlight the importance of adopting realistic assumptions about compliance, particularly amongst regulatees who are unable to pass on costs and have a strong incentive to adopt cost-minimising strategies. Compliance with the letter of a regulation can be significantly different, and has different cost implications, from complying with the spirit.

13.1 BACKGROUND

The Welfare of Farmed Animal (England) (Amendment) Regulations 2003 (S.I. 2003 No. 299) established specific rules intended to set minimum standards for the welfare of pigs. The Regulations arose in response to the European Commission Directives 2001/88/EC and 2001/93/EC and had to be transposed into national law by 1 January 2003. In England, this was achieved by amending the Welfare of Farmed Animals (England) Regulations 2000 (S.I. 2000 No. 1870). The key provisions that had to be implemented are summarised in Table 13.1.

Table 13.1   Summary of the key provisions

Measure	Date of implementation	Estimated *ex ante* annual cost/ charge (£)
1. Permanent access to manipulable materials[1]	14 Feb. 2003	2 119 900 – 8 796 000
2. Raising the minimum weaning age to 28 days	14 Feb. 2003	4 397 000
3. Providing permanent access to water for all pigs over two weeks of age	14 Feb. 2003	502 000
4. Minimum space requirements for group housed sows and gilts	Existing buildings have until 1 Jan. 2013 to comply	783 000
5. Minimum continuous 'solid' lying area for sows and gilts	Existing buildings have until 1 Jan. 2013 to comply	76 000

Note: 1. Environmental enrichment through the provision of manipulable materials 'provides pigs with the opportunity to root, investigate, chew and play and thus helps reduce stress and minimise aggressive behaviour' (Defra 2002). Manipulable materials can be in the form of straw (or a similar material), or specialised equipment such as chains or footballs.

13.2   METHODOLOGY

This case study examines the provisions introduced on 14 February 2003 (provisions 1–3 in Table 13.1). It focuses primarily on baseline and compliance issues for two reasons:

- The overall accuracy of the *ex ante* estimates in industries undergoing rapid change depends to a large extent on the accuracy of the baseline used. This case study therefore represents an opportunity to examine the effects of the baseline on overall costs in a rapidly changing sector.
- In order to assess comprehensively and accurately the direction and magnitude of all the errors in the unit costs, a great deal of data is required. Although there may well be errors in some of unit costs used, the absence of significant scope for innovation and of sustained lobbying during the drafting of the regulations means that any errors are less likely to be systematic. It was therefore decided to limit the discussion of unit costs to cases where there was evidence that they had had significant impact on the overall costings.

13.3   THE BASELINE

The accuracy of the *ex ante* estimates depends upon the extent to which the baseline data used to calculate the *ex ante* costs reflect the actual *ex post* situation. The most important of the baseline data are the breeding herd size and the distribution of the breeding herd between indoors and outdoors, as these affect the total costs of three and two of the measures introduced in 2003 respectively. The *ex ante* baseline data (based on data from the June 2001 Agricultural Census) and *ex post* baseline data (based on the June 2003 Agricultural Census) are compared in Table 13.2. This shows that there are considerable discrepancies between the *ex ante* and *ex post* baselines in terms of the sizes of the herds. These differences are particularly pronounced for the indoor and outdoor breeding herds due to the different assumptions regarding the distribution of the breeding herd between indoor and outdoor production.

The percentage of the breeding herd outdoors in 2003 was estimated by plotting a best fit line using the data in Table 13.3. This gave a result of 30.5 per cent compared to the *ex ante* estimate of 25 per cent. It should be noted that the herd sizes cited in the RIA (see table 13.2 of Defra 2002) imply that around 20 per cent of the breeding herd are indoors, rather than 25 per cent. The reason for this discrepancy is not clear (it could be due to, for example, simplification and rounding errors, different definitions of 'breeding herd' or double counting); however, the effect is to exaggerate the difference between the *ex ante* and *ex post* outdoor herd estimates. The effects of these baseline discrepancies on cost estimates are examined below.

13.4   PROVISION OF MANIPULABLE MATERIALS

This provision is intended to improve the welfare of pigs by providing them with some form of environmental enrichment. Such enrichment enables pigs to satisfy their natural desire to 'root, investigate, chew and play' (Defra 2002, p 3), and there is evidence that this can reduce aggressive behaviour (see for example, Beattie *et al.* 2001). The regulations state that: 'all pigs must have permanent access to a sufficient quantity of material such as straw, hay, wood, sawdust, mushroom compost, peat or a mixture of such which does not adversely affect the health of the animals'.This requirement implies implementation costs for slurry-based systems. The requirement can be met by either (a) providing straw or a similar material via a dispenser, or (b) providing some form of specialist equipment suspended over the pen. As this part of the regulations only applies to the indoor herd, the smaller than predicted size of the indoor herd (see Table 13.2) implies that, in the absence

Table 13.2   Comparison of the ex ante *and* ex post *baseline data*

Data		Ex ante	Source	Ex post	Source	Ex ante:ex post (%)
1. Herd size		**5 000 000**	RIA – from June 2001 Agricultural Census	**4 075 423**	June 2003 Agricultural Census	+18
2. Breeding herd size		**489 000**	RIA p 5	**418 071**	June 2003 Agricultural Census	+14
3. % of breeding herd outdoors		25%	RIA p 2, p 5	30.5%	See text	−22
4. Indoor herd size		**400 000**	RIA p 18	418 071 × 0.695 = **290 559**		+27
5. Outdoor herd size	5a	**89 000**	Implied by 2 and 4	**127 512**		−43
	5b	**100 000**	RIA p 19			−28
	5c	**122 250**	Implied by 2 and 3			−4

Table 13.3   *Estimates of the percentage of the breeding herd produced outdoors*

Year	% of breeding herd outdoors	Source
1996	20	Webster and Dawkins (2000)
2001	25	RIA (Defra 2002)
2005	35	British Pig Executive (2005)

Table 13.4   *Cost of providing manipulable materials*

	Total annual cost
(a) if all use straw or equivalent	£8 795 990
(b) if all use specialised equipment	£2 119 100

Table 13.5   *Cost increases per pig for straw or equivalent*

	Annual cost increase per pig
Purchasing straw or equivalent	£860 000/1.96m = £0.44
Labour costs	£5 722 500/1.96m = £2.92

of other changes, the *ex post* total cost will be proportionately smaller. However, the total cost of providing manipulable materials depends largely on whether straw or specialist equipment is used (Table 13.4).

If we assume that the unit costs in the RIA are accurate, then the adoption of option (a) implies the cost increases per pig listed in Table 13.5. Actual changes in variable and fixed costs for a sample of the indoor herd are reported in the *Pig Yearbooks* (see Figures 13.1a and 13.1b). These graphs do not show any significant increase in either straw/bedding or labour costs in and after 2003 when the regulations were introduced. While any increase may be obscured by other cost changes (for example, increased use of artificial insemination may have reduced labour costs), the graphs suggest that either most farms have opted to use specialised equipment, or the unit costs of using straw have turned out to be much lower than anticipated. In either case, the total costs of providing manipulable materials are likely to be at the low end of the predicted range of annual costs (£8 795 990–£2 119 100) or lower.

Anecdotal evidence[1] suggests that in many cases compliance through the use of 'specialised equipment' is met by simply hanging an infrequently replenished tyre or chain in the pen. If this approach, based

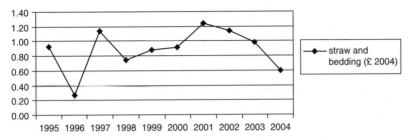

Source: British Pig Executive and Meat and Livestock Commission *Pig Yearbooks.*

Figure 13.1a   Annual cost per pig from indoor herd sample

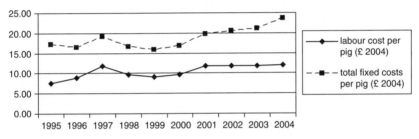

Source: British Pig Executive and Meat and Livestock Commission *Pig Yearbooks.*

Figure 13.1b   Costs per pig from indoor herd sample

on compliance with the letter rather than the spirit of the regulation, is widespread, then the *ex post* unit costs of providing 'specialised equipment', and consequently the overall cost of the manipulable materials provision, will be considerably lower than the *ex ante* estimates.

13.5   MINIMUM 28 DAY WEANING

This provision raised the minimum weaning age from 21 days to 28 days, apart from in systems using all-in/all-out farrowing accommodation[2] where the 21 day minimum weaning period was retained. It was estimated that this change would lead to three sources of increased costs (see Table 13.6). The RIA estimated that the 28 day period would apply to 20 per cent of the indoor breeding herd, or 80 000 sows. Assuming that the assumption of 20 per cent is correct, this overestimates the number of sows, and hence the total costs, by 27 per cent (see Table 13.2). In addition, it is possible that the figure of 20 per cent is higher than the actual percentage, and hence that

Table 13.6   Ex ante *total costs of raising the minimum weaning age to 28*
              days

Measure	Estimated *ex ante* annual cost (£)
Providing new farrowing places	927 700
Increased labour	1 150 000
Cost of lost production	2 320 000

Source: Defra (2002).

the *ex ante* estimate of total costs exceed the turnout costs by more than 27 per cent. There are three reasons why the proportion of the indoor herd affected by this measure may be less than 20 per cent:

1. There may have been an increase in the proportion of farms using an all-in/all-out system in order to reduce labour costs.
2. Some farms may have (inaccurately) claimed to be using an all-in/all-out system in order to avoid the increased minimum weaning age.
3. There is a potential loophole in paragraph 46 of the regulations – piglets may be weaned at less than 28 days if 'the welfare or health of the dam or piglets would otherwise be adversely affected' – and some farms may have avoided the increased minimum weaning age by claiming this.

The RIA estimated that increasing the weaning age would decrease sow productivity by 0.9 pigs/sow/year for the 80 000 sows affected by the regulations. This amounts to a reduction of 0.15 pigs/sow/year averaged over the whole breeding herd. Trends in sow production are shown in Figure 13.2. There is no decrease in sow production between 2002 and 2003 and the predicted change does not appear to have occurred. However, the predicted change of 0.15 is small and could be obscured by other trends, notably industry responses to post-weaning multi-systemic wasting syndrome. It is worth noting that in its review of 2003 market trends and sow productivity, the British Pig Executive (2004, p 9) did not refer to the regulations, which one would expect it to do if the regulations had had a marked impact. It could therefore be argued that the regulation's effects on productivity (and hence cost in terms of lost production) are likely to have been less than the 0.9 pigs/sow/year predicted in the RIA.

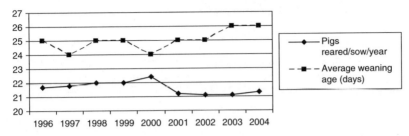

Source: British Pig Executive and Meat and Livestock Commission *Pig Yearbooks.*

Figure 13.2   UK weaning age and sow production rates

13.6   PERMANENT ACCESS TO WATER

The cost of providing permanent access to water was estimated to be a minor cost relative to the overall total cost of the regulations (from 3–6 per cent of the total annual cost). While it is therefore unlikely to affect the overall cost of the regulations, it provides a useful illustration of the ways in which errors can combine to produce misleading results. The *ex ante* and *ex post* costs are compared in Table 13.7.

The *ex ante* and *ex post* total costs are very similar, but this is despite, rather than as a result of the baseline assumptions. The cost effect of the lower than forecast breeding herd size is negated by that of the higher than forecast proportion of the breeding herd reared outdoors, for which

Table 13.7   Comparison of ex ante *and* ex post *costs of providing access to water*

	Ex ante (Defra 2002)	**Ex post (Cost from Defra 2002; herd sizes from Table 13.2)**
Indoor breeding herd	Herd size = 400 000 Farrowing places without water = 400 000×0.20×0.40 = 32 000 Cost = 32 000×£35 = **£1 120 000**	Herd size = 290 559 Farrowing places without water = 290 559×0.20×0.40 = 23 200 Cost = 23 200×£35 = **£812 000**
Outdoor breeding herd	Herd size = 100 000 Cost = £10×100 000 = **£1 000 000**	Herd size = 127 512 Cost = £10×127 512 = **£1 275 000**
Total cost	**£2 120 000**	**£2 087 000**

the unit cost of providing permanent access to water is higher (see Table 13.8).

The fact that the *ex ante* and *ex post* total costs are in agreement is an interesting result as it demonstrates that simple comparisons of *ex ante* and *ex post* costs are not necessarily good indicators of the validity of the original assumptions, and reveal little about the accuracy of the predicted cost distributions within firms and industries.

Table 13.8   Unit cost of providing access to water

	Indoor	**Outdoor**
Unit cost (per pig) of providing access to water	£1 120 000/400 000 = £2.8	£10

13.7   CONCLUSIONS

An overview of the relationship between *ex ante* and *ex post* costs is presented in Table 13.9.

13.7.1   Baseline Errors

The *ex ante/ex post* discrepancies in this case study are dominated by baseline errors that are the inevitable result of not attempting to account for

Table 13.9   Comparison of the ex ante *and* ex post *costs*

Element	***Ex ante: ex post***	**Explanation**
1. Provision of manipulable materials	+	*Ex ante/ex post* likely to be higher than turnout due to a combination of baseline errors, under-compliance/'innovation'.
2. Minimum weaning age	+	*Ex ante/ex post* likely to be higher than turnout due to a combination of baseline errors and under-compliance.
3. Permanent provision of water	0	Significant baseline errors cancelling each other out
Overall	+	**Likely to be higher overall as main cost elements (1 and 2) are overestimated.**

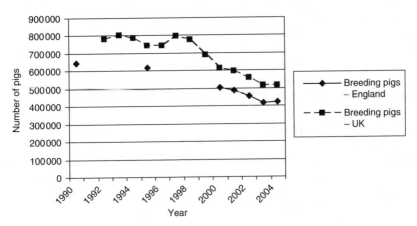

Sources: Defra's Agricultural Census (English data); BPEX's *Pig Yearbooks* (UK data).

Figure 13.3   Breeding pig numbers in England and the UK

temporal variation in an industry undergoing rapid change. This failure to adopt dynamic assumptions is somewhat surprising given the high profile and rapid change in the pig industry in recent years. For example, Figure 13.3 shows the dramatic change in the breeding herd since the late 1990s. There have also been significant changes in pig productivity and the proportion of the herd reared outdoors (see Table 13.2). However, it is easy to be wise after the event: what may seem like an unreasonable assumption now – that the decline in the pig industry was bottoming out in 2001 – may have been justified when the RIA was being written. Superimposed on these trends have been significant one-off events, notably the foot and mouth (FMD) outbreak in 2001. It has been suggested that the breeding herd figures for 2001, the year that was used as the baseline, were inflated 'due to movement restrictions and the lack of an export market for cull sows as a result of the Foot and Mouth disease outbreak' (Defra/National Statistics 2005, p 18). These raise doubts about the suitability of using data from 2001 as a baseline from which to predict future costs.

13.7.2   Compliance Issues

Realistic assumptions about compliance should be adopted, particularly amongst regulatees who are unable to pass on costs and have a strong incentive to adopt cost-minimising strategies. Compliance with the letter of a regulation can be significantly different, and has different cost implications, from complying with the spirit. Discrepancies are more likely where the regulation does not have the widespread support of the regulatees and there is a light-touch enforcement regime. These conditions apply to some agricultural regulations where the regulatee typically has limited scope to pass increased costs on and where, as a consequence, a small cost increase can represent a significant reduction in profit margins (or in many cases, an increase in losses). In addition, the dispersed and often remote character of farming can raise logistical problems in terms of monitoring and enforcement.

13.7.3   Effect of Lobbying

The effect of lobbying on behalf of the regulatees is commonly cited as a reason for errors in *ex ante* estimates. It is possible that these regulations may have been seen as going some way to levelling the animal welfare playing field within the EU and therefore being potentially advantageous to the UK pig industry. In a survey of pig production in 12 countries, the UK had the highest cost of production and the highest variable costs – these were attributed in part to 'additional bedding costs relating to higher welfare loose straw finishing systems' (Knowles 2002, p 6). Although this doesn't help the pig industry compete with other meats, the prospect (although distant) of reducing the cost disadvantage of the UK pig industry relative to other EU producers may have limited industry opposition to the regulations, and hence the bias associated with lobbying and asymmetric correction of errors. However, the National Pig Association response to the provisional RIA – and the upwards revision of most costs between the provisional and final RIA – would seem to contradict this (National Pig Association 2002).

13.7.4   Lessons from the Case Study

The lessons drawn from this study are broadly similar to those from the Groundwater Regulations study in Chapter 12, that is, both show the importance of adopting dynamic assumptions (and suitable baselines) when developing cost estimates for rapidly changing sectors. Furthermore, this study re-emphasises the need to make realistic assumptions about patterns of compliance, particularly where regulatees are unable to pass on costs and have a strong incentive to adopt cost-minimising strategies.

NOTES

1. Interview with Susan Jarvis, Scottish Agricultural College, 14 October 2005.
2. A system of management in which the barn is completely filled at one time and then completely emptied at one time to allow for cleaning and disinfecting between groups of pigs. (http://isu.porkgateway.com/web/guest1/definitions accessed 22 April 2008.)

REFERENCES

Beattie, V.E., Sneddon, I.A., Walker, N. and Weatherup, R.N. (2001) Environmental enrichment of intensive pig housing using spent mushroom compost, *Animal Science*, 72, 35–42.

British Pig Executive (2004) *Pig Yearbook 2004*. Milton Keynes: BPEX.

British Pig Executive (2005) *Pig Yearbook 2005*. Milton Keynes: BPEX.

Defra (2002) *Final Regulatory Impact Assessment: The Welfare of Farmed Animals (England) (Amendment) Regulations 2003*. London: Defra.

Defra and National Statistics (2005) *Pig Statistics 28/10/2005*, London: DEFRA.

Knowles, A (2002) *EU Cost of Production Project*. Milton Keynes: BPEX/MLC.

National Pig Association (2002) *Response to the Partial RIA for the Welfare of Farmed Animal (England) (Amendment) Regulations 2002*, London: National Pig Association.

Webster, S. and Dawkins, M. (2000) The post-weaning behaviour of indoor-bred and outdoor-bred pigs, *Animal Science*, 71, 265–71.

14. The Food Safety (General Food Hygiene) (Butchers' Shops) Amendment Regulations 2000 (UK)

Michael MacLeod

Regulations designed to reduce the risk of *E. Coli* 0157 food poisoning are examined in this chapter. These regulations are somewhat unusual in that they have been the subject of several *ex post* analyses. The evidence suggests that the *ex ante* costs were underestimated because of incorrect assumptions that (a) the regulations would not impose any one-off implementation costs on business, and (b) that the costs to Local Authorities of administering the licensing scheme would be largely offset by license fee revenue. The study highlights the difficulties of attributing costs to specific regulatory measures. It also raises questions about the ways in which time spent complying with regulations is measured and valued.

14.1 BACKGROUND

In 1996 there was a serious outbreak of *E. Coli* 0157 in North Lanarkshire, which led to the deaths of 17 people and the illness of another 500. The subsequent inquiry carried out by the Pennington Group traced the outbreak to the food handling practices at a butcher's shop. The Pennington Group produced a set of recommendations, one of which was to introduce a licensing scheme for butchers in the UK. The Food Safety (General Food Hygiene) (Butchers' Shops) Amendment Regulations 2000 (Statutory Instrument 2000 No. 930) introduced the licensing scheme as recommended.

The regulations require that butchers' shops handling and selling unwrapped raw meat and ready-to-eat foods from the same premises hold a licence issued by the Local Authority (LA). In order to qualify for a licence, shops need to satisfy a number of conditions, including (Food Standards Agency 2000, para. 10):

- compliance with existing relevant food hygiene and temperature control legislation;
- the operation of a documented Hazard Analysis Critical Control Point (HACCP) food safety management system. This builds on the requirement in existing legislation for hazard analysis under the Food Safety (General Food Hygiene) Regulations 1995, which require food hazards to be identified and controlled, and procedures reviewed;
- enhanced hygiene training for food handlers and supervisory staff over and above the provisions of the 1995 general hygiene regulations.

14.2   METHODOLOGY

The Butchers' Regulations are unusual in that there is significant *ex post* data available, notably three studies carried out by Walker and Jones (2002), Gaze *et al.* (2003) and Griffith *et al.* (2003). The data collected in these surveys are used as the basis for estimating the *ex post* costs of the regulations.

14.3   BASELINE AND COMPLIANCE ISSUES

The meat retail mix in Britain has been undergoing a period of rapid change in response to changing consumer preferences and shopping patterns. Between 1994 and 2004, the number of butchers' shops in Britain fell from 11 793 to 7300, a drop of 38 per cent (Cullen 2004). Although there was a marked reduction in butchers' shops during the year when the regulations were introduced, the short time gap between the creation of the Regulatory Impact Assessment (RIA) and the implementation of the regulations means that underlying trends in the baseline are unlikely to have made much impact.

Another potential source of error is that of bias created by the selective removal of less competitive, higher-cost butchers in response to the cost increases arising from the regulations. Wheelock (2002, p 38) noted that 'independent butchers have been under intense competition from the multiples for many years, and consequently many of them have closed. Therefore, those that have survived must provide a good service and be efficient.' While Wheelock (2002) did report that some butchers had ceased trading as a result of the regulations, he also noted that it was not simply a matter of the least (cost) efficient closing – factors such as age and willingness to retrain or change practice also played a part.

Finally, levels of compliance with the regulations appear to be high. The Food Standards Agency (2001) reported that (in November 2000): 'approximately 86% of butchers would have licences by the beginning of December, and that only 4% had been refused licences. The remaining 10% of butchers were working closely with their local authorities to ensure full compliance.'

14.4 COMPARISON

The *ex ante* cost estimates given in the RIA are summarised in Table 14.1 and Table 14.2. These estimates were based on the assumption that 'the licensing Regulations will not introduce significant new costs for businesses other than for those associated with training and the licence application fee' (RIA para 25 – Food Standards Agency 2000). This is because it was thought that most of the operating and structural requirements of HACCP had already been introduced under the 1995 Hygiene Regulations. Another key assumption was that the costs to Local Authorities of administering the licensing scheme were expected to be largely offset by the licence fee revenue. These assumptions are examined below.

14.4.1 Implementing HACCP Procedures

The RIA estimated the one-off cost of implementing the regulations to be £4.5m and the recurring costs (excluding licensing) to be £2.6–2.7m (see Table 14.2).

14.4.2 One-Off Costs

The one-off *ex ante* cost is attributed to the funding of the Government initiatives in support of the regulations: the costs to business are predicted to be £0. There is little reason to doubt that the cost of Government support was significantly different from the *ex ante* estimate. Indeed, the Food Standards Agency (2004) reported that 'Approximately 7,500 butchers in England received support to implement HACCP through a £4.5 million Government training and consultancy initiative delivered by the Meat and Livestock Commission (MLC).' However, the *ex ante* estimate of no significant one-off costs for business is a potential source of error. Three *ex post* studies of the Butchers' Regulations have been carried out: Walker and Jones (2002); Gaze *et al.* (2003), and Griffith *et al.* (2003). Gaze *et al.* (2003) and Walker and Jones (2002) specifically asked butchers how much the regulations had cost to implement, and their findings are summarised in Tables 14.3 and Table 14.4.

Table 14.1　Summary of the ex ante *cost estimates by sector*

Sector		Ex ante cost estimates
Business		Recurring costs of around £3.3m, no significant one-off costs
Charities		None
Citizens		Difficult to determine, likely to be negligible
Government	Central	£4.5m one-off cost for a support initiative
	Local	Extra costs offset by the licence fee

Source:　Food Standards Agency (2000).

Table 14.2　Summary of the ex ante *cost estimates by cost type*

Cost		Ex ante cost estimates
One-off implementation costs	Business	0
	Government	£4.5m
Recurring implementation costs to business (not inc. licensing)		£2.6m – £2.7m
Licensing	Cost to business (recurring)	£670 000
	Cost to LAs (recurring)	minimal
Total one-off		£4.5m
Total recurring		£3.3m – £3.4m

Source:　Food Standards Agency (2000).

The results in Table 14.3 are based on a survey by Gaze *et al.* (2003) of 202 butchers in three selected regions of England (the South West, the Midlands and Yorkshire) and the results in Table 14.4 are based on a survey by Walker and Jones (2002) of 29 butchers in Derby. The results are based on specific questions that asked how much it had cost their shop to implement HACCP. If we assume that the costs are the same throughout the rest of England, then these results imply that the cost of implementing HACCP in England was between £3.5m and £6.9m. Assuming that the cost to the Government was £4.5m, then this gives one-off *ex post* costs in the range £8.0–11.4m compared with the *ex ante* estimate of £4.5m.

Table 14.3   HACCP implementation costs based on Gaze et al. *(2003)*

Implementation cost (£)	Assumed average cost	% of respondents[a]	Cost for all butchers in England (no of butchers×%×cost)
<500	300	65	6 700×0.65×300 = 1 306 500
500–1000	750	27	6 700×0.27×750 = 1 356 800
>1000	1 500 or	8	6 700×0.08×1 500 = 804 000
	3 000		6 700×0.08×3 000 = 1 608 000
		Total	**£3 467 300** (assuming 1500)
			£4 271 300 (assuming 3000)

Note: a excluding don't knows.

Table 14.4   HACCP implementation costs based on Walker and Jones
           (2002)

Implementation cost (£)	Assumed average cost	% of respondents	Cost for all butchers in England
<100	50	5	16 750
100–200	150	23	231 150
300–400	350	11	257 950
400–500	450	5	150 750
500–1000	750	33	1 658 250
1000–5000	3000	23	4 623 000
		Total	**£6 937 850**

14.4.3   Recurring Implementation Costs to Business (Not Including Licensing)

The RIA identified training and licensing as the two main recurring costs of the regulations. The RIA estimated that training would cost £2.6m per year. In their survey, Gaze *et al.* (2003) asked a sample of butchers to esti- mate how much it cost them to maintain their shops' HACCP. These results can be used to estimate the ongoing cost of the regulations throughout England (see Table 14.5).

Again, if we assume that the costs are the same throughout the rest of England, then the cost would be in the range £1.8–2.1m, compared to the *ex ante* estimate of £2.6m. However, this comparison needs to be treated with some caution, as Gaze *et al.* (2003, p 60) found that in their assess- ment of costs, many butchers 'had not considered the cost of their time, spent for example in attending training courses, developing the HACCP

Table 14.5   *Recurring costs to business based on Gaze* et al. *(2003)*

Implementation cost (£)	Assumed average cost	% of respondents	Cost (no of butchers×%×cost)
<100	50	25	6 700×0.25×50 = 83 750
100–500	300	66	6 700×0.66×300 = 1 326 600
>500	700 or	9	6 700×0.09×700 = 422 100
	1000		6 700×0.09×1000 = 603 000
		Total	**£1 832 450** (assuming £700)
			£2 013 400 (assuming £1 000)

Notes:
1. Percentage of respondents excludes 'don't knows'.
2. Table excludes cost of licensing.

Table 14.6   *Recurring costs to business based on Griffith* et al. *(2003)*

Item	% of butchers reporting an increase	Mean time increase (hours)	Mean weekly cost increase (£)	Annual cost increase for England (£)[b]	Mean time increase[a] (hours)
Time cleaning	38.0	2.0	17.0	2 250 664	0.8
Cleaning materials	46.8	na	9.0	1 467 461	na
Monitoring HACCP	76.5	3.4	28.9	7 702 601	2.6
HACCP record keeping	73.2	2.5	21.3	5 419 362	1.8
Checking products	48.3	2.3	19.6	3 289 819	1.1
Total				**20 129 907**	
Cost per shop[a]				**3004**	**6.3**

Notes:
a   Averaged over all butchers.
b   Calculated as col.2/100 × col. 4× 52 × 6700 (number of butchers), e.g. 0.38 × 17 × 52 × 6700.
Table excludes cost of licensing.

documentation and training staff. The costs provided, therefore, are not reliable estimates.' It is interesting to compare these results with those of Griffith *et al.* (2003), who specifically asked butchers to estimate the additional time burden of the regulations (see Table 14.6).

The costs reported in Table 14.6 are very high and it is doubtful that an average increase in working time of 6.3 hours and a cost of £3000 per shop would have resulted in the fairly sanguine attitudes regarding the costs of the regulations reported in other parts of the survey (for example 54 per cent of the respondents agreed with the statement 'Although HACCP has cost money it is outweighed by the benefits' (Griffith *et al.* 2003, p 54). There are two reasons why the reported increases may be higher than the actual increases. Firstly, although Griffith *et al.* (2003) specifically asked respondents to 'report whether requirements for licensing have had the direct effect of either increasing or decreasing the time and money spent on managing food hygiene from week to week', it may have been difficult for respondents to distinguish between general hygiene improvement costs and the additional costs arising from the regulations. It is therefore possible that not all the cost increases reported are attributable to the regulations. Secondly, respondents may be engaging in strategic behaviour, for example, they may be deliberately overestimating the costs in order to reduce the scope of future measures. Despite these caveats, the scale of the costs implied by the results of Griffith *et al.* (2003) suggest that there is a significant ongoing cost, particularly in terms of staff time, resulting from the regulations, and the cost is almost certainly significantly higher than the £2.6m training-related costs reported in the RIA.

14.4.4 Cost of Licensing

Licensing involves inspection of premises by Local Authority Environmental Health Officers, who check that shops are complying with the regulations and provide advice on HACCP implementation. Butchers pay an annual fee of £100 to the LA, which is intended to (substantially) offset the costs incurred by the LA during the licensing process. The RIA estimated that licensing would cost butchers £670 000 per annum and that the cost of licensing to LAs would effectively be zero due to the extra costs being offset by the licence fee.

Cost of licensing to butchers
The total cost to butchers depends on the number of butchers being licensed and the fee paid. There is little reason to believe that the *ex post* cost would be significantly different from the *ex ante* estimate for two reasons:

1. The *ex post* fee of £100 is as predicted in the RIA.
2. There was only a short period of time between the RIA and the implementation of the regulations so, even though there was a large fall in the number of butchers' shops in the UK during 2000, this should not have had a significant effect on the total costs.

Cost of licensing to the LA

The RIA implies that the cost of licensing the regulations to LAs will be offset by the licence fee – the fact that no costs for this are included in the total costs implies that the costs not offset by the licence fee were expected to be minimal. However, there is evidence that the costs to LAs are significantly greater than the licence fee revenue. Walker and Jones (2002) reported that 'to successfully license all 29 premises has cost the City [Derby] Council approximately £22,000', compared to an annual license revenue of £2900. This equates to a net cost to the council of £666 per business. At this rate, the total net cost to LAs in England would be £4.46m per annum. This is a highly significant cost, given that the total recurring costs were estimated to be only £3.3–3.4m in the RIA. However, it should be noted that this cost, while recurring, is likely to reduce with time as licence renewals require less work by LAs than initial applications (Gaze *et al.* (2003, p v).

14.5   CONCLUSIONS

The results of the *ex ante* and *ex post* analyses are summarised in Table 14.7. They suggest that both the one-off and the recurring costs of the regulations were underestimated *ex ante*. While there is considerable uncertainty in the *ex post* estimates, particularly regarding the recurring costs to business, the *ex ante* estimates seem to be underestimated by at least a factor of two. The main reasons for the apparent errors in the *ex ante* estimate are the assumptions that (a) the regulations would not impose any one-off implementation costs on business, and (b) the costs to Local Authorities of administering the licensing scheme would be largely offset by license fee revenue.

The *ex ante/ex post* comparison was complicated by uncertainty regarding which costs the *ex post* estimates were measuring. The *ex post* surveys asked slightly different questions and these may well have been interpreted in differing ways by the respondents. It could therefore be argued that the *ex post* and *ex ante* estimates of costs to business are not exactly comparing like with like. A related problem is that of distinguishing additionality. Can we be confident that the costs arising from the regulations cited by respondents in the *ex post* surveys are actually additional, that is, they do not include the costs of hygiene-related measures that the regulatees would have undertaken anyway, either voluntarily or in response to other legislation? Colatore and Caswell (reported in Romano *et al.* 2005) distinguish between three types of compliance cost: (a) total cost of the actual HACCP system adopted; (b) minimum HACCP costs required to comply with the

Table 14.7 Comparison of the ex ante and ex post cost estimates

Cost		Ex Ante (RIA)	Ex Post			
			(based on Gaze et al. 2003, p57)	(based on Griffith et al. 2003, p18)	(based on Walker and Jones 2002)	(as in ex ante estimates)
One-off implementation costs	Business	0	£3.5m – £4.3m		£6.9m	
	Govt	£4.5m				£4.5m (FSA 2004)
Recurring implementation costs to business (not inc. licensing)		£2.6m – £2.7m	£1.8m – £2.0m	£20.1m		
Licensing	Cost to business (recurring)	£670 000				£670 000
	Cost to LAs (recurring)	minimal			£4.5m	
Total one-off		**£4.5m**	**£8.0m – £11.4m**			
Total recurring		**£3.3m – £3.4m**	**£7.0m – £25.3m**			

regulations; and (c) incremental cost of HACCP (the minimum cost net of voluntary adoption of HACCP, that is, the additional cost of the regulation). Despite these issues, the direction of variance between the *ex ante* and *ex post* estimates is consistent.

The difference between the *ex ante* and *ex post* estimates of the cost of licensing is important because it (a) led to significant errors in the total recurring cost of the regulations, and (b) led to errors in the distribution of costs. Given the results from Walker and Jones (2002), it seems strange that the RIA predicted that no net cost would arise to LAs as a result of licensing. However, this assumption may have been reasonable in the light of the consultation responses. The RIA consulted widely and reported that 'The proposal for a £100 licence fee appeared to be non-contentious' (Food Standards Agency 2000, para 34). The RIA did not report any concerns raised by LAs during the consultation regarding the costs of administering the licensing scheme. There are several potential explanations for the difference between the *ex ante* and *ex post* estimates of licensing costs:

1. Administering the licensing scheme took considerably more time than expected.
2. LAs overcomplied with the regulations.
3. LAs were reluctant to argue for a higher licence fee in case it created problems of non-compliance.
4. LAs were broadly in favour of the regulations and were therefore reluctant to be critical during the consultation.
5. The estimates in Walker and Jones (2002) may be inflated as a result of the respondents engaging in strategic behaviour.

Whatever the actual reasons for the discrepancy, the effect appears to have been to impose a significant opportunity cost on LAs:

> The shortfall of £19,300 [the net cost of administering the licensing scheme] has impacted on the City Council's routine food hygiene inspection figures with these premises being removed from the risk-based inspection programme and placed on their own separate schedule. (Walker and Jones 2002)

14.5.1 Lessons from the Case Study

This study shows the importance of accounting for the value of the time people spend in complying with regulations. Time can be a significant cost element – where applicable, specific information on it should be sought at an early stage so that it can be valued and included in the cost calculations. This study also highlights the problems associated with defining costs consistently and identifying actual additional costs. Regulations are often implemented in complex, rapidly changing areas of policy, which makes it difficult to attribute particular actions (and associated costs) to particular regulations. However, efforts should be made to establish clear lines of sight between regulations and actions in order to minimise the risk of double counting.

REFERENCES

Colatore, C. and Caswell, J.A. (2000), 'The cost of HACCP implementation in the seafood industry: A case study of breaded fish', in L. Unnevehr (ed.), *The economics of HACCP costs and benefits*, St Paul, MN: Eagan Press, pp. 45–79.

Cullen, R. (2004) *Where Will Independent Butchers Be in 10 Years Time?* Milton Keynes: Meat and Livestock Commission.

Food Standards Agency (2000) *Regulatory Impact Assessment: The Food Safety (General Food Hygiene) (Butchers' Shops) Amendment Regulations 2000*. London: Food Standards Agency.

Food Standards Agency (2001) *Paper Note 01/01/02: Report on Progress on Butchers' Licensing in England*. London: Food Standards Agency (available at: http://www.food.gov.uk/multimedia/pdfs/note010102, accessed 22 April 2008).

Food Standards Agency (2004) *Evaluation of Butchers' Shop Licensing in England Wednesday 08 September 2004* (available at: http://www.food.gov.uk/foodindustry/guidancenotes/meatregsguid/butcherslicensing/butcherseural, accessed 22 April 2008).

Gaze, R., Everitt, M., Goode, J., Allchurch, E., Chappell, A. and Walker, S.J. (2003) *Evaluation of the Butchers' Licensing Initiative in England*. Chipping Campden: CCFRA.

Griffith, C.J., Hayburn, G. and Clayton, D. (2003) *An Evaluation of the Butchers' Licensing Initiative in England; Final Report,* Contract Reference: ZB00036. Cardiff: Food Research and Consultancy Unit (FRCU), University of Wales Institute.

Romano, D., Cavicchi, A., Rocchi, B. and Stefani, G. (2005) Exploring costs and benefits of compliance with HACCP regulation in the European meat and dairy sectors, *Acta Agricultura Scand Sinavica Section C*, 2, 52–9.

Walker, E. and Jones, N. (2002) The good, the bad and the ugly of butchers' shops licensing in England: one local authority's experience, *British Food Journal*, 104 (1), 20–30.

Wheelock, J.V. (2002) *Final Report: Evaluation of Butchers' Shop Licensing Initiative in Scotland Prepared for the Food Standards Agency Scotland* (available at: http://www.food.gov.uk/multimedia/pdfs/S01011finalreport.pdf, accessed 22 April 2008).

PART III

Synthesis and conclusions

15. Assessing innovation dynamics induced by environmental policy

Paul Ekins and Andrew Venn

The evidence presented in the case studies and review provides a number of reasons why *ex ante* and *ex post* costs may differ. In the last chapter, these will be brought together into a number of overall conclusions of this book, together with recommendations for the estimation of such costs in the future.

First, however, it seems desirable to investigate in more detail one of the main reasons that has emerged for the divergence between *ex ante* and *ex post* estimations – the extent to which innovation is stimulated and employed to meet regulatory and other policy goals.

15.1 INTRODUCTION

Environmental technologies are a key element in the quest for sustainable development. They have the potential to sidestep the classic dilemma between economic growth and environmental improvement. In the past, numerous new technologies have been introduced in Europe that have contributed to pollution prevention, environmental clean-up and the conservation of energy and resources.

Many of the new technologies recently introduced in Europe have led to reductions in costs and/or reinforced the competitive strength of European industry. This is because 'clean' technologies developed in Europe have become successful export products on the world market. The important role of eco-innovation is recognised by the European Commission. In January 2004, the Environmental Technologies Action Plan (ETAP, COM(2004)38 final) was published. The ETAP aims to harness the full potential of environmental technologies to reduce pressures on natural resources, improve quality of life and stimulate economic growth.

Despite the recent introduction of the ETAP, there is a need for illustrated examples of the mechanisms behind the development and diffusion of cleaner technologies in industry today. In particular, the actual and potential role of environmental policies (including the specific influence of EU policy) deserves closer investigation.

This chapter draws on the results of the project 'Assessing innovation dynamics induced by environment policy', which was carried out in 2006 for the European Commission, DG Environment, by a consortium comprising the Institute for Environmental Studies (IVM), the Institute for European Environmental Policy (IEEP), the Policy Studies Institute (PSI) and the Netherlands Environmental Assessment Agency (MNP).[1] The objective of the project was twofold: first, to analyse (using specific case studies) how different environmental policy instruments induce innovation and to provide an analysis of the dynamics of this innovation; secondly, to analyse the extent to which market-driven innovation can lead to lowering the environmental impacts of products and processes. The project involved undertaking a literature review and five case studies. This chapter draws on the literature review (Oosterhuis and ten Brink 2006) to discuss how eco-innovation has been conceptualised and analysed, and then provides brief summaries of the case studies, drawing together their conclusions.

15.2 CONCEPTUALISING ECO-INNOVATION

15.2.1 A Model of Technical Change

Technologies do not exist in a vacuum. They are a product of the social and economic context in which they were developed and which they subsequently help to shape. There is now a large literature that seeks to understand how technological change occurs, and its driving forces. One relatively simple model set out in Foxon (2003) assesses the drivers, barriers and policies related to inducing innovation for a low carbon future.

The model differentiates between drivers of technical change according to whether they are 'technology push' or 'market pull', as illustrated and discussed in Figure 15.1. This shows how technologies are developed through basic and applied research and development (R&D), through to demonstration and commercialisation and thereby diffusion into society. Although for ease of illustration the process is depicted as a linear, sequential chain of events, in reality it is characterised by multiple feedbacks, overlapping stages and interactions, involving research, the existing body of scientific and technological knowledge, the potential market, invention, and the various steps in the production and commercialisation processes (Kline and Rosenberg 1986; OECD 1992).

The first, pre-market phases of the process are described as 'technology push', because the principal drivers are the business and policy decisions

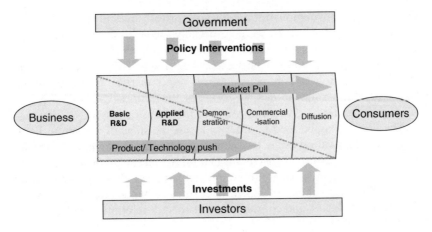

Notes:
1. The innovation process involves the development and deployment of new technologies, products and services by business in order to meet the needs of consumers. To achieve this, funding is required from a variety of investors, such as insurance companies, banks, private equity houses and angel investors.
2. In the early stages of the market, take-up is largely driven by the product/technology push. As consumer awareness builds, the rate of deployment is accelerated as consumer demand grows.
3. Government can make various policy interventions at various stages of the innovation chain to overcome barriers to the development of various technologies, products and services.

Source: Foxen (2003, p 18). Reproduced by kind permission of the Carbon Trust from Carbon Trust (2002).

Figure 15.1. Role of innovation chain actors

that cause the technology to be developed. The commercialisation and diffusion processes are much more driven by consumer demand-pull in the markets which have been targeted or into which the technologies will by then have penetrated to some extent. Clearly, as shown, both sets of drivers are present to some extent in all phases: even at the earliest phases of technology R&D, potential market demand is a major interest, and even during diffusion, research-driven technological change may occur. For the process to take place successfully, continuous learning from and feedback between these processes are required.

Each stage of the process may require, or be subject to, private investments or policy interventions (which may include government investments). At the R&D stages, at least for technologies which are thought to be of major potential public benefit, public investment and other policy interventions are likely to be relatively important (shown by the length of the arrows). From demonstration onwards, private investments are likely to be relatively important. However, especially for technologies of potential public benefit but uncertain market demand, it is likely that public support and policy interventions will be necessary both to help the technology from the demonstration to commercialisation stages (a risky transition sometimes called the 'valley of death' because of the business casualties which it often induces) and even right through to the diffusion stage.

The model may be used in order to assess the stage of a given technology in the innovation cycle. Its distinction between research, commercial, market and institutional (f)actors is helpful in analysing how a technology has got to a particular stage, and to project how it might progress to future stages. The case studies examined later in this chapter focus on a varied mix of technologies, and consideration of their development in the context of the model should reveal the diversity of incentives, motivations and actions that always underpin the widespread diffusion of a technology in society.

Oosterhuis and ten Brink (2006) note that new technologies, when they are successful in being applied and finding their way to the market, often follow a pattern in which the uptake starts at a low speed, then accelerates and slows down again when the level of saturation approaches. This is reflected in the well-known logistic or S-curve (see Figure 15.2). The acceleration in uptake is not only because the technology is becoming more widely known, but also due to improvements and cost reductions occurring in the course of the diffusion process because of economies of scale and learning effects. Cost reductions as a function of the accumulative production (or sales) of a particular technology can be represented by 'learning curves' or 'experience curves'. Figure 15.3 shows a learning curve for photovoltaic (PV) energy technology. The 'learning rate' is the percentage cost reduction with each doubling of cumulative production or sales.

IEA (2000) has assessed the potential of experience curves as tools to inform and strengthen energy technology policy. It stresses the importance of measures to encourage niche markets for new technologies as one of the most efficient ways for governments to provide learning opportunities. McDonald and Schrattenholzer (2001) have assembled data on experience accumulation and cost reduction for a number of energy technologies (including wind and solar PV). They estimated learning rates for the resulting 26 data sets, analysed their variability, and evaluated their usefulness for applications in long-term energy models. Junginger (2005) applied a learning curve approach to investigate the potential cost reductions in renewable electricity production technologies, in particular wind and biomass based. He also addressed a number of methodological issues related to the construction and use of learning curves.

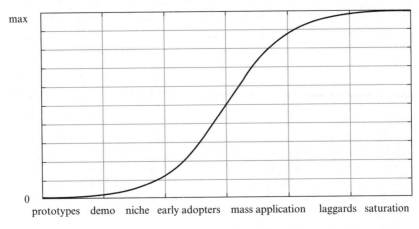

prototypes   demo   niche   early adopters   mass application   laggards   saturation

Figure 15.2   Stages in the introduction of new technology; the S-curve

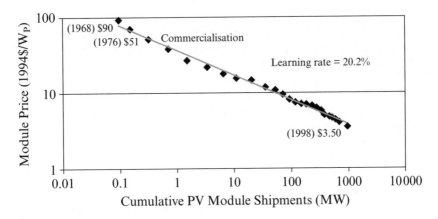

Source: Harmon (2000). Reproduced by kind permission of the Institute for Applied Systems Analysis.

Figure 15.3   Learning curve of PV-modules, 1968–1998

Several studies have been carried out to assess the quantitative rela-tionship between the development of costs of environmental technologies and time. A TME study (1995) pioneered this, and RIVM (2000) further explored the consequences of this phenomenon. Several other studies address this issue (for example, Anderson 1999; Touche Ross 1995).

Table 15.1   Annual decrease in cost of applying environmental technologies

Technology / Cluster	Annual cost decrease		
	Min.	**Average**	**Max.**
Dephosphating sewage	3.8%		6.7%
Desulphurisation of flue gas at power stations	4%		10%
Regulated catalytic converter	9%		10.5%
Industrial low NO$_x$ technologies	17%		31%
1. High efficiency central heating		1.4%	
2. Energy-related technologies		4.9%	
3. End-of-pipe, large installations		7.6%	
4. End-of-pipe, small installations (catalysts)		9.8%	
5. Agriculture low emission application of manure		9.2%	

Source: TME (1995, p. vi); RIVM (2000, p. 13), cited in Oosterhuis (2006a, p.26).

Both RIVM and TME conclude that the reduction of unit costs of environmental technologies goes faster than the – comparable – technological progress factor that is incorporated in macro-economic models used by the Netherlands Central Planning Bureau. In these models the average factor is about 2 per cent annually. The results of both the RIVM and TME studies for the annual cost decrease of environmental technologies are presented in Table 15.1. Both studies show comparable results: the annual cost decrease is mostly between 4 and 10 per cent. Therefore, when modelling environmental costs for the longer term, some form of technological progress needs to be taken on board in addition to what is assumed in the macro-economic model.

In the TME and RIVM studies no attempt was made to differentiate between two types of technological progress (see Krozer 2002):

1. Gradual improvements of already existing technologies (which Krozer assumes will mainly lead to cost savings and not so much to increased reduction potential);
2. Innovations (or 'leap technologies') for technologies which are new and can compete with existing technologies in both efficiency (lower costs) and effectiveness (larger reduction potential).

This distinction is important, especially concerning the development of the reduction potential, because this will enable a greater reduction in pollution in the future than currently thought.

The anecdotal evidence on waste water treatment and low NO_X technologies in industry actually shows both developments:

1. Increasing reduction potential (to almost 100 per cent theoretical) in a period of about 30 years;
2. Decreasing unit costs.

So from the empirical point of view both developments are important enough to be separately considered when estimating the future costs of environmental technologies.

15.2.2 Characterising Eco-innovation

Oosterhuis and ten Brink (2006) show that there is widespread agreement in the literature that environmental policies have the potential to exert a strong influence on both the speed and the direction of environmental innovation. Rather than being an autonomous, 'black box' process, technological development is nowadays acknowledged (as illustrated in the previous section), to be the result of a large number of different factors that are amenable to analysis. Environmental policy can be one of these factors, even though its relative importance may differ from case to case. This section focuses specifically on innovation in respect of environmental technologies. Such innovations ('eco-innovations') display many features of 'ordinary' innovations, but they have an additional characteristic in that their application may reduce certain negative environmental impacts (including resource use), and this is often the main reason for their introduction.

A general feature of innovations that is also relevant for eco-innovation is the extent to which the innovation implies changes in inputs, capital goods, skills required, organisational routines, links with suppliers and customers and so on. Innovation may also be incremental (small changes to an existing process or product, not affecting existing routines), or it may have a breakthrough character, implying fundamental changes in an existing system. Obviously, these are two extreme types and many innovations will be somewhere in between them.

A specific feature of environmental technology is the particular mechanism by which the environmental impact is reduced. The following types are often distinguished:

1. 'End-of-pipe' technology (isolating or neutralising polluting substances after they have been formed). End-of-pipe technology is often seen as undesirable because it may lead to waste that has to be disposed of.[2]

2. 'Process-integrated' technology, also known as 'integrated' or 'clean' technology. This is a general term for changes in processes and production methods (that is, making things differently) that lead to less pollution, resource and/or energy use.
3. Product innovations, in which (final) products are developed or (re)designed that contain less harmful substances (that is, making different things), use less energy, produce less waste and so on.

It is often argued that there is a 'natural' tendency for environmental technology to develop from abatement (end-of-pipe) to 'integrated' (clean) technologies. This view is, however, challenged by Berkhout (2005). Frondel *et al.* (2004) also point out that a certain amount of end-of-pipe technology will remain necessary to curb specific emissions which cannot easily be reduced with cleaner production measures.

As noted above, environmental innovations can be policy-driven or business-driven. Obviously, end-of-pipe technology will usually be primarily policy-driven. Process and product innovations, however, usually come about as part of the normal business cycle. For such innovations, environmental policy tends to be just one among the many factors that steer, accelerate, or set the conditions for the innovation process.

15.2.3   The Counterfactual

Because technological innovation is a normal ongoing part of business activity and economic development, it is far from easy in evaluating a policy that is intended to stimulate eco-innovation to establish what would have happened had the policy not been introduced, that is, the baseline or counterfactual. There are essentially two possibilities. First, as noted above, it is possible for 'normal' innovation to result in increased resource efficiency and environmental improvement, so that the policy may not be responsible for all the environmental improvement that may be observed. On the other hand, it is possible that 'normal' innovation may involve the development of processes or technologies that throw up new hazards for human health or the environment, or intensify old ones. In this case an evaluation against the state of the environment at the time of policy implementation may understate its environmental gains.

There is no clearcut methodology that can assess the 'without policy' counterfactual. Essentially each case study must proceed to estimate it as best it can in order to arrive at the best possible assessment of policy effectiveness (see 3.3 in Chapter 3).

15.2.4 Different Types of Policy Instruments

In a market economy, the basic motivation of innovation among market players (whether making things differently or making different things) is to make financial profits or otherwise strengthen market position. Policies succeed in inducing eco-innovation when they change the investment/ return equation in favour of environment-improving innovation, rather than other innovation or no innovation at all.

There are various types of policy instruments which a national government can employ in an attempt to improve the environment, perhaps through inducing eco-innovation. Such instruments may be grouped under four generic headings (see Table 2.2 in Chapter 2 and Jordan *et al.* (2003):

1. Market- or incentive-based (also called economic) instruments (see EEA 2006 for a recent review of European experience). These instruments include 'emissions trading, environmental taxes and charges, deposit-refund systems, subsidies (including the removal of environmentally-harmful subsidies), green purchasing, and liability and compensation' (EEA 2006, p.13). Except for green purchasing, these instruments change the investment/return equation directly, by changing the relative prices and costs of inputs or processes in favour of those with less environmental impact. These instruments are often perceived to give a positive incentive in favour of eco-innovation.
2. Classic regulation instruments, which seek to define legal standards in relation to technologies, environmental performance, pressures or outcomes. Kemp (1997) has documented how such standards may bring about innovation. These instruments change the investment/return ratio by imposing penalties on actors who fail to meet the standards, which is sometimes perceived as giving a less positive incentive signal than a market-based instrument.
3. Voluntary or self-regulation (also called negotiated) agreements between governments and producing organisations (see ten Brink 2002 for a comprehensive discussion). These change the investment/return ratio either by forestalling the introduction of market-based instruments or by regulation (that is, they are more profitable than the counterfactual, which is perceived to involve more stringent government intervention, rather than necessarily the status quo). They can also lead to greater awareness of technological possibilities for eco-innovation that increase profitability as well as improving environmental performance (see Ekins and Etheridge 2006 for a discussion of this in relation to the UK Climate Change Agreements).

4. Information- and education-based instruments (the main example of which given by Jordan *et al.* (2003) is eco-labels, but there are others), which may be mandatory or voluntary. These change the investment/ return ratio sometimes by promoting more eco-efficient products to consumers. They can also improve corporate image and reputation.

It has been increasingly common in more recent times to seek to deploy these instruments in so-called 'policy packages' which combine them in order to enhance their overall effectiveness across the three (economic, social and environmental) dimensions of sustainable development.

The rest of this section is taken from the discussion of the effects of different types of environmental policy on innovation in the literature review by Oosterhuis and ten Brink (2006). They note that the impact of environmental policy on innovations in environmental technology has been studied in various ways, both theoretically (often using models) and empirically.

Jaffe *et al.* (2002) distinguish two major strands of thought regarding the determinants of innovative activity: the 'induced innovation' and the 'evolutionary' approach. They argue that only the second approach allows for 'win-win' solutions according to the Porter hypothesis.[3] They state that empirical analysis of policy impact on innovation mainly exists in the area of energy efficiency. Berkhout *et al.* (2003) conclude that many of the main provisions of the REACH (Registration, Authorisation and Evaluation of Chemicals) proposals will tend to promote innovation, both within the EU chemicals sector and more widely.

Krozer (2002) investigated the extent to which environmental innovations can be introduced at socially acceptable costs, and what policies are needed to stimulate this. He developed a method to estimate cost functions and to identify (using these functions) areas where R&D investments in cost-reducing innovations will be attractive. The importance of policy features that create better sales conditions for environmental innovations is emphasised. These include timely announcement, the assurance of strict demands and fast implementation.

Montalvo (2002) addresses the subject from a firm-behaviour perspective. Leaning upon Ajzen's 'Theory of Planned Behaviour' (Ajzen 1991) he distinguishes three types of factors determining a firm's willingness to invest in cleaner technology: its attitude (determined by perceived risks), social pressures (including regulation) and control (the technological and organisational capabilities of the firm). His findings (based on a study of the *maquiladoras* firms located near the Mexico–US border) suggest that the third factor has the biggest influence, which would imply that reinforcing the cleaner technology knowledge base in enterprises should be the main policy priority.

The significance of environmental policies in driving eco-innovation is usually confirmed by empirical studies. Lanjouw and Mody (1996) presented evidence on environmental innovation and diffusion over the 1970s and 1980s. In the United States, Japan and Germany, the share of environmental patents in all patents was higher than the corresponding share of pollution abatement expenditure in GDP. Across these three countries and over time, innovation responded to pollution abatement expenditure, an indicator of the severity of environmental regulations.

Pickman (1998) conducted an empirical study of the US manufacturing industry's environmental patent activities and environmental regulation as measured by pollution abatement and control expenditure (PACE) data. She found a statistically significant positive relationship between environmental regulation and innovation when estimated by ordinary least squares (OLS). However, the OLS coefficient of pollution abatement costs was inconsistent because of a correlation between the explanatory variable and unobservable variables. Two-staged least squares addressed the inconsistency problem, resulting in positive and significant PACE coefficients. Thus, there is evidence in this case that innovation is a response to environmental regulation.

Kemp (2000) concluded from the available literature that the technology responses to environmental policy range from the diffusion of existing technology, incremental changes in processes and product reformulation to product substitution and the development of new processes. The most common responses to regulation are incremental innovation in processes and products and diffusion of existing technology (in the form of end-of-pipe solutions and non-innovative substitutions of existing substances). Often, the new technologies are developed by firms outside the regulated industry. The studies reviewed by Kemp also showed, unsurprisingly, that the stringency of the regulation is an important determinant of the degree of innovation, with stringent regulations such as product bans being necessary for radical technology responses. Technology-forcing standards appear to be a necessary condition for bringing about innovative compliance responses.

Newell *et al.* (2002) used a 'product characteristics' approach to analyse the influence of energy prices and other factors on the energy efficiency of air conditioners and water heaters. Besides energy prices, government energy efficiency standards also had a significant impact on the average energy efficiency of the models offered for sale. Similä (2002) showed that regulation (gradually tightening of emission limit values) has had an observable impact on the diffusion of technology in the Finnish pulp and paper industry, particularly with respect to end-of-pipe technology.

Results from a survey by Becker and Englmann (2005) suggest that the chemical industry's reactions to environmental regulations seem to be by far the most important reason for carrying out both end-of-pipe and pro-duction-integrated innovations. Popp (2006) examined the innovation and diffusion of air pollution equipment, using patent data. He concluded that investors respond to domestic, but not to foreign regulatory pressures. The results suggest that transfers of environmental technologies across borders will be slowed by the need for domestic R&D to adapt these technologies to local markets.

Finally, it should be noted that environmental policies can also have a counterproductive impact on innovations in environmental technology. For example, Strasser (1997) argues that traditional environmental regulation has often discouraged innovation and diffusion of cleaner technology. He states that the extent to which a business is likely to develop or embrace new technologies in response to regulatory stimuli is a reasonably knowable and predictable process, and therefore regulators can craft environmental poli-cies that will be consciously supportive of environmental technology. A change in regulatory culture is needed, as well as a multimedia and sector-oriented approach. A familiar type of the possible 'anti-innovation' impact of environmental policy is the so-called 'new source bias', which results from regulations which impose stricter demands on new sources than on existing sources (see for example, Stanton 1993).

There is no unanimity in the literature about the kinds of policy instru-ments that are best suited to support the development and diffusion of environmental technology. Some general observations, however, can be made.

Economic instruments (charges, taxes and tradeable permits) are often seen as superior to direct regulation (command-and-control), because they provide (if designed properly) an additional and lasting financial incentive to look for 'greener' solutions. For example, Jaffe *et al.* (2002) conclude that market-based instruments are more effective than command-and-control instruments in encouraging cost-effective adoption and diffusion of new technologies. Requate (2005), in a survey and dis-cussion of recent developments on the incentives provided by environ-mental policy instruments for both adoption and development of advanced abatement technology, concludes that under competitive condi-tions, market-based instruments usually perform better than command and control. Moreover, taxes may provide stronger long-term incentives than tradeable permits if the regulator is biased towards short-term considerations. Johnstone (2005) also presents some arguments from literature suggesting that taxes are more favourable to environmental innovations than tradeable permits.

Nevertheless, direct regulation was shown to work well in Germany when applying air emissions standards to power plants when the energy sector was still not liberalised and the energy companies had the possibility of passing through the costs. The context was important in having parties accept the required command and control. Evidence suggests that the instrument and context reduced German emissions very quickly, and faster than countries where economic instruments were used. This gives one counter example to the oft-quoted position that market-based instruments are more effective. Direct regulation may also be a powerful instrument in spurring eco-innovation (provided that the standards set are tight and challenging) because firms may have an interest in developing cleaner technology if they can expect that technology to become the basis for a future standard (for example, Best Available Technology – BAT), so that they can sell it on the market.

Ashford (2005) argues that a command-and-control type of environmental policy is needed to achieve the necessary improvements in eco and energy efficiency. According to Ashford, the 'ecological modernisation' approach, with its emphasis on cooperation and dialogue, is not sufficient. Economic instruments may also be less appropriate if the main factor blocking eco-innovation is not a financial one. For instance, simulations with the MEI Energy Model (Elzenga and Ros 2004), which also takes non-economic factors into account, suggest that voluntary agreements and regulations may be more effective than financial instruments (such as charges and subsidies) in stimulating the implementation of energy-saving measures with a short payback period.

Some authors, such as Anderson *et al.* (2001) stress that 'standard' environmental policy instruments are not sufficient to induce eco-innovation, and that direct support for such innovation is also needed. The main reasons for this are the positive externalities of innovation and the long time lag between the implementation of a standard policy and the market penetration of a new technology.

The appropriateness of particular instruments (or instrument mixes) may depend on the purpose for which they are used (such as innovation or diffusion) and the specific context in which they are applied (see for example Kemp 2000). Finally, the design of an instrument may be at least as important as the instrument type. One type of instrument can produce widely different results when applied differently. For example, Birkenfeld *et al.* (2005) show remarkable differences in the development of trichloroethylene emissions in Sweden and Germany. Both countries used direct regulation, but in Sweden this was done by means of a ban with exemptions, whereas Germany opted for a BAT approach. The latter proved to be much more effective in terms of emission reduction.

There were four groups of research questions that the Innovation Dynamics project on which this chapter is based sought to answer:

1. What are the key stages and cycles in the dynamics of environmental technology innovation? How is the transition made from pre-commercialisation to commercialisation? How is the transition made from niche to main markets? What types of innovation exist (that is, incremental and breakthrough) and how does technology maturity affect the situation?
2. What have been the different experiences gained through the implementation of different policy types? Which policy instruments have been most successful? Are specific policy instruments useful for specific stages in the innovation process?
3. Are there any guidelines or trends which can be interpreted or extrapolated from the case study findings? Are there any general rules of thumb? What are the implications for environmental policy (especially learning curves and economies of scale)?
4. How can the influence of environmental policy be related to the 'ordinary' innovation activities of firms (that is, baseline innovation)?

The rest of this chapter explores these questions through the insights gained from the case studies, in order to gain further understanding of how regulation might stimulate innovation and therefore reduce the costs that might be associated with it. Each innovation case study is very briefly reviewed in terms of what type(s) of policies were assessed and the conclusions about the policy influence on innovation, if any.

15.3   CASE STUDY SUMMARIES

This section of the chapter summarises the main findings of the innovation case studies. Section 15.4 provides a synthesis of the findings and pulls together some broader conclusions.

15.3.1   Case Study 1: Car Fuel Economy / CO_2 Emissions[4]

What type(s) of policies were assessed?
Three attempts to improve fuel efficiency in cars are addressed by the case study.

Firstly the European experience is focused on. One important element of Europe's strategy to reduce CO_2 emissions from passenger cars and to improve fuel efficiency is the voluntary agreements that were brokered with the automobile industry to reduce total new passenger fleet average CO_2 emissions according to specific targets and timetables.[5] The voluntary agreements were concluded in 1998 with the European Automobile

Manufacturers' Association (ACEA), the Japan Automobile Manufacturers Association (JAMA) and the Korea Automobile Manufacturers Association (KAMA). The agreements are collectively labelled the ACEA Agreement. The target for new passenger fleet average CO_2 emissions is 140g CO_2/km by 2008/9.[6] The Community's target for 2012 is 120g CO_2/km. This longer-term target has not yet been included in any formal agreement with the car industry. The Commission has stated on several occasions that a failure of the car industry to meet the 2008/9 target might lead to mandatory regulation in the future.

Secondly the United States (US) Corporate Average Fuel Economy (CAFE) programme is studied. In 1975 the CAFE programme was initiated by the US Congress as a measure to conserve petrol and reduce US reliance on imported oil (Gerard and Lave 2003). The CAFE programme set mandatory average fuel economy standards for car manufacturers for passenger cars and light-duty trucks. For passenger cars, the standards increased from 18 miles per gallon (mpg) in 1978 to 27.5 mpg in 1985. For light-duty trucks, the standard is 20.7 mpg. These standards have not been raised since 1985.

Thirdly, the Japanese Top Runner Programme is investigated. This was introduced in Japan in 1999 as part of the revision of the Law on the Rational Use of Energy, addressing many sectors, including the car manufacturing sector (Naturvårdverket 2005). Among the targeted product groups (for example, passenger cars), the most energy-efficient product (the 'Top Runner') becomes the basis of the regulatory standard in 3 to 12 years time, taking into account the potential for technological innovation and diffusion. The standards in the Top Runner Programme are also used in the green purchasing law and the green car tax scheme. Additionally, there is an annual award for the most energy-efficient products and systems.

Policy influence on innovation
The ACEA programme in Europe and the Top Runner Programme in Japan are more ambitious in their targets for innovation than the CAFE programme in the US. A further difference is that the Japanese and US programmes are mandatory, while the EU programme is voluntary (although with the threat of regulation if EU targets are not met).

In inducing innovation, the EU and Japanese policy instruments perform better than the US CAFE programme. This is not surprising, given the large gap between the stringency of fuel-efficiency standards in Europe and Japan versus the US. None of the standards, however, are expected to give incentives for radical or breakthrough innovations. Both the ACEA and the Top Runner Programmes seem to be focusing more on the rapid diffusion of already available technologies and incremental innovations. To date, however, the ACEA agreement has not been very successful in stimulating promising newer technologies such as direct injection in petrol cars and the production of hybrid cars.

It is not yet clear whether there is a discernable difference between mandatory and voluntary types of policy instruments and their respective effects. Further, it is not yet known whether the car industry will meet the final ACEA standards in 2008, or how the European Commission will react if the targets are not met. The US CAFE programme has mandatory standards, but it also has legal loopholes, and according to some observers, the non-compliance penalties are too small to make a big impression on car manufacturers.

One interesting distinction between the European ACEA approach and the Japanese Top Runner approach is that ACEA sets standards at the industry level, while the Top Runner Programme sets standards at the company level. Perhaps this latter approach has the advantage that companies are more directly involved in the process. It is, for example, remarkable that only half of the European car manufacturers mentioned the ACEA standard in their annual reports (WRI 2005).[7]

15.3.2   Case Study 2: Energy Efficiency of Electronic Appliances[8]

What type(s) of policies were assessed?
Three experiences of attempts to improve ICT energy efficiency in different areas are addressed by the case study.

Firstly the European experience is focused on. The EU supports the use of energy efficiency criteria in public tenders. However, it has not yet made such procurement practices mandatory. For example, the recent Directive on energy end-use efficiency and energy services (2006/32/EC) includes an article (5) obliging Member States to 'ensure that energy efficiency improvement measures are taken by the public sector, focussing on cost-effective measures which generate the largest energy savings in the shortest span of time'. They should use at least two out of a list of six measures (set out in Annex VI of the Directive), one of which is the requirement 'to purchase equipment that has efficient energy consumption in all modes, including in standby mode, using, where applicable, minimised life-cycle cost analysis or comparable methods to ensure cost-effectiveness'. It seems therefore that the EU currently gives more weight to the 'other measures' if they are considered to be more cost-effective.

Secondly, the American ICT energy efficiency programme is addressed. This is a case of an extremely simple use of centralised powers. In 1993, President Clinton signed Executive Order 12845 requiring Federal agencies to purchase computer equipment, specifically personal computers, monitors and printers that met the Energy Star requirements. Largely due to this, as we shall see below, Energy Star labelled products soon came to dominate the market.

Thirdly, the Japanese Green Procurement Law and Top Runner Programmes are studied. Both of these programmes are mandatory. Japan can be considered to be the international leader in green purchasing of office equipment and electronics. Führ (2001) considers this to be one reason for the advanced position Japanese electronics companies have, even in other markets, when it comes to environmental compliance. In 2001 the Law concerning the Promotion of Public Green Procurement (Green Procurement Law) came into force. As far as energy efficiency criteria are concerned, the Green Procurement Law incorporates the standards developed in the Top Runner Programme, under which energy efficiency standards are formulated for various product groups, including copiers and computers. These standards have to be met within 3 to 12 years, depending on the product group, and they are based upon the most energy-efficient model on the current market: 'today's best model sets tomorrow's standards' (IEA 2003). There are currently 12 ICT product groups included in both the Top Runner Programme and the Green Procurement Law.

Policy influence on innovation
In the European case, it seems that the policy for encouraging innovation in energy efficiency of ICT has been incoherently applied in the past. Because a non-mandatory approach has been employed, it can be said that out of the three territories which were investigated, it is the European approach which has inspired the least amount of innovation in energy efficient ICT.

Experience from the US shows that the Executive Order was extremely influential in encouraging innovation in the ICT sector. Indeed as a direct result of the Order, it is estimated that in 1999, 95 per cent of monitors, 85 per cent of computers and 99 per cent of printers sold were Energy Star compliant (Webber *et al.*, 2000). According to Siemens (2001), the Executive Order was crucial in creating awareness and the public market for Energy Star products, particularly office equipment. Moreover, extensive promotion efforts to all government levels, tools to demonstrate cost and greenhouse gas emission savings, and integration within government procurement catalogues, appear also to have been key to promoting Energy Star procurement.

The Japanese policy approach was also highly successful. Until 2004, computers were included in the Green Procurement Law. The success of the policy approach is illustrated by the fact that since all of the computers in the market have met the set energy efficiency criteria, they have been collectively taken off the list of green procurement items. With the introduction of new Top Runner standards however, computers will be reintroduced into the Green Procurement Law again, in order to improve energy efficiency gains further.

15.3.3   Case Study 3: Photovoltaics (PV)[9]

What type(s) of policies were assessed?
This case study addresses the policy promotion of solar PV in Germany, the UK and Japan. The main policies associated with solar PV support in each country are as follows:

1. Germany: principally feed-in tariffs (guaranteed payments for power output above market rates), but also investment subsidies, soft loans and R&D;
2. Japan: R&D, installation subsidies, Renewable Portfolio Standard (RPS, an obligation to install a certain proportion of renewables);
3. UK: demonstration projects, installation subsidies, Renewables Obligation (similar to RPS), and exemption from the climate change levy (a business energy tax).

Policy influence on innovation
In the German case, the introduced policy measures have yielded increases in the innovation, production and application of PV technology. In 2004, Germany became the world leader in terms of yearly installed PV. Furthermore, a drop in prices for PV systems in Germany of almost 40 per cent has been observed since 1995. According to a 2003 report of BMU (the German Environment Ministry), however, the price decrease in that year reflects market dynamics (increased competition by foreign producers) rather than cost reductions resulting from technology innovation (BMU 2003).

In the Japanese case, policy aimed at inducing innovation in the PV sector seems also to have been successful. Much of Japan's PV development to date has been driven by specific large programmes such as the solar roofs initiative. In contrast, their recent RPS initiative is not expected to yield historical levels of PV deployment (as the RPS aims at raising the proportion of energy from renewables for electricity generation to only 1.35 per cent by 2010, much less than Europe's 12 per cent).

Lastly in the UK case, policy support for either innovation or diffusion of PV has been relatively weak. The implemented Renewables Obligation has done little to promote PV development as it does not differentiate between the technologies at different stages of development, and tends to promote those closest to the market (that is, not PV). Deployment levels have also been relatively small through other subsidy schemes.

By comparing Germany, the UK and Japan in the above context, lessons emerge. The feed-in tariff's main advantage is that it guarantees sustained above-market payments for the still-costly PV technologies – the guaranteed feed-in tariffs for electricity from PV are considerably higher than for the other technologies (50.62 cents/kWh for electricity from PV as opposed to 8.7 cents/kWh for wind energy). Ten Brink *et al.* (2006) argue that the UK policy approach of using the Renewables Obligation and exemptions from the climate change levy, have been more expensive per unit of renewable power produced and less effective than other policy mechanisms (such as those in Germany, Luxembourg and Austria).

15.3.4 Case Study 4 – Emissions from Pulp and Paper Production[10]

What type(s) of policies were assessed?
Pulp and paper is a mature industry, industrialised paper manufacturing in Europe dating from the early 19th century (Berkhout, 2005).

Rather than investigate policies on a country-by-country basis, the pulp and paper case study summarises previous research studies which focus on technological advances, with some policy analysis, in a number of countries.

Reinstaller (2005) investigates the differences in responses to the market demand for chlorine-free paper in Sweden and the United States. The most advanced (but also most costly) technology for producing chlorine-free paper was observed to have taken more of a market share in the Swedish case when compared to the US market. This is mainly attributed to Europe having two distinct features which the US lacked. These differences were in the public perception of the health risks of dioxins[11] and the strong role of Greenpeace as a 'policy entrepreneur' in Europe.

Blazejczak and Edler (2000) examined differences between trends in innovations in energy consumption in the pulp and paper industry and waste paper recycling in various nations. It was found that Swedish policy is most innovation-friendly as it is characterised by a search for consensus in combination with ambitious long-term goals. Japan's policy with respect to the pulp and paper industry is considered to be less innovation-friendly, mainly because its pulp and paper industry is not considered to be a 'strategic' sector in industrial policy. Finally, environmental policy in the United States is considered to be least innovation-friendly as it relies too much on particularly inflexible technology standards.

Hildén *et al.* (2002) investigate the Finnish pulp and paper industry. There is no analysis in the case study of specific types of policies which have been applied, only analysis of the impact on inducing innovation. This will therefore be dealt with below in the policy influence on innovation section.

Chappin (2005) examines the impact of environmental regulations on innovation activity in waste water, solid waste and energy efficiency in the paper and board industry in the Netherlands from 1980 to 2003. The Netherlands distinguishes between top-down instruments (command-and-control), economic instruments (taxes and subsidies), and interactive instruments. The interactive instrument used in the Netherlands is known as the Target Group Policy, where collective environmental targets for industry sectors are set through an interactive process between government and the industry associations. Once these collective targets are set, the industry association co-ordinates the abatement efforts of its members.

Policy influence on innovation
Reinstaller (2005) concluded that environmental policy may have played a role in the diffusion of chlorine-free paper in Sweden, but only indirectly, as firms might have innovated due to anticipating stricter standards in the future. Blazejczak and Edler (2000) found that Swedish policy was most innovation-friendly in the pulp and paper sector as it was characterised by a search for consensus in combination with ambitious long-term goals.

Hildén *et al.* (2002) analysed the impact that Finnish policy has had on innovation in the Finnish pulp and paper sector. Concerning air and water pollution regulation, the regulatory practice used has not induced the development of new technologies, it is argued, as the approach and targets set (using BAT – Best Available Technology – and limits to emission values) could be met by existing abatement technology. Secondly, an integrated pollution prevention and control (IPPC) permit requirement for operators to assess recycling of water and materials may have induced some innovation, but it is concluded that it remains an 'open question' as to whether the innovation occurred as a result of normal commercial practices or as a result of the Finnish policy. Thirdly, although the diffusion of abatement technology was achieved, such diffusion trends were achieved in other nations by other means (such as effluent charges). The regulatory framework therefore seemed to give no benefits over other forms of environmental policy. Finally, it is concluded that R&D requirements in IPPC permits have not had any discernable impact on innovation and diffusion.

Chappin (2005) found no association between the implementation of policy measures and the number of innovation research projects in the areas studied, with the exception of research projects on energy efficiency that increased in number in the period 1994–5 after the signing of the first

Long Term Agreement on energy efficiency between government and the industry in 1993 (an interactive policy instrument). Kuik (2006b) argues that one of the reasons for the lack of association that is suggested by Chappin (2005) is that because of the steady accumulation of new policy measures applicable to the sector, it is difficult to link research and specific policy measures directly.

Finally, Kuik (2006b) argues that the evidence on the relationship between environmental policy instruments and innovation in the pulp and paper sector suggests that of the instruments assessed, none have forced radical innovation. Of the evidence reviewed, it suggests that in practice, the type of policy instrument that is applied matters less; it is the other characteristics of the instruments (intensity, flexibility, dynamic orientation) that matter more.

15.3.5   Case Study 5 – Substitution of Hazardous Chemical Substances[12]

What type(s) of policies were assessed?
The replacement of chlorinated solvents in Sweden, Denmark, the US and Germany by less hazardous alternatives is used as an exemplary case for substitution in general. However, prior to assessing policy instruments in these countries, it is noted that only Sweden and Denmark have introduced an 'environmental' substitution obligation in their legislation (as current European legislation only mandates the substitution principle for occupational and safety cases, that is, excluding environmental protection).

Firstly the Swedish experience is focused on, where the substitution principle had already become part of chemicals legislation in 1973 (Löfstedt 2003). Since 1999 it has been known as the 'product choice principle', one of the cornerstones of the Swedish Environmental Code. A famous example of the application of the substitution principle in Sweden is the ban on trichloroethylene (tri) which was introduced in 1996. The European Court of Justice found this ban to be in agreement with EU law (case C-473/98). Nevertheless, the ban has met with a lot of opposition, on the one hand because a total ban was considered to be disproportional given the relatively minor harmful properties of tri, and on the other hand because many industries argued that they had no substitute for it. Exemptions from the ban were made possible for the latter cases.

Secondly the Danish policy approach is assessed. Danish occupational health and safety legislation, enacted in 2001, requires the replacement of hazardous substances or materials by less hazardous ones. This substitution is compulsory even if the effects of the hazardous substances are insignificant. The law provides for exemptions if substitution is technically impossible or prohibitively expensive. In addition, the Danish

Environmental Protection Agency has published a 'List of Undesirable Substances'. These substances (more than 8000) are not banned, but their substitution is being encouraged. In 2003, a website was launched[13] containing more than 200 examples of substitutions in different companies. Replacement of hazardous chemicals in Denmark is also promoted by means of economic instruments. For example, environmental taxes are levied on pesticides, chlorinated solvents, CFCs, nickel-cadmium batteries, soft PVC and phthalates.

Thirdly, the American Massachusetts Toxics Use Reduction Act (TURA) is studied. The 1989 TURA legislation requires that manufacturing firms using specific quantities of approximately 900 industrial chemicals undergo a biennial process to identify alternatives to reduce waste and the use of those chemicals. Through the toxics use reduction planning process, firms understand why they use a specific chemical (what 'service' it provides), and how it is used in the production process. They also conduct a systematic search for viable alternatives and a comprehensive financial, technical, environmental and occupational health and safety analysis of them. The act instructs firms to identify ways to redesign production processes and products and provides six different methods that count as toxics use reduction (Tickner *et al.* 2005).

Finally the German experience in applying the substitution principle is investigated. The German Ordinance on dangerous substances (*Gefahrstoffverordnung*) states (in 9(1)) that employers should prevent or minimise the dangers to the health and safety of their employees caused by hazardous substances, preferably by replacing the relevant substance. A decision not to substitute has to be justified. The German substitution principle is therefore primarily based on occupational health and safety considerations.

Policy influence on innovation

In the Swedish case, when compared to the approaches in other countries, the Swedish tri ban may not have been very effective, as a large number of exemptions were granted. In Germany, where the emphasis has been on technical standards for equipment and emissions, industry has invested in modern, 'closed' systems for tri use. As a result, the specific emissions of tri per euro of value-added in the metal industry in Sweden is now 90 times higher than in Germany, whereas in 1993 it was only 9 times higher (Birkenfeld *et al.* 2005). Major reductions in tri use have also been achieved in Norway, where a tax on tri and other chlorinated solvents was introduced in 2000. Purchases of tri in Norway fell from more than 500 tonnes in 1999 to 82 tonnes in 2000 and 139 in 2001 (Sterner 2004). This reduction is thought to have been driven by efforts to cut leakage and boost recycling, as well as through substitution (ENDS 2003). The tri example from Sweden thus suggests that imposing chemical substitution by means of a general ban with exemptions may lead to less environmental innovation than stimulating substitution by means of financial incentives or regulations aimed at limiting exposure and emissions. However, it is of note that Sweden and Denmark, the two EU countries applying the substitution principle, also have the highest rate of R&D in their respective chemical industries.

In the Danish case, regarding the environmental taxes which are levied on hazardous chemicals, there is some evidence for the effectiveness of these taxes (Ecological Council 2002). According to a Danish cable producer which has replaced PVC with phthalates by halogen-free polymers in part of its products, the taxes on PVC and phthalates have helped to lessen the price difference (Ecological Council 2006). The tax on chlorinated solvents, though much lower than the Norwegian tax on the same substances, contributed to a decrease in the use of these substances by 60 per cent (Sterner 2004).

In the case of the US TURA experience, between 1990 and 2000, some 550 firms that continuously participated in the programme had reduced the use of the targeted toxic chemicals by 40 per cent (Tickner and Geiser 2004, Appendix A). According to O'Rourke and Lee (2004), mandatory planning, new mechanisms of accountability and improved processes of learning have all been critical to TURA's success in motivating firms to innovate for the environment. The TURA programme has designated tri as one of five high-priority substances that are to receive special attention, with the aim of attaining significant reduction in use. In 2004 a project was started, targeted at smaller businesses using tri which do not have direct access to pollution prevention information and resources (TURI 2006). Spin-off programmes with the aim of widening participation can be seen as being a testament to the successful nature of the TURA programme.

As indicated above, the German approach to chlorinated solvents has differed from the approach taken in Sweden (a ban with exemptions) and Denmark (taxation). Rather than seeking a reduction in the use of the hazardous substances *per se*, the German approach focused on risk reduction through the introduction of 'closed' systems for the use of chlorinated solvents. As a result of this policy, Germany not only achieved substantial decreases in solvent use, but also became a leading exporter of high-quality closed-loop degreasing equipment (Sterner 2004). This can be seen as an illustration of 'first mover advantages' and the famous 'Porter hypothesis' (Porter and van der Linde 1995; see Example 2B, Chapter 2).

15.4   SYNTHESIS OF CASE STUDY FINDINGS

15.4.1   Summary of Findings

The headline conclusions of the case studies may be summarised as follows:

1. **Automotive industry** – Innovation levels differed greatly between the three countries studied. Japan had incentivised the most innovation, although there was little information about the development of its standards, the USA set standards unambitiously low, and Europe had induced 'modest' levels of innovation. In the European case, other trends (such as dieselisation) had influenced the EU car manufacturing sector more.
2. **Office appliances** – Innovation levels as identified in Japan and the USA were high and directly correlated to the respective policies which were implemented, in both cases strict public procurement policies. In Japan, these were combined with increasingly stringent standards. The European case study saw that there was an uneven use of energy efficiency criteria in Member States' public ICT tenders. This is coupled with the fact that the EU still tends to shy away from mandatory energy efficient public procurement despite industry support.
3. **Photovoltaics** – This sector has undergone rapid and innovative development in recent years. Japan and Germany have both encouraged significant expansion and development of the sector through substantial financial incentives and R&D support. With far lower financial commitment, the UK has not managed to achieve substantial deployment of installed PV capacity.
4. **Pulp and paper** – In Europe there has been innovation with respect to abatement technologies, but the extent to which this has been induced by policy is not clear. Insofar as an effect is discernible, it seems to be more due to the characteristics of the instrument (for example, its stringency) than to the nature of the instrument itself.
5. **Hazardous chemicals** – In general there has been success in encouraging innovation or diffusion of existing technology. Policy approaches in Sweden, Denmark and Germany have in different ways all been influential in encouraging innovation and reducing environmental impact. There is an interesting contrast between approaches that seek to reduce the use of hazardous substances (Sweden, Denmark) and those that seek to contain them (Germany). It is of note that Sweden and Denmark, the two EU countries applying the substitution principle, also have the highest rate of R&D in their respective chemical industries.

Table 15.2 shows the findings of the case studies in more detail.

Table 15.3 categorises the environmental policy instruments used, as revealed by the case studies, in terms of the typology in section 15.2.4, and shows the type of innovation which seems to have been primarily induced (see section 15.2.2). It also provides an overall indication of the success of the policy in inducing eco-innovation. The table shows that a wide range of different environmental policies has been used in different countries, ranging in Europe across voluntary approaches, directives, investments, grants, bans, taxes and technical standards. In the USA, classic regulation, that is, command and control, appears most common.

In the case studies, there is only one example of environmental taxes (5 – Denmark), which seems to have had a good impact. The two examples of voluntary measures (1 and 2 – both Europe) do not seem to have performed particularly well. Nor do other instruments where their stringency is simply inadequate to drive changes in the market (1 – USA, 3 – Europe). All the excellent results have been induced by strong policies, whether mandatory public procurement (2 – USA and Japan), in Japan's case combined with increasing standards; strong market incentives combined with large R&D budgets (3 – Japan); or stringent regulation (5 – Germany). In respect of PV (case study 3), Germany seems to have matched Japan's market incentives, but not the R&D, which may go some way to explaining Japan's leadership in manufacturing.

In terms of the innovation type experienced, to some extent this depended on the choice of case study. Case studies 1, 2 and 3 were all product-related (though the changes in products may also have involved process changes), while 4 and 5 were a mixture as shown. No evidence emerges from the case studies as to whether certain types of instruments are more likely to bring about certain kinds of innovation. Classic regulation, sometimes combined with public procurement, emerges in these case studies as the most popular way to encourage eco-innovation. In fact, some kind of classic regulation appears to have been involved in all cases rated 'excellent', and in most rated 'good' (the exceptions here being 3 – Germany and 5 – Denmark, which are examples of strong economic instruments).

Only one clear example emerges in favour of the Porter hypothesis (5 – Germany), although other possible examples are 3 – Japan (it is still too early to say whether market leadership in PV will translate into commercial success, to repay the considerable up-front investment in securing it), and 1 – Japan (where the policy-induced high energy efficiency of Japanese cars may give them an advantage, especially if high oil prices persist) compared to the lower efficiencies achieved by US car makers.

The case studies also give different illustrations of the possible contributions and combinations of 'technology push' and 'market pull' in

Table 15.2 Overall case study finding.

Case study	Country/Area	Policy Instrument	Shortcomings or virtue of policy in inducing innovation
1	Europe	Voluntary agreement	'Modest' contribution in terms of induced technological innovation in the car making sector. Market, other green policies stronger drivers.
1	USA	Fuel economy standards	Poor choice of instrument. Unambitious standards not increased since 1985. Little innovation.
1	Japan	Standards	Good. Results of innovation exceeded expectations. Targeted sectors. Cross-sectoral application. Dynamic incentives.
2	Europe	Directive obligations	Wide differences via transposition into MS law. No mandatory procurement requirements. Low innovation impact.
2	USA	Green purchasing law (Executive Order)	Order transformed the market. Critical role in innovation and raising benchmark in energy efficiency.
2	Japan	Green purchasing law	Japan now international forerunner in innovative energy-efficient electronics.
3	Germany	Investment subsidy, feed-in tariff, soft loans	Significantly stimulated innovative development of PV technology. Corresponding drop in prices. However, other external factors also at play.
3	Japan	Research, subsidies, legislation	Significant expansion of installed PV capacity through policy-driven deployment. Combined with R&D to make Japan one of the market leaders.
3	UK	Relatively small grants, weak obligations	No strong commitment to innovation or promotion of technology. UK 'missed the boat'.

4	Various	Legislation	Impact of policy weak as other factors explain differential uptake rates of pulp and paper technologies. Trends of increasing innovation by industry in deployment of abatement technologies. But policy influence not clear.
5	Sweden	Ban with exemptions	Successful ban, yet undermined by wide-ranging exemptions.
5	Denmark	Taxes	Diffusion of existing (less hazardous) technology aided by taxes. Taxes reduced price difference between used cheaper (hazardous) chemicals and other more expensive (less hazardous) chemicals.
5	USA	Legislative requirement to review chemical use	Participating firms reduced toxic chemical use by 40% (1990–2000). Spin off schemes targeting SMEs.
5	Germany	Technical standards	Successful. Industry innovated and developed 'closed system' for chemical use, now exporting new technology.

Table 15.3 Comparisons of observed innovation

Case Study	Country or Area	Policy Result in Inducing Innovation	Policy Type				Innovation Type Experienced		
			Incentive/ Market-Based	Classic Regulation	Voluntary	Information-Based	End of Pipe	Process-Integrated	Product Innovation
1	Europe	*Medium*			X				X
1	USA	*Poor*		X					X
1	Japan	*Good*	X	X					X
2	Europe	*Poor*			X[1]	X			X
2	USA	***Excellent***	X	X					X
2	Japan	***Excellent***	X	X		X			X
3	Germany	*Good*	X						X
3	Japan	***Excellent***	X	X					X
3	UK	*Poor*	X	X					X
4	Various	*Unclear*		X			X		
5	Sweden	*Good*		X			X		X
5	Denmark	*Good*	X					X	X
5	USA	*Good*		X				X	
5	Germany	***Excellent***		X				X[2]	

Notes:

1. Although a Directive is used and an obligation is present, other considerations supersede obligations making the approach voluntary. The option of mandatory public procurement is being discussed at the time of writing by the European Community Energy Star Board.
2. Although there has been product innovation, the main success of the policy has been the eco-innovation of new processes and capital stock together with a reduction in the use of hazardous chemicals.

inducing innovation, discussed here for the four examples of 'excellent' innovation.

In the USA electronic appliances case (case study 2) the Executive Order by President Clinton was introduced in 1993. Energy efficiency improvements were already developing, yet the Executive Order acted as a catalyst for faster change, with the government policy acting as a 'market pull' force on the technology. In the same case study related to Japan, the Green Procurement Law was introduced in 2001, later than the USA, but in this case the 'market pull' factor of public procurement was supplemented by knowledge that the standards would be increasingly tightened through the Top Runner Programme, giving an impetus to 'technology push' through R&D as companies sought to get their products into the favoured Top Runner position. Despite its later start than the US in this area, this is considered to be one reason why Japanese ICT companies have strong positions when it comes to environmental performance.

Similar forces were at work in Japan in the PV sector (3 – Japan), financial support for which has been in place since 1974. Initially the support was clearly located at the basic R&D stage ('technology push'), and this lasted a long time before the new technology was ready for wide deployment. More recently, the 'technology push' has been supplemented by ambitious 'market pull' deployment programmes, which have enabled Japanese companies to achieve the cost reduction shown in the learning-curve graph (Figure 15.3). As noted above, it remains to be seen whether this large investment over a long period will achieve real commercial success through the emergence of non-subsidised markets for PV.

Finally, in Germany in the hazardous chemicals sector (case study 5) the German ordinance on dangerous chemicals policy was adopted in 1998. The policy has resulted in the eco-innovation of new processes such as high-quality closed-loop degreasing equipment. In Figure 15.1, eco-innovation would seem to be located in the applied R&D stage, achieving market success (and investment mobilised by 'market pull') once successful closed-loop processes had been developed. As a result of this policy, as noted, Germany has not only achieved substantial decreases in solvent use, but has also become a leading exporter of high-quality closed-loop degreasing equipment. The case study is a classic example of the outcome of regulation forecast by the Porter hypothesis.

15.4.2 Cross-Cutting Themes

Across the case studies there are a number of cross-cutting themes with policy implications:

1. **Technological development** – One assumes that most regulatory approaches seek to allow for technological development and increasing efficiencies over a time period. However, the technical expertise required to understand all factors at play in such sectors as the hazardous chemicals sector or the PV sector is formidable, and there are bound to be problems of asymmetric information (see section 3.1, Chapter 3) between industry and the policy maker.

2. **Commercial factors** – Many levels of innovation are affected by commercial learning curves and economies of scale associated with the production and development of new technologies and processes. These developments will rarely be disclosed due to their sensitive commercial nature – making it hard for the policy maker to predict accurately potential rates of innovation, as they will rarely be party to such sensitive information.

3. **Standards** – It seems from analysis in case studies 1, 2 and 5 that setting standards for industry can work effectively. This incentivised approach, with technical standards and green procurement plans, allowed firms to approach the target flexibly and innovate to meet it. However, when standards are set low (such as in case study 1 – USA) unsurprisingly there is little incentive to exceed the benchmark.

4. **Focus** – It is apparent that unless actions are targeted to specific areas and take into account external trends, as they were in Japan with the Top Runner Programme, policies will generally not aid in encouraging innovation. This was seen in the UK PV market where policies failed to take account of external developments in the global market, the focus of policy in the UK; also, the low levels of funding attached were insufficient to allow for significant levels of innovation or deployment.

5. **Historical trends** – There can be historical factors at play which present barriers to innovation in certain sectors or geographical locations. For example, in the pulp and paper industry, innovation is low because the industry is mature and the median age of paper machines in Europe is 23 years. In the USA, the historical setting of low levels for fuel economy improvements in automobiles encouraged a poor performance in the sector.

It seems therefore that there are a range of factors involved, at the generic level, which influence the rate at which innovation dynamics are influenced. And although one must be careful when comparing directly the effectiveness of each approach, these factors do indeed lend insights into how policy makers may better innovation proof future policies.

15.5   CONCLUSIONS

We now turn to address the issues raised at the start of this chapter, answering each group of questions as they appear in section 15.2.4.

1.   **What are the key stages and cycles in the dynamics of technology innovation? How is the transition made from pre-commercialisation to commercialisation? How is the transition made from niche to main markets? What types of innovation exist (that is, incremental and breakthrough) and how does technology maturity affect the situation?**

In the model in section 15.2.1 there are five stages of innovation: Basic R&D, applied R&D, demonstration, commercialisation and diffusion. Case study 2, in respect of Japan and the USA, offers the clearest example of transition from pre-commercialisation to commercialisation, driven by aggressive public purchasing, which has so far been conspicuously missing in Europe. Japanese support for PV (case study 3) has demonstrated how support of innovation can be implemented through all the stages 1 to 5 of the innovation process. The only issue now is whether further support for PV will enable the technology to expand from market niche status (in a few products and off-grid applications) to a main market without the support of public subsidy. Of the observed case studies, most experienced incremental innovation. The case study closest to a breakthrough form of innovation was case study 2 – where the US and Japanese policy approaches acted as rapid catalysts for the eco-innovation of new ICT products. Technology maturity as seen in case study 4 (pulp and paper) acted as a barrier to breakthrough forms of innovation, although certain eco-innovations were achieved.

2.   **What have been the different experiences gained through the implementation of different policy types? Which policy instruments have been most successful? Are specific policy instruments useful for specific stages in the innovation process?**

As shown in Table 15.2, classic command-and-control regulation has been the most often implemented policy approach, sometimes in combination with other policies, and has been associated with the best examples of eco-innovation. Incentive-based measures have been implemented far less often, but seem to have performed relatively well. In contrast, voluntary agreements in these case studies have not been implemented often, and have not performed well where they have been implemented. No case study looked primarily at the performance of an information instrument. The principal evidence of policy success in relation to a particular stage in the innovation process is in respect of public purchasing, which can clearly be a very effective form of 'market pull' for technologies which are ready for mass diffusion. With regard to Europe, which has yet to implement strong public purchasing requirements to drive eco-innovation, this is probably the single most important lesson of this project. Public support for R&D is obviously most important in relation to 'technology push', although the German chemicals experience shows how policy can also drive applied R&D and take it through to commercialisation. A number of successful approaches combined different types of policies, and this seems especially important when it is desired to influence more than one of the stages of innovation (for example, case study 3 – Japan).

3. Are there any guidelines or trends which can be interpreted or extrapolated from the case study findings? Are there any general rules of thumb? What are the implications for environmental policy (especially learning curves and economies of scale)?

A number of lessons can be learned from the case studies, some of them already mentioned above:

1. Inducing innovation requires strong policy. Weak policy, whether in terms of weak standards (for example, 1 – USA), or low levels of expenditure (3 – UK) will not be likely to achieve it.
2. Classic regulation was the single most important type of policy in the case studies where eco-innovation was stimulated, sometimes combined with market-based instruments (especially public purchasing or subsidies).
3. Regarding learning curves and economies of scale, case studies 2, 3 and 5 all found that when policy, or external factors, encouraged innovation, positive relationships between increases in production and reduction in costs were found. The PV case study noted that it was not merely learning curves of PV which must be taken into account, but also learning curves of associated infrastructural technology.

4. How can the influence of environmental policy be related to the 'ordinary' innovation activities of firms (baseline innovation)?

History shows that innovation is one of the normal characteristics of markets and capitalist economic development, and current innovation rates are, in historical terms, very high. However, normal innovation is driven by a desire for market success, which may have little to do with environmental impacts. In fact, normal innovation may increase or decrease environmental impacts. The environmental policy makers' task is to seek to harness normal innovation forces in order to achieve win-win outcomes, that is, environmental improvements as well as improvements in products and processes from a market point of view. Because innovation is inherently unpredictable, and there is no methodology that can reliably assess the 'without policy' counterfactual, there is an inherent problem in assessing the results of policy in terms of eco-innovation. However, as this project has shown, careful case study comparisons can generate insights as to whether and how eco-innovation has been achieved.

NOTES

1. See http://ec.europa.eu/environment/enveco/others/index.htm#innodyn, http://ec.europa. eu/environment/enveco/pdf/paper 1.pdf, and http://ec.europa.eu/environment/enveco/pdf/ workshop_report.pdf for documents from the project.
2. This is not necessarily the case, though. For example, reducing nitrogen oxides at the end of a smokestack or car exhaust produces the harmless substances nitrogen and oxygen, which are natural components of air (although even then particles from the platinum catalyst from the vehicle's catalytic converter may cause pollution).
3. The thinking being that if there are win-wins potentially available, then there would be no need for inducements. Others argue that there are win-wins that are not picked up without external help given information barriers or other barriers (time, limits to reward systems).
4. Kuik (2006a).
5. Other elements include fuel-economy labelling on cars and the promotion of car fuel efficiency by fiscal measures (EC 2005).
6. The target year is 2008 for ACEA and 2009 for JAMA and KAMA.
7. Only BMW included detailed information in its 2003 annual report on its strategy to meet the ACEA standard (WRI 2005).
8. Oosterhuis (2006b).
9. ten Brink et al. (2006).
10. Kuik (2006b).
11. Health risks were especially feared in Germany, the biggest export market for Swedish paper. A main event in the German sensitivity to the risks of dioxin was the Seveso incident (1976) in Italy, where dioxins were released to the environment after an accident in a chemical plant (Reinstaller 2005).
12. Oosterhuis (2006c).
13. www.catsub.dk.

REFERENCES

Ajzen, I. (1991), The theory of planned behaviour. *Organizational Behaviour and Human Decision Processes*, 50, 179–211.
Anderson, D. (1999), *Technical Progress and Pollution Abatement: An Economic View of Selected Technologies and Practices*. draft. London: Imperial College of Science, Technology and Medicine.
Anderson, D., Clark, C., Foxon, T., Gross, R. and Jacobs, M. (2001), *Innovation and the Environment: Challenges and Policy Options for the UK*. London: Imperial College Centre for Energy Policy and Technology and the Fabian Society.
Ashford, N.A. (2005), Government and Environmental Innovation in Europe and North America. In: M. Weber and J. Hemmelskamp (eds), *Towards*

Environmental Innovation Systems. Berlin/Heidelberg/New York: Springer pp. 159–174.

Becker, F. and Englmann, F.C. (2005), Public Policy, Voluntary Initiatives and Water Benign Process Innovations: Empirical Evidence from the West German Chemical Industry during the Mid-1990s. In: M. Weber and J. Hemmelskamp (eds), *Towards Environmental Innovation Systems.* Berlin/Heidelberg/New York: Springer pp. 137–157.

Berkhout, F., Iizuka, M., Nightingale, P. and Voss, G. (2003), 'Innovation in the chemicals sector and the new European Chemicals Regulation', A report for WWF-UK, September SPRU – Science and Technology Policy Research, University of Sussex, Falmer.

Berkhout, F. (2005), Technological Regimes, Environmental Performance and Innovation Systems: Tracing the Links. In: M. Weber and J. Hemmelskamp (eds), *Towards Environmental Innovation Systems.* Berlin/Heidelberg/New York: Springer pp. 57–80.

Birkenfeld, F., Gastl, D., Heblich, S., Maergoyz, M., Mont, O. and Plepys, A. (2005), *Product Ban versus Risk Management by Setting Emission and Technology Requirements: The Effect of Different Regulatory Schemes Taking the Use of Trichloroethylene in Sweden and Germany as an Example.* Diskussionsbeitrag Nr. V-37-05, October. Passau: University of Passau, Wirtschaftswissenschaftliche Fakultät.

Blazejczak, J. and Edler, D. (2000), Elements of Innovation-friendly Policy Regimes: An International Comparative Study for the Paper Industry. In: J. Hemmelskamp, K. Rennings and F. Leone (eds), *Innovation-Oriented Environmental Regulation: Theoretical Approaches and Empirical Analysis.* ZEW Economic Studies 10. Heidelberg/New York: Physica Verlag.

BMU (2003), *National Survey Report of PV Power Applications in Germany 2003.* Berlin: BMU.

Carbon Trust (2002), *Submission to Energy White Paper Consultation Process.* London: Carbon Trust.

Chappin, M.M.H. (2005), Environmental Regulation and Environmental Innovation: The Case of Wastewater Treatment, Waste and Energy-Efficiency in the Dutch Paper and Board Industry. *Proceedings of the 11th Annual International Sustainable Development Research Conference*, 6–8 June 2005, Tampere, Finland.

EC (2005), *Implementing the Community Strategy to Reduce CO_2 Emissions from Cars: Fifth Annual Communication on the Effectiveness of the Strategy.* Communication from the Commission to the Council and the European Parliament, COM(2005)269 final. Brussels: European Commission.

Ecological Council (2002), *Environmental Budget Reform in Denmark.* Copenhagen: The Ecological Council.

Ecological Council (2006), *Hazardous Chemicals Can Be Substituted.* Copenhagen: The Ecological Council.

EEA (European Environment Agency) (2006), *Using the Market for Cost-Effective Environmental Policy: Market-Based Instruments in Europe.* EEA Report No.1/2006. Copenhagen: EEA.

Ekins, P. and Etheridge, B. (2006), The environmental and economic impacts of the UK climate change agreements. *Energy Policy*, 34, 2071–2086.

Elzenga, H. and Ros, J. (2004), *MEI-Energie: RIVM's energiebesparingsmodel* (MEI Energy: RIVM's energy savings model). *Kwartaalschrift Economie*, 1 (2), 168–189.

ENDS (2003), *Norwegian solvent tax slashes consumption. Environment Daily*, 1413, 26 March.

Foxon, T. (2003), *Inducing Innovation for a Low-Carbon Future: Drivers, Barriers and Policies.* London: Carbon Trust.

Frondel, M., Horbach, J. and Rennings, K. (2004), *End-of-Pipe or Cleaner Production? An Empirical Comparison of Environmental Innovation Decisions Across OECD Countries.* ZEW Discussion Paper No. 04-82. Mannheim: Zentrum für Europäische Wirtschaftsforschung.

Führ, V. (2001), Japan. In: C. Erdmenger and V. Führ (eds) *The World Buys Green: International Survey on National Green Procurement Practices.* Freiburg: International Council for Local Environmental Initiatives (ICLEI).

Gerard, D. and Lave, L.B. (2003), *The Economics of CAFE Reconsidered: A Response to CAFE Critics and a Case for Fuel Economy Standards.* Regulatory Analysis 03-10. Washington: AEI-Brookings Joint Center for Regulatory Studies.

Harmon, J. (2000), *Experience Curves of Photovoltaic Technology.* Interim Report IR-00-014. Laxenburg: International Institute for Applied Systems Analysis (IIASA).

Hildén, M. Lepola, J., Mickwitz, P., Mulders, A., Palosaari, M., Similä, J., Sjöblom, S. and Vedung, E. (2002), Evaluation of environmental policy instruments: a case study of the Finnish pulp and paper and chemical industries. *Monographs of the Boreal Environment Research* 21.

IEA (2000), *Experience Curves for Energy Technology Policy.* Paris: International Energy Agency.

IEA (2003), *Cool Appliances: Policy Strategies for Energy Efficient Homes.* Paris: International Energy Agency.

Jaffe, A.B., Newell, R.G. and Stavins, R.N. (2002), Environmental Policy and Technological Change. *Environmental and Resource Economics*, 22, 41–69.

Johnstone, N. (2005), The Innovation Effects of Environmental Policy Instruments. In: J. Horbach (ed.), *Indicator Systems for Sustainable Innovation.* Heidelberg/New York: Physica Verlag, pp. 21–41.

Jordan, A., Wurzel, R. and Zito, A. (eds) (2003), *'New' Instruments of Environmental Governance? National Experiences and Prospects.* London: Frank Cass.

Junginger, M. (2005), *Learning in Renewable Energy Technology Development.* PhD Thesis, Utrecht: Utrecht University.

Kemp, R. (1997), *Environmental Policy and Technical Change: A Comparison of the Technological Impact of Policy Instruments*, Cheltenham: Edward Elgar.

Kemp, R. (2000), Technology and Environmental Policy: Innovation Effects of Past Policies and Suggestions for Improvement. In: OECD, *Innovation and the Environment.* Paris: OECD pp. 35–61.

Kline, S.J. and Rosenberg, N. (1986), An Overview of Innovation. In: R. Landau and N. Rosenberg (eds), *The Positive Sum Strategy.* Washington D.C.: National Academic Press.

Krozer, Y. (2002), *Milieu en innovatie* (Environment and innovation). PhD Thesis, Groningen: Groningen University. http://dissertations.ub.rug.nl/faculties/jur/2002/y.krozer, accessed 22 April 2008.

Kuik, O. (2006a), *Environmental Innovation Dynamics in the Automotive Industry.* Amsterdam: The Institute for Environmental Studies (IVM), Vrije Universiteit Amsterdam.

Kuik, O. (2006b), *Environmental Innovation Dynamics in the Pulp and Paper Industry.* Amsterdam: The Institute for Environmental Studies (IVM), Vrije Universiteit Amsterdam.

Lanjouw, J.O. and Mody, A. (1996), Innovation and the international diffusion of environmentally responsive technology. *Research Policy*, 25 (4), 549–571.

Löfstedt, R.E. (2003), Swedish chemical regulation: an overview and analysis. *Risk Analysis*, 23 (2), 411–421.

McDonald, A. and Schrattenholzer, L. (2001), Learning rates for energy technologies. *Energy Policy*, 29, 255–261.

Montalvo Corral, C. (2002), *Environmental Policy and Technological Innovation: Why Do Firms Adopt or Reject New Technologies?* Cheltenham: Edward Elgar.

Naturvårdverket (2005), *The Top Runner Program in Japan: Its Effectiveness and Implications for the EU*. Stockholm: The Swedish Environmental Protection Agency.

Newell, R.G., Jaffe, A.B. and Stavins, R.N. (2002), The Induced Innovation Hypothesis and Energy-Saving Technological Change. In: A. Grübler, N. Nakicenovic and W.D. Nordhaus (eds), *Technological Change and the Environment*. Washington D.C.: Resources for the Future and Laxenburg: IIASA, pp. 97–126.

OECD (1992), *Technology and the Economy: The Key Relationships*. Paris: OECD.

Oosterhuis, F. (ed.) (2006a), *Innovation Dynamics Induced by Environmental Policy: Final Report to the European Commission DG Environment*. IVM Report E-07/05, November. Amsterdam: The Institute for Environmental Studies (IVM), Vrije Universiteit Amsterdam.

Oosterhuis, F. (2006b), *Energy Efficient Office Appliances*. Amsterdam: The Institute for Environmental Studies (IVM), Vrije Universiteit Amsterdam.

Oosterhuis, F. (2006c), *Substitution of Hazardous Chemicals*. Amsterdam: The Institute for Environmental Studies (IVM), Vrije Universiteit Amsterdam.

Oosterhuis, F. and ten Brink, P. (2006), *Assessing Innovation Dynamics Induced by Environment Policy: Findings from Literature and Analytical Framework for the Case Studies*. Amsterdam: The Institute for Environmental Studies (IVM), Vrije Universiteit Amsterdam.

O'Rourke, D. and Lee, E. (2004), Mandatory planning for environmental innovation: Evaluating regulatory mechanisms for toxics use reduction, *Journal of Environmental Planning and Management*, 47(2).

Pickman, H.A. (1998), The effect of environmental regulation on environmental innovation. *Business Strategy and the Environment*, 7 (4), 223–233.

Popp, D. (2006), International innovation and diffusion of air pollution control technologies: the effects of NO_x and SO_2 regulation in the US, Japan, and Germany. *Journal of Environmental Economics and Management*, 51 (1), 46–71.

Porter, M.E. and van der Linde, C. (1995), Green and competitive: ending the stalemate. *Harvard Business Review*, 73 (5), 120–133.

Reinstaller, A. (2005), Policy entrepreneurship in the co-evolution of institutions, preferences, and technology: comparing the diffusion of totally chlorine free pulp bleaching technologies in the US and Sweden. *Research Policy*, 34 (9), 1366–1384.

Requate, T. (2005), Dynamic incentives by environmental policy instruments: a survey. *Ecological Economics*, 54 (2–3), 175–195.

RIVM (2000), *Techno 2000; Modellering van de daling van eenheidskosten van technologieën in de tijd*. Rapportnummer 773008003, April. Bilthoven: RIVM.

Siemens, R. (2001), A Review and Critical Evaluation of Selected Greener Public Purchasing GPP Programmes and Policies. Paper for the *Workshop on Financial, Budget and Accounting Issues in Greener Public Purchasing*, Vienna, 29–31 October.

Similä, J. (2002), Pollution regulation and its effects on technological innovations. *Journal of Environmental Law*, 14 (2), 143–160.

Stanton, T.J. (1993), Capacity utilization and new source bias: evidence from the US electric power industry. *Energy Economics*, 15 (1), 57–60.

Sterner, T. (2004), Trichloroethylene in Europe: Ban versus Tax. In: W. Harrington, R.D. Morgenstern, and T. Sterners (eds), *Choosing Environmental Policy: Comparing Instruments and Outcomes in the United States and Europe.* Washington D.C.: Resources for the Future, pp. 206–221.

Strasser, K. (1997), Cleaner technology, pollution prevention, and environmental regulation. *Fordham Environmental Law Journal*, 9 (1), 1–106.

ten Brink, P. (ed.) (2002), *Voluntary Environmental Agreements: Process, Practice and Future Use.* Sheffield: Greenleaf Publishing.

ten Brink, P., Anderson, J., Bassi, S. and Stantcheva, E. (2006), *Innovation Case Study: Photovoltaics.* Brussels: Institute for European Environmental Policy.

Tickner, J.A. and Geiser, K. (2004), The precautionary principle stimulus for solutions- and alternatives-based environmental policy. *Environmental Impact Assessment Review*, 24, 801–824

Tickner, J.A., Geiser, K. and Coffin, M. (2005), The U.S. experience in promoting sustainable chemistry. *Environmental Science and Pollution Research*, 12 (2), 115–123.

TME (1995), *Technische vooruitgang en milieukosten, aanzet tot methodiekontwikkeling* (Technological progress and environmental costs, initiative for methodological development). The Hague: TME.

Touche Ross (1995), *A cost-effectiveness study on the various measures that are likely to reduce pollutant emissions from road vehicles for the year 2010.* Final report to the CEC, DG III, November 1995. Brussels: European Commission.

TURI (2006), *Trichloroethylene and chlorinated solvents reduction.* http://www.turi.org/content/view/full/2652/ accessed 13 June 2006.

Webber, C.A., Brown, R.E. and Koomey, J.G. (2000), Savings estimates for the Energy Star voluntary labeling program. *Energy* Policy, 28, 1137–1149.

WRI (2005), *Transparency Issues with the ACEA Agreement.* Washington: WRI.

16. Conclusions and recommendations
Paul Ekins and Michael MacLeod

16.1 CONCLUSIONS FROM THE CASE STUDIES

As discussed in Chapter 3, a number of earlier studies have identified substantial differences between *ex ante* and *ex post* estimates of the costs of policies. It was seen that overestimation of *ex ante* costs seems to be common, but it is not a universal rule.

The case studies reported in this book seem to confirm this mixed picture, with *ex ante* overestimation of compliance costs occurring frequently, but not consistently. With regard to the European case studies (see Table 16.1), in a number of cases, the *ex ante* estimates were about twice as large as the *ex post* results. In some cases, however (Large Combustion Plants in the UK; specific elements of the ozone depleting substances case) much higher *ex ante*: *ex post* ratios were found. On the other hand, the IPPC case showed no large differences between *ex ante* and *ex post* estimates.

Table 16.2 shows the extent of *ex ante* overestimation in the UK case studies, and compares this with the studies reviewed in Harrington *et al.* (1999). It seems that in the UK case studies reviewed in this book, the relative occurrence of overestimates to underestimates was less than in either the European studies or the studies reviewed in Harrington et al. (1999), but even so overestimates were twice as common as underestimates.

The headline conclusion of this book is therefore that *ex ante* estimates of the costs to business of environmental legislation often (though not always) exceed the *ex post* estimates by a substantial margin. A large variety of factors can be responsible for the observed differences between *ex ante* and *ex post* estimates. Moreover, even if the overall difference in the estimates is small, these factors may still be at work if they tend to neutralise or counteract each other (as was for instance observed in the IPPC case).

Many of the factors cannot be easily influenced. It is therefore reasonable to expect that the gap between *ex ante* and *ex post* costs is here to stay. Therefore, even though there is room for improvement in the quality and accuracy of cost estimates, it is equally important to be aware of the factors behind the gap. Indeed, Harrington *et al.* (1999) argue that *ex ante* esti-

Table 16.1 Ex ante /ex post *ratio for European case studies*

Case study chapter	European Directive (sector)	*Ex ante/Ex post* ratio	
		Upstream	Consumers
6	Road transport (Netherlands)	2 (1.4−6)	−
7	Large Combustion Plant Directive (LCPD) (Power sector)	2 (Germany)	6−10 (UK)
9	Integrated Pollution Prevention and Control (IPPC)	>1.2 (operational costs) ~ 1.1 (capital costs)	−
10	Ozone deleting substances (ODS)	2.5 (1.4−125)	1.25
11	The Nitrates Directive (Agriculture)	~ 2	−

Table 16.2 *Results of the UK studies and comparison with Harrington* et al. *(1999)*

	Total costs				Unit costs			
	+	0	−	?	+	0	−	?
UK case studies	4	0	2	0	4	0	2	0
Harrington *et al.* 1999	12	6	2	6	12	8	6	0

Notes:
+ *Ex ante* costs overestimated compares with *ex post* costs.
0 *Ex ante* costs accurate.
− *Ex ante* costs underestimated.
? Comparison of costs uncertain.
Results are defined as inaccurate if *ex ante* and *ex post* costs differ by more than 25%.

mates can be useful in the development of environmental regulations without necessarily providing good predictions of *ex post* costs. In their view, cost estimates should be seen as making an input into environmental regulatory decision making and not as a forecast intended to be judged in isolation.

In the European case studies, Oosterhuis (2006) identified the following four factors as the principal causes of *ex ante/ex post* differences, together with the case studies in which they were most apparent.

16.1.1 Factors Related to the Definition and Measurement of Costs

The importance of distinguishing between aggregate costs and unit costs is illustrated by the study of the Large Combustion Plants Directive (LCPD) case. This showed that in the UK, the costs of complying with the Directive have been much lower than anticipated. However, this was mainly due to unforeseen responses (fuel switching instead of end-of-pipe measures). In Germany, where implementation was mainly effected by means of end-of-pipe measures, *ex ante* and *ex post* estimates did not differ that much. In other words, the costs per unit of emission reduction (at power plants that did not switch fuels) did not deviate much, whereas aggregate costs for all power plants were considerably lower *ex post* than *ex ante*.

The LCPD case also shows the importance of technology suppliers as a source of cost data. Whereas the power sector (having little experience with desulphurisation) overestimated *ex ante* costs, the *ex ante* estimates by the German Umweltbundesamt were close to the *ex post* costs because they were based on interviews with technology providers. These had made lots of tenders for building desulphurisation plants, so had worked quite extensively on cost estimates.

In the case study of Integrated Pollution Prevention and Control (IPPC), it was concluded by comparing the *ex ante* and the *ex post* cost data that *ex ante* estimates of investment costs of the Best Available Technology (BAT) options based on suppliers' information were reasonably realistic (within a range of 20 per cent). However, the operational costs of the flue gas treatment options were overestimated. The analysis also revealed that the emission reduction efficiency for SO_X realised by flue gas cleaning was lower than the *ex ante* estimates of emission reductions based on the suppliers' information. These two opposing errors more-or-less neutralised each other.

The nitrates case study provides another example of the issue of attributing costs. Some measures taken in agriculture have multiple objectives (for example, nitrates, ammonia, phosphorus and greenhouse gas reduction), causing ambiguity as to what part of the costs should be allocated to what policy. The nitrates case also revealed large differences between Member States in methods to assess costs. However, the extent to which these differences influenced the accuracy and reliability of the estimates remains unclear.

16.1.2 Factors Related to Baseline Assumptions, Counterfactual Scenarios, Differences Between Planned and Implemented Policies, and Business (or Market) Response

All the case studies to some extent illustrate the difficulties involved in constructing counterfactual scenarios. The complexities of business and market responses to regulations are very evident in the ozone depleting substances (ODS) case study. This shows that the businesses which helped generate the estimates would not have been the ones which ultimately paid any additional cost. The mandatory nature of the Montreal Protocol often provided a way for business to pass the costs on to the user sectors, and ultimately to the consumers. In addition to this, those companies which led in the development of CFC substitutes achieved a market rent so long as their competitors were in the process of catching up. These lead companies also opposed legislation, but only until they had managed to develop substitutes, after which they moved to encourage the regulations which they then gained from. The laggards were the European companies which therefore lost out due to their delay in innovation.

16.1.3 Differences Between Planned, Adopted and Implemented Policies

In the CFC case, compliance was not always achieved in the way anticipated during *ex ante* estimates. For example, regulators moved their focus from the use sectors, as anticipated, to producers and importers, which proved to be a significantly more cost-effective approach. Also, the Montreal Protocol later changed to permit the interim use of HCFCs.

The nitrates case study illustrates the importance of adequacy of implementation. In the Netherlands, the method of implementing the Directive (by means of the 'MINAS' system) was considered to be inappropriate in a Court ruling. Therefore, the *ex post* costs of implementing the MINAS system cannot be regarded as reflecting the costs of the Nitrates Directive in the Netherlands.

16.1.4 The Potential for Innovation, Economies of Scale and other Cost-Reducing Dynamics

This issue was examined in detail in Chapter 15 and little further therefore needs to be said here. However, with regard to the European case studies, the LCPD case clearly demonstrates the impact of unforeseen technological developments on eventual compliance costs. In the UK, power producers complied with LCPD requirements by switching massively to gas fired combined cycle gas turbine (CCGT) plants, making further expensive investment in flue gas desulphurisation (FGD) largely unnecessary. In the Netherlands, the overestimation of *ex ante* LCPD cost estimates is believed to be because these estimates were made in the late 1980s, on the basis of data about first small-scale applications of desulphurisation and denitrification technologies, that is, emerging technologies that improved in the following years.

In the CFC case study, it was concluded that the failure to predict compliance costs correctly was likely to be due to conservative assumptions by some within the industry in the face of uncertain future technological developments and a lack of incentive to provide realistic predictions. As long as the sectors' interest lies in talking down the prospects of innovation, it is likely that only detailed external reviews of industry assumptions can critically challenge *ex ante* cost estimates.

In the car emissions case study, the main reason for overestimation was the *ex ante* assumption about the unit costs of environmental equipment and measures. The *ex post* cost estimates often tend to decrease over time due to improvements in technology and efficiency. The *ex ante* estimates fail to consider these effects. Unit costs of environmental technology have the tendency to decrease over time, with annual changes of around 10 per cent. The additional costs to comply with regulations concerning diesel vehicles were especially overestimated. In reality, the automobile industry was able to supply complying cars at much lower costs than initially thought.

In the Nitrates Directive case study, the comparison of *ex ante* and *ex post* estimates of the MINAS policy in the Netherlands suggested that for some sectors (such as the dairy sector), manure and fertiliser policies have resulted in efficiency gains due to more rational fertiliser management that offset part of the *ex ante* expected costs. The extent of these efficiency gains will in general depend on the initial situation (how rational it is) and the design of the policy instruments and associated advisory initiatives around these instruments.

The importance of each of the above four factors differs from case to case. However, evidence from the literature and other case studies suggests that, in particular, the potential for (unanticipated) innovations and cost reductions often plays a major role. Large differences between *ex post* and *ex ante* estimates are usually due to the introduction of new technologies (after the introduction of the legislation) with low or even negative net cost, as with the LCPD (CCGT technology) and the ODS (CFC substitutes) cases above. Considerable underestimates of the cost reduction potential of innovation may also occur if *ex ante* costs are based on data for prototypes or first applications that have not yet benefited from economies of scale and 'learning curve effects'.

There seems to be little evidence of industry knowingly providing biased cost estimates. However, in the face of uncertain future technological development, the affected industry will tend to be conservative, that is, to come up with relatively high cost figures. They may also be reluctant to make cost data publicly available, as this is often commercially sensitive information. Suppliers of environmental technology may have an incentive to be over-optimistic and give low cost estimates in order to influence decision making. On the other hand, technologies eventually delivered to the market usually have a 'safety margin', that is, a guaranteed minimum efficiency level, whereas the 'real' efficiency is higher. The involvement of independent experts may provide additional, relatively 'neutral' cost information.

The often substantial time lag between the stage at which *ex ante* cost estimates are made (during the preparation of the legislation) and the time when the costs are actually incurred by business implies that many of the assumptions on which the *ex ante* estimates were based may no longer be valid. In addition to the policy itself, market conditions and contextual factors may have changed. Moreover, the response by business may be quite different from what was expected. Cost assessment procedures will have to deal with this inherent and largely inevitable uncertainty. Sensitivity analyses and explicit consideration of the assumptions and the extent to which they turned out to be false are therefore needed.

Differences in implementation are in fact not a separate source of divergence between *ex ante* and *ex post* costs, but rather a specific case of assumptions not becoming reality (the assumption in this case being full implementation and enforcement of the originally proposed legislation by means of a particular policy).

Relatively reliable predictions of compliance costs might be conceivable in the case of detailed technical prescriptions, uniformly required from all actors involved in the EU. However, the tendency in environmental policy is towards more flexibility, leaving Member States and firms as much room as possible to find their own solutions for meeting the requirements and objectives. From that perspective, the scope for making precise *ex ante* cost estimates is not likely to become larger. This does not mean though that estimates are not useful and do not give a very good feel for the costs.

With regard to the UK case studies, Table 16.3 shows whether the costs were overestimated or underestimated, and summarises the apparent reasons for this. The results in Tables 16.3 and 16.4 summarise, and unavoidably simplify, six stories of cost overestimation, cost underestimation and uncertainty. Initially, the *ex ante* estimates were categorised using the same criterion as Harrington *et al.* (1999), that is, they were defined as inaccurate if they differed from the *ex post* estimate by more than 25 per cent (see Table 16.2). Using this criterion, two-thirds of the UK case studies

Table 16.3   UK case study results: summary comparison of ex ante and ex post costs

Chapter number and case study	Ex ante costs compared to ex post costs	Confidence in ex ante/ex post assessment	Summary of findings
4. Air Quality Strategy: road transport	+	Medium	Industry tends to overestimate costs of vehicle regulations and underestimate innovation. Regulators also tend to overestimate, but to a lesser extent.
5. Air Quality Strategy: electricity generation	+	Low	The Air Quality Strategy Evaluation indicates overestimates.
8. Control of Major Accident Hazards (COMAH) Regulations 1999	–	High	Underestimated due to baseline and compliance issues. Asymmetric correction of (ex post) errors.
12. The Groundwater Regulations 1998	+	Medium	Overestimated due to compliance issues and post-implementation changes in the regulation
13. The Welfare of Farmed Animals (England) (Amendment) Regulations 2003	+	High	*Ex ante* likely to be higher than turnout due to a combination of baseline errors, and under-compliance/'innovation'.

14. The Food Safety (General
Food Hygiene) (Butchers'
Shops) Amendment
Regulations 2000 SI
930

High

−

Errors due to incorrect *ex ante*
assumptions that: (a) there would be
no implementation costs on business,
and (b) that the costs to Local Authorities
of administering the licensing scheme
would be largely offset by license fee
revenue.

Notes:
1. Note that a distinction is made between (a) non-compliance (i.e. not meeting the legal/technical requirements of a regulation) and (b) undercompliance (i.e. satisfying the legal/technical requirements of a regulation in a way that is unlikely to satisfy the spirit of the regulation and
achieve its objectives).
2. + = overestimate; − = underestimate.

Source: adapted from MacLeod *et al.* 2006.

Table 16.4   UK case study results and reasons for divergence of ex ante/ex post cost estimates

Reason for *ex ante/ex post* discrepancy		Chapter number of case study						Systematic (S) or random error (R)
		4	5	8	12	13	14	
Ex ante overestimated	Post-estimate changes in the regulation	X						R
	Uncertainty/lack of information/incorrect assumptions/baseline errors		X		X	X		R
	Lower than predicted compliance rates (non-compliance or under-compliance)				X	X		S
	Strategic behaviour by regulatees, e.g. lobbying, overestimating costs leading to estimates of maxima rather than means	X						S
	Asymmetric correction of errors							S
	Static assumptions leading to the underestimation of innovation/adaptation	X			X	X		S
Ex ante underestimated	Post-estimate changes in the regulation							R
	Uncertainty/lack of information/incorrect assumptions/baseline errors			X			X	R
	Overcompliance			X				S
	Strategic behaviour by regulators							S
	Cost turbulence and selection bias			X				S
	Asymmetric correction of errors							?

in this book came to the conclusion, albeit with varying degrees of confidence, that the *ex ante* costs had been overestimated compared to the *ex post* estimates. However, there were two cases where it was concluded, with a high degree of confidence, that the *ex ante* costs had been significantly underestimated. Table 16.2 showed that these results are comparable to the findings of Harrington *et al.* (1999), who examined 25 (mainly US) regulations, and exhibit the following important similarities:

1. *Ex ante* costs (unit and total) were overestimated for over half the regulations studied.
2. While *ex ante* costs are most often overestimated, they are also occasionally underestimated.

It could be argued that the criterion used to define accuracy (+/−25 per cent or more) is too strict. Recently, Medhurst (2005) commented that he believed 'a factor of two error (i.e. +/−100%) was pretty reasonable . . . and would be acceptable to most policy-makers'. Obviously if this higher error margin were to be accepted, the number of *ex ante* estimates considered accurate would increase and the confidence with which estimates are defined as inaccurate would decrease.

In Table 16.4, the most common reasons for overestimating the *ex ante* costs were (a) the adoption of static assumptions and the consequent underestimation of innovation, and (b) uncertainty. Compliance issues, strategic behaviour by regulatees, and post-estimate changes in the regulation were also identified. For *ex ante* underestimation, uncertainty was indentified twice, while compliance issues and asymmetric correction of errors were indentified once each. Both of the case studies where *ex ante* underestimation occurred were characterised by mistaken *ex ante* assumptions. One of these, the COMAH case study, was unusual in that the *ex post* data gathered were also going to be used for future regulatory appraisal and were in some respects, *ex ante*. Not surprisingly perhaps, these reasons are similar to the reasons for divergence in the cost estimates cited by Oosterhuis (2006) and discussed above.

The results in Table 16.4 suggest that there may be systematic bias in favour of overestimating *ex ante* costs, because more of the overestimates are the result of systematic errors than the underestimates. The remaining reasons for *ex ante/ex post* discrepancies are random and could therefore result in either over- or underestimation.

It is also worth examining the potential sources of error discussed in Chapter 3 and shown in Table 16.4 that did *not* appear to play a part in the case studies (for example, asymmetric correction of errors was not identified as a cause of overestimation). This does not mean that they are unimportant. The results in any study of this type depend to an extent on the choice of case studies. For example, it could be argued that the estimates for regulations amenable to technical solutions, such as air pollution control measures, are more likely to exhibit errors relating to technological innovation. In addition some sources of error, such as baseline errors, tend to be easier to identify than the subtler and somewhat diffuse influence of the process of asymmetric error correction.

16.2 POLICY IMPLICATIONS AND RECOMMENDATIONS

Oosterhuis (2006) drew the following conclusions from the European case studies, arguing most importantly that, even though the hope for perfect *ex ante* cost estimates is illusory, it should at least be possible to set out some guidelines which might lead to better accuracy and comparability.

The main challenges for the improvement of cost estimates and for the convergence of *ex ante* and *ex post* estimates include the following:

1. The need for clear definitions and consistency in the use of the term 'costs'.
2. The construction of counterfactual scenarios and addressing the question of the extent to which the real developments differed from that scenario.
3. Taking due account of the complexities involved in environmental regulation (that is, the difficulty of attributing costs to one particular policy measure).
4. Distinguishing between estimates of unit and total costs.
5. Dealing with the fact that *ex ante* estimates are often done on early proposals that are changed in the subsequent legislative process, and even later, in the implementation phase.
6. Coping with the bias caused by *ex ante* estimates that are done to fit in with lobbying, and may therefore not be entirely neutral.
7. Trying to obtain information on costs from a wide range of sources (including for example potential suppliers of implementing technology).
8. Investigating the mechanisms behind innovation and cost decreases due to environmental policy. This may provide the necessary tools to take these factors into account so as to obtain more realistic *ex ante* cost estimates.

Some amplifications and discussion of these points now follows.

16.2.1   Ex Ante Estimates

The reliability of *ex ante* cost data can be improved by carefully selecting and evaluating the information sources. Ideally, data from different sources (suppliers, operators, researchers and so on) should be analysed to arrive at a reliable range of cost figures.

Legislation can lead to benefits in the form of 'avoided costs' (for example, lower energy costs due to energy saving). Avoided costs are likely to be at least as challenging to estimate as conventional costs of compliance, but their inclusion in the *ex ante* estimate is essential to prevent overestimation of net cost.

Ex ante estimates should keep track of the development of the policy process, as changes in the policy proposals will inevitably imply changes in the estimates. Ideally, each amendment should be accompanied by a revision of the estimated costs.

The construction of the counterfactual scenario (what would have occurred in the absence of regulation) is a difficult part of cost estimation. If one wants to be less dependent on the use of rather complex scenarios vulnerable to many external variables or factors, it is necessary to gain a better understanding of business behaviour and the likely response to a given policy measure.

The issue of strategic versus marginal responses needs to be examined in much more detail, with consideration of the heterogeneity of businesses and of their likely responses (especially where policy impacts on SMEs), and of the genuine technological uncertainties that surround these responses.

Cost assessment procedures will have to deal with many uncertainties, which are to a large extent inevitable. Sensitivity analyses and explicit consideration of the assumptions and the extent to which they turned out to be false are therefore needed. The sensitivity analyses should identify the key parameters that are expected to influence costs, and assess how changes in these parameters affect expected costs. Identifying the key determinants of costs *ex ante* helps when designing *ex post* evaluation.

Further research should reveal whether it is possible to formulate general 'rules of thumb' regarding the extent to which cost decreases can be expected as a result of unanticipated substitution options, innovation, economies of scale and learning curve effects. This might lead to some standard reduction factors to be applied in *ex ante* cost estimates, dependent upon the specific technology and context at hand.

16.2.2   Estimating *Ex Post* Costs and Comparing Them with *Ex Ante*

The planning of *ex post* estimates needs to be built into regulations in order to generate learning about the degree to which they have succeeded.

It would seem sensible to develop guidelines for *ex post* cost estimates and measurements, as there is no structured framework yet to measure the realised costs to business. If such measurements are to be carried out, a common set of indicators and quality standards should be developed. This would enable *ex post* cost assessments at a much more detailed level than currently is the case.

Comparisons of *ex ante* and *ex post* estimates should ask whether entities complied as they were expected to, and aim to find out why (or why not). *Ex post* assessments should also take account of how the regulation changed during the period of its negotiation and implementation. Obviously, changes in contextual factors should also be considered. However, as *ex ante* estimates are intended to make the policy-making process more transparent (by revealing potential trade-offs and so on) *ex ante* and *ex post* assessments should be kept as simple as possible.

When comparing *ex ante* and *ex post* annualised cost estimates of (in principle) the same phenomenon (or technology), the following should be carefully considered to arrive at comparable figures:

1. exchange rates and the price basis;
2. the number of units *ex post* and *ex ante*;
3. unit costs *ex post* and *ex ante*;
4. the way in which costs are estimated or expressed: annualised costs, investments, net present value;
5. interest rates and discount rates applied in the calculation of costs;
6. depreciation periods;
7. treatment of operating and administrative costs;
8. the inclusion or exclusion of indirect or 'welfare costs' (such as the attributed loss of market share) in the calculation.

For a policy instrument in which targets are periodically revised, it should be possible to establish a feedback process that draws on the *ex ante* and *ex post* evaluations of each stage. 'Learning loops' that involve progressive tuning of the assessment method and benefit from the improvements in the data should facilitate more accurate estimation of compliance costs for target revisions over time. This could also benefit, for example, the assessment of future costs by EU accession countries adopting measures some time after existing Member States.

Investments in costs estimates will usually be very small relative to the cost of implementation. It would be interesting to investigate the potential efficiencies provided by high-quality cost estimates (in terms of better policy measures). This would require an in-depth analysis of cases in which not only the results of *ex ante* and *ex post* cost estimates are compared, but also differences in investment in the estimation and the methodology used, as well as the role of the estimates in the decision-making process.

On the basis of the UK case studies, MacLeod *et al.* (2006) came to very similar conclusions to Oosterhuis (2006) on the way the accuracy of cost estimates could be improved, while also agreeing that not all the discrepancies between the *ex ante* and *ex post* cost estimates are the result of avoidable shortcomings in the *ex ante* estimates. As has already been noted, post-estimate changes in the regulations, or unforeseeable events affecting the baseline could render the most rigorous *ex ante* estimate inaccurate. Also innovation, by its very nature, is hard to predict with any certainty. Despite these caveats, MacLeod *et al.* (2006) set out a series of practical recommendations for improving the accuracy of *ex ante* cost estimates based on the findings of the UK case studies. These are summarised in Table 16.5.

It is clear that, despite the differences between the UK and European studies (that is, in terms of remit and types of regulation examined), there are common conclusions regarding, for example, the importance of the ways in which costs are defined and attributed to specific regulations; the importance of establishing accurate baselines and making valid assumptions; and the difficulty of predicting the role of innovation and of obtaining objective data.

Eliminating bias arising from the strategic behaviour of interest groups is difficult given the asymmetry of knowledge: regulators often have to rely on those they are regulating for much of their data. Where there is reason to believe that data are being manipulated, then they should ideally be checked by an independent expert in the field. Another approach is to carry out some form of pilot study. Although they will not always be practical or appropriate, pilot studies are a potentially rich source of data.

Most of the *ex ante* estimates could have been improved through the examination of trends and adoption of dynamic assumptions. It is therefore recommended that anyone undertaking an *ex ante* analysis should ask the following questions: (a) Does the regulation apply to a rapidly changing sector? (b) Is there likely to be a significant time gap between the *ex ante* estimate and implementation? If the answer to these questions is yes, then historic trends should be examined and forecasts made of variables that will affect the costs. Particular challenges are posed by sectors that, while not appearing dynamic *ex ante*, undergo significant change in response to the regulation. Such changes, often involving innovation and cost reduction, are difficult to predict with any degree of certainty.

Table 16.5   Recommendations from UK case studies for improving the accuracy of ex ante estimates

Recommendation	Case study chapter number					
	4	5	8	12	13	14
1. Examine validity of data provided by groups with vested interests in the regulation.			×			
2. Examine baseline trends, particularly when (a) attempting to forecast for a rapidly changing sector; and (b) there is a significant time gap between the *ex ante* estimate and implementation.		?	×	×	×	
3. Examine the potential for innovation and adopt dynamic assumptions where appropriate.	×			×	×	
4. Make pragmatic assumptions about compliance, particularly where regulatees have a strong incentive to adopt cost-minimising strategies, or where overcompliance is likely.			×	×	×	
5. Business survey results should be treated with caution, particularly when based on small samples providing non-anonymous responses on sensitive issues.				×		
6. Distinguish between expenditures and costs and try to include all major cost elements, including those often overlooked, e.g. time.	×		×			
7. Analyse total costs *and* unit costs.	×					
8. For *ex ante* pilot studies/surveys: obtain an adequate sample and design them with the possibility of follow-up work in mind.						×

One often asked question is whether the *ex ante* cost estimates developed by regulated industries are so predictably biased that one could apply some generalised correction factor. The conclusion of this book is that neither the nature nor the extent of the bias are predictable enough to permit this, as innovation can involve a variety of responses, including: economic restructuring; shifts in production; the introduction of end-of-pipe technologies and/or process changes; and cosmetic changes. The only plausible approach to dealing with such estimates is to examine them on a case-by-case basis. In that regard, analysts should demand full transparency of the data and assumptions used and then scrutinise them carefully to assess their overall quality. Perhaps it would be worthwhile to undertake a study of historical evidence of innovation in response to regulation in order to identify the types of sectors and regulations that are most likely to reduce costs through innovation. While quantifying the likely effect of innovation would still be very difficult, such an analysis would enable regulators to provide a qualitative assessment (for example, low, medium or high) of the likelihood of cost reduction through innovation.

As has been seen, compliance levels can have profound effects on the accuracy of *ex ante* costs, especially total costs. It is therefore important that pragmatic assumptions about compliance are adopted, particularly where regulatees have a strong incentive to adopt cost-minimising strategies, or where overcompliance is likely. When regulations are identified where compliance (under or over) is likely to be an issue, it is recommended that some form of sensitivity testing is carried out for the costs under different levels of compliance. The identification of regulations where compliance may be an issue would be aided by a wider study that investigated historic levels of compliance in terms of sector, unit cost (as a proportion of margin), type of measure, type of monitoring and enforcement and so on.

A related question to whether *ex ante* cost estimates reflect *ex post* estimates is: to what extent do cost estimates, whether *ex ante* or *ex post*, reflect the actual cost of a policy? Estimates depend on where the system boundaries are drawn (for example, farm, sector or economy), how costs are defined (partial equilibrium, full equilibrium or social cost-benefit analysis) and which costs are included, as discussed in Chapter 3. Time is often difficult to quantify and can easily be overlooked, even when it is a major cost. Cost estimation is complicated by the difficulties involved in precisely identifying the additional actions, and hence costs, arising as a result of a regulation. To what extent are measures required by a regulation likely to be the measures that the regulatees would have undertaken anyway, either voluntarily or in response to other legislation?

Finally, the studies on which this book is based have highlighted the lack of comparable *ex ante* and *ex post* data sets. This is primarily because few *ex post* analyses are carried out, despite official guidance recommending periodic reviews of regulations (for example, in the UK, Regulatory Impact Unit 2003, p.29). The dearth of rigorous *ex post* analyses is not surprising. It is easy to understand why a detailed analysis of an implemented regulation is unlikely to seem an attractive proposition: it is potentially costly and time-consuming; the criticism generated by a result showing inaccuracy of *ex ante* estimates is likely greatly to exceed any praise which accurate estimates (which will to some extent be the expectation) may attract; and there will be new legislative priorities to formulate and assess. It may therefore be worth considering the needs of any *ex post* analysis at an early stage and integrating them into the assessment process. This could include actions such as keeping a detailed record of all the key assumptions made during an impact assessment, or establishing a Quality Assurance procedure to record information in a standard format. Anything that can be done to simplify the implementation of *ex post* analyses should be encouraged in order to increase the number of *ex ante/ex post* comparisons undertaken and, in so doing, improve the accuracy of *ex ante* estimates and, therefore, the quality of the legislation to which they relate.

REFERENCES

Harrington, W., Morgenstern, R.D. and Nelson, P. (1999) *On the Accuracy of Regulatory Cost Estimates*, Washington D.C.: Resources for the Future, available at: http://www.rff.org/Documents/RFF-DP-99-18.pdf, accessed 14 April 2008.

MacLeod, M., Moran, D., Aresti, M.L., Harrington, W. and Morgenstern, R. (2006) *Comparing the Ex ante and Ex post Costs of Complying with Regulatory Changes*, Final Report to DEFRA, contract number EPES 0405-19, London: Defra, available at: http://www.defra.gov.uk/science/project_data/ Document Library/SD14011/SD14011_3366_FRP.pdf, accessed 5 April 2008.

Medhurst, J. (2005) Ex-post estimates of costs to business of EU environmental policies. Presentation given at the *European Commission Workshop*, Brussels 10 October 2005.

Oosterhuis, F. (ed.) (2006) *Ex post Estimates of Costs to Business of EU Environmental Legislation*, Final Report to DG Environment, March, available at: http://ec.europa.eu/environment/enveco/policy/pdf/2007_final_report_conclutions.pdf, accessed 5 April 2008.

Regulatory Impact Unit (2003) *Better Policy Making: A Guide to Regulatory Impact Assessment*, London: Cabinet Office.

Index